PRAYERFUL RESPONSIBILITY

Prayer and Social Responsibility in the Religious Thought of Douglas Steere

JOHN D. COPENHAVER, JR.

foreword by
E. Glenn Hinson

UNIVERSITY
PRESS OF
AMERICA

Lanham • New York • London

BX
7795
.S74
C67
1992

Copyright © 1992 by
University Press of America®, Inc.
4720 Boston Way
Lanham, Maryland 20706

3 Henrietta Street
London WC2E 8LU England

Library of Congress Cataloging-in-Publication Data

Copenhaver, John D., 1949-
Prayerful Responsibility : Prayer and Social Responsibility
in the religious thought of Douglas Steere / John D. Copenhaver, Jr. ;
foreword by E. Glenn Hinson.
p. cm.
Revision of the author's thesis (Ph. D.)
—Catholic University of America, 1986.
Includes bibliographical references and index.
1. Steere, Douglas Van, 1901- .
2. Spirituality—History—20th century.
3. Prayer—History,20th century.
4. Sociology, Christian—History—20th century.   I. Title.
BX7795.S74C67   1992   248—dc20   91-38167 CIP

ISBN 0-8191-8530-2 (cloth : alk. paper)

TO MY PARENTS

whose steadfast love has been a source of
inspiration and encouragement.

ACKNOWLEDGEMENTS

I deeply appreciate the assistance I have received while working on this project. Paul J. Philibert, O.P., S.T.D., the dissertation director, provided patient and painstaking supervision of the organizing and writing of the dissertation; he also offered support and encouragement at several critical moments. The other readers (Raymond Studzinski, O.S.B., Ph.D., William Dinges, Ph.D., and James C. Logan, Ph.D.) have each made valuable critical suggestions that have strengthened the thesis. My sister, Mary Stone Klingelhofer, studied the manuscript for infelicities in style and made numerous suggestions that have made the text more readable.

I thank my friend Father Conrad Hoover, a Roman Catholic priest and former retreat director for the Church of the Saviour, for first impressing upon me the important contribution that Douglas V. Steere has made to contemporary Christian spirituality.

As I was developing my bibliography of Steere's writings, the staff of The Quaker Collection at Haverford College, especially Ms. Eva Walker Myer, provided valuable assistance.

The Elizabeth Ann Bogert Fund for the Study and Practice of Christian Mysticism awarded the dissertation a grant that helped defray the expenses of research and travel. The grant also provided important "moral" support.

Even before the dissertation proposal was approved, Dr. and Mrs. Steere offered me the warmest hospitality on my many trips to Haverford College. Dr. Steere generously set aside several afternoons to answer patiently my questions about his life and his spiritual theology, and made available to me some of his less accessible writings. He also graciously agreed to read the dissertation as it progressed. The dissertation has been immeasurably enriched by his co-operation.

My wife, Marsha A. Childs, while pursuing her own career, has managed to offer me the most crucial support. When we were married in 1979, one of the vows we made to each other was "I will honor your goals and dreams and help you to fulfill them." She has been unfailingly faithful to that vow, and has shared ungrudgingly in the sacrifices involved in a prolonged academic program, as well as in the writing of this book. I am profoundly grateful for her companionship, support, and love.

The author gratefully acknowledges the use of material from the following books and articles:

Excerpts reprinted with permission of Trinity University Press from *Character and Christian Life: A Study in Theological Ethics* by Stanley Hauerwas. Copyright 1975,

CONTENTS

FOREWORD

All who know and love Douglas V. Steere will rejoice that a part of his exceptional contribution to spirituality has received the fine and sensitive appraisal John D. Copenhaver, Jr. has given it in these pages. Although Dr. Copenhaver has not had the advantage long term personal acquaintance would supply, he has done a masterful job of research and presented a clear and cogent set of theses vis-a-vis the relation of prayer and social responsibility in the thought of Douglas Steere. These theses do justice to the complexity and subtlety of Steere's thought and demonstrate its integrity and value. Copenhaver's analysis of sources and critique confirm what many of Douglas Steere's friends and readers have known all along, that is, that Douglas Steere speaks not just from, to, and for his own Quaker tradition but from, to, and for the Church universal, and indeed even all seekers of truth.

The author makes a solid case for five theses from several major books and articles by Steere.

1.) Prayer (especially corporate prayer) deepens an awareness of creatureliness and evokes a consciousness of solidarity with all persons and all creation. Out of this perceived solidarity "seeds of concern" surface in the consciousness of the one who prays.

2.) Prayer nurtures an awareness of God's infinite concern for every person and fosters a willingness to participate in God's redemptive order.

3.) Prayer cleanses action, work, and service of their repetitive nature and restores their frame of meaning.

4.) Acts of social responsibility clarify and test the genuineness of prayer.

5.) Both prayer and social responsibility are incomplete in themselves. They are partially integrated through alternation and fully integrated through simultaneity.

Although not all points appear in each of the writings examined, most turn up with consistency from the outset of Steere's writing career with his highly popular *Prayer and Worship*, published in 1938. The rather explicit way in which Steere developed some of them leaves little room to doubt the accuracy of Copenhaver's conclusion.

I hope this study of a central facet of Douglas Steere's thought and contribution will awaken others to a person of great religious importance whose work has thus far received less attention than it deserves. Many of the great and near great thinkers, and just ordinary saints, of this century have sought his company and reveled in his companionship and conversation. If this book challenges you to join that privileged company of friends, you will be fortunate indeed, for you will not go away without being blessed.

E. Glenn Hinson

PREFACE

As I have had to run this book through three different word processing systems in order to obtain the desired format, I have had to read it over and over. Regardless of how many times I read it, I always find Douglas Steere's writings spiritually nourishing. I expected to tire of them, but his writings always "speak to my condition," as the Quakers say. For those who are not familiar with Steere's work, the textual analysis will offer frequent opportunities to sample his writings. On the other hand, those who have read and reveled in his writings will be able to examine the way his religious thought has developed.

This book is essentially an updated version of my 1986 doctoral dissertation at the Catholic University of America. For some time I considered "popularizing" the work for broader consumption, but upon further reflection, I decided to publish it in its present format. I believe Steere's work deserves the serious theological analysis that this approach allows. On the other hand, Steere does not write as an academic theologian (i.e., he does not write primarily for the academy or for other theologians) so his writings have an accessibility that is rare in someone of his intellectual stature. For this reason, the educated layperson should be able to benefit from this work, as well as the religious or theological scholar.

Five theses presented in the Introduction of the book serve as a device for organizing the investigation of Steere's approach to the relation of prayer and social responsibility. In the second chapter, which examines Steere's writings over a period of fifty years, some variation on the theses occurs in each work. For readers so inclined, that chapter may serve as a type of *lectio divina* (spiritual reading) on the theme of prayer and action. For the more analytical reader, it offers insight into the development of Steere's approach to the problem.

Steere wrote most of his books and articles before the current sensitivity about gender exclusive language. I have decided to quote him just as he wrote, but, in all my writing, I have sought to use gender inclusive language.

It is my hope that this work will prove useful for a variety of purposes. First, for readers interested in Douglas Steere's thought, the book reveals the key sources for his thought and the way in which his ideas have developed over the course of his writing career. Second, for readers interested in Quaker spirituality, the work offers a critical examination of the spiritual writings of a key twentieth century Quaker thinker and creates a dialogue between a classical Quaker and a liturgical approach to spiritual formation. Third, as Steere has been a pioneer in ecumenical spirituality, the book provides insights into the theology that underlies his ecumenical and interfaith initiatives and evaluates his ecumenical leadership. Fourth, for those readers involved in giving and receiving spiritual direction, the book conveys Steere's wise spiritual guidance on a key concern of contemporary Christian spirituality. Fifth, for those teaching courses in Christian spirituality or American religious thought, the book may supplement a more general text as a case study of a perennial problem for Christian spirituality. The analysis of Steere's key sources (von Hügel, Woolman, and Kierkegaard) has the value of situating Steere's spirituality in the broad stream of Christian spirituality that nourished him. Finally, for all seekers of truth, Steere's life and writings offer companionship and counsel for the long journey.

INTRODUCTION

A perennial problem of Christian spirituality has been that of relating prayer and social responsibility. Although there are few examples[1] of a complete disjunction of these two elements of Christian existence, a functional disjunction is fairly common. There are Christians who appear to feel that their entire social responsibility is fulfilled by periodic financial contributions to the church, obeying the laws of the land, and caring for those within their immediate network of relations. They emphasize the importance of orthodoxy, worship, and personal devotions. On the other hand, there are those Christians who have little or no time for prayer or worship because they feel they love and serve God best by working for justice for the oppressed. Prayer and worship are a waste of time and are, in fact, offensive to God as long as injustice exists. Of course, both these descriptions are caricatures of two approaches to Christian life, but they are not so distorted that one cannot recognize certain forms of evangelical piety[2] in the former and the more extreme forms of social activism in the latter.

As these approaches to Christian discipleship represent two poles of Christian existence, this study will sketch briefly their historical development in the twentieth century. Until the early part of the twentieth century the majority of North American Protestants practiced an evangelical or holiness piety. Using Urban Holmes' phenomenology of prayer, this spirituality can be described as highly affective and kataphatic.[3] In some cases this piety was wedded to efforts for social change, e.g., the abolitionist movement.[4] More often it divorced personal piety from the struggle for social justice.[5] With the rise of liberalism and the social gospel, evangelical piety lost much of its power and influence. Protestantism was roughly divided into two camps: the liberals, who embraced Biblical criticism and the social gospel; and the evangelicals (including the Fundamentalists) who rejected Biblical criticism and emphasized personal piety. A further setback for evangelical piety was occasioned by the triumph of neo-orthodoxy in the nineteen-thirties.

In its concern to move Protestant theology beyond the subjectivity of liberalism as it had developed in the theology of Schleiermacher and Ritschl, neo-orthodoxy often viewed efforts aimed at personal sanctity as superfluous, if not dangerous.[6] Neo-orthodoxy focused its attention on the revelation of God's saving action in Jesus Christ rather than the human religious experience. In spite of the valuable works by Barth, Brunner, and Bonhoeffer on the spiritual life,[7] neo-orthodoxy created a climate of suspicion concerning experiential Christianity.

This attitude reigned in mainline Protestantism until the late nineteen-sixties. During the nineteen-sixties, when liberal social activism reached its apex, a resurgence of evangelical piety began and expressed itself in the Jesus movement and the charismatic renewal. During the nineteen-seventies a major shift occurred in the way these two camps expressed themselves. The evangelicals, who previously emphasized personal piety, began to express a more active interest in social issues. The formation of Evangelicals for Social Action and the Sojourners community are two examples of this shift among the "new" evangelicals.[8] Among conservative evangelicals, the Moral Majority exemplified the new political activism. On the other hand, the liberals who had been emphasizing the social agenda of Christian faith displayed a growing appetite for experiential religion. The establishment of the Shalem Institute for Spiritual Formation and the Upper Room's Academy for Spiritual Formation provides evidence of this shift in liberal Protestantism. Although the political activism of socially conservative evangelicals has waned somewhat in the late eighties and early nineties (as seen in the demise of the Moral Majority), these broad trends have continued. The mainline fascination with spirituality (seen in the growing number of courses in spirituality offered at mainline seminaries) shows no signs of abating. Today evangelicals call for social responsibility and socially concerned liberals call for a renewal of spirituality. "Few Christians today defend either a personal piety that does not express itself in active concern for others or a social activism that is not nourished by a personal faith."[9]

From this brief historical survey, one may be tempted to think that the problem has been solved now that there appears to be a near universal concern for a Christianity that includes both the personal and social dimensions of the faith. The danger remains, however, that these two movements in the Christian life may be conceived as "mutually supplementary, as if Christian life were a matter of putting together two aspects that are inherently unrelated."[10] In such a bifurcation the true wholeness of Christian existence is destroyed, and it is not restored when the two are put together.[11]   Although there have been efforts to define this relation, it appears that this remains one of the major theological tasks of this era.[12] As long as this relation remains amorphous or confused, the potential for mutual enrichment will be diminished.

The way in which people pray is indicative of their whole religious attitude. Gordon Allport has distinguished two types of religious attitudes. Urban Holmes has summarized Allport's thesis in this way:

> Intrinsic religion is characterized by health. Religious faith is a source of the growth and expansion of the horizons of our knowing. It enables risk. Extrinsic religion is defensive. It encourages a person to exclude others and may even breed a kind of paranoia, as exemplified in the mass suicides of the People's Temple in Guyana in November of 1978.[13]

Prayer may also be intrinsic or extrinsic. Another way of expressing this is to say that prayer may be transformative (changing values and broadening social vision) or manipulative (seeking divine support for one's own convictions, leading to a restricted social vision). Here the relatedness of prayer and social responsibility becomes clearer, but the relationship is still amorphous. How does prayer transform values and broaden social vision?

This study will contribute to a more adequate understanding and explication of the relation of prayer and social responsibility through an analysis and critical evaluation of Douglas V. Steere's treatment of this problem. Most of Steere's writings occur between 1938 and 1973, a period when mainline Protestantism eschewed personal piety. In spite of this, Steere's work has had broad ecumenical appeal. He is one Protestant leader who has been able to articulate a spiritual theology that weds contemplative prayer with a responsible social vision. As his theology draws deeply on his own Quaker tradition, this Introduction will describe briefly the Quaker contribution in this area.

Since its beginning in the mid-seventeenth century, the Religious Society of Friends has been known for its interest in experiential religion and its prophetic social engagement. Louis Bouyer describes early Quaker spirituality in this way:

> Intrepid submission to the letter of the gospel; truthfulness, nonviolence, a permanent disposition . . . to devote themselves to the unfortunate with the same humble simplicity as their waiting for the Spirit--alike in silence and solitude as in communal recollection: these things were their great safeguards.[14]

Although it would be unwieldy to describe here the Quaker influence in social reforms, even a partial list would include its work for prison reform, humane treatment of the mentally disturbed, freedom of religion, the abolition of slavery, and just dealings with Native Americans. During the twentieth century the American Friends Service Committee (AFSC) has been the social action agency of American Quakers and it has had a distinguished record. The AFSC, along with its British counterpart, received the 1947 Nobel Peace Prize for its relief efforts during the two world wars. It is in this tradition that Steere has developed his treatment of the relation of prayer and social responsibility.

Although Steere is firmly grounded in the Quaker tradition, he draws deeply on his studies in Roman Catholic spiritual theology and Western philosophy (especially existentialism as it is expressed in the writings of Pascal, Kierkegaard, Marcel, Maritain, and Unamuno). His deep appreciation for Roman Catholic spirituality is not uncommon in the Quaker community.

> It may seem surprising, but is not really so very odd, that Quakerism has provided the environment in the heart of Protestantism in which people have been most ready to give a warm and instinctive welcome to the highest teachings of the Catholic mystics . . .[15]

Steere is indeed one in whom the highest teaching of the Catholic mystics is welcomed. He is especially influenced by Friedrich von Hügel, whose work was the subject of his doctoral dissertation at Harvard University. He frequently utilizes these sources (Catholic spiritual theology and Western philosophy) in developing his approach to the problem of relating prayer and social responsibility.

As Steere's theological and literary sources will be the subject of later chapters, this Introduction seeks to give only the briefest background on these sources. It will also provide some indication of Steere's aptitude for dealing with this problem, though a more complete treatment of his career will follow in the next chapter.

Parker Palmer has noted, in his brief biography of Douglas and Dorothy Steere, that the three areas where Douglas Steere has made his greatest contributions are ecumenical relations, spiritually-rooted social concerns, and scholarship and publication. Although this paper will show that Steere's spiritual theology grounds his approach to ecumenism and interfaith encounter, the key interest here is with his efforts to unite contemplative prayer and a responsible social vision. The purpose here is to establish that the problem of relating prayer and social responsibility has been a major concern in his writing and that, in theory and practice, he has articulated and embodied an approach that has earned him great respect.

Steere has been a career professor of philosophy at Haverford College, but the overwhelming majority of his writings have been in the area of spirituality. Elton Trueblood, in his book *A People Called Quakers* (1966), described Steere as the leading living Quaker devotional writer and noted his reputation as scholarly interpreter of devotional classics.[16] Elizabeth Gray Vining, an important Quaker author, has written in the preface to *Quaker Spirituality*, one of the volumes in the Paulist Press series of Classics in Western Spirituality, that

> No other modern Friend is so well qualified as Douglas Steere to make this selection or to write the Introduction that opens up Quaker thought and practice and explains its varying elements, its ways of worship and action.[17]

These comments reflect Steere's reputation within the Religious Society of Friends.

Steere has also held many important positions and received honors that indicate his intellectual, organizational, and spiritual gifts. He was appointed a Rhodes Scholar in 1925, graduated with a Ph.D. in philosophy from Harvard University via Oxford in 1931, and assumed Rufus Jones' chair in philosophy at Haverford in 1934. He helped found Pendle Hill (a Quaker center for religious and social studies) in 1930 and, in the nineteen-fifties and sixties, chaired its board for sixteen years. He acted as president of the American Theological Society in 1945-46, taught as Harry Emerson Fosdick Visiting Professor at Union Theological Seminary in 1961-62, and served as the official Quaker Observer at three sessions of Vatican II and at the Anglican Lambeth Conference in 1968. He was a member of the Board of Managers of the American Friends Service Committee for fifteen years (serving ten years as chairman of the Work Camp Committee and organizing Quaker relief work in Finland in 1945). He acted as chairman of the North American Committee of the International Fellowship of Reconciliation for twelve years and worked on committees of the National and World Council of Churches. He chaired the Friends World Committee for Consultation from 1964-1970, established (with Godfrey Diekmann) the Ecumenical Institute for Spirituality, and convened the first Zen-Christian Colloquium in Japan and a similar Hindu-

Christian Colloquium in India.

Steere has been in great demand as a lecturer. Some of his more important lectures include: the 1942 Ingersoll Lecture and the 1943 William Belden Noble Lectures at Harvard, the Swarthmore Lecture in 1955 for the London Yearly Meeting, the Rauschenbusch Lectures (lectures in Christianity in its social expression and application) at Colgate-Rochester Divinity School, and the Stone Lectures at Princeton Theological Seminary in 1957. For his record of service and publication, he has received honorary doctorates from five institutions of higher education and the 1981 Upper Room Citation.

This impressive record of service and honors gives some indication of Steere's aptitude for dealing with the problem at hand and reveals how central social responsibility is in his life work. Although most of his writings and lectures deal with the "intensification of the life of God in the individual hearts of men,"[18] a large part of his organizational energies have been invested in social concerns. This apparent dichotomy disappears when it is realized that Steere never writes about prayer or contemplation without relating it to a costly engagement of social responsibility. In a review of Steere's 1982 book, *Together in Solitude*, Wendy Wright notes that, "Steere is steeped in both the quiet attentiveness to divine inspiration and the responsible social vision that characterize the best of Quaker thought."[19] Steere's influence, and the centrality of his concern to relate personal and social religion, is visible in the choice of topics for the first Zen-Christian Colloquium in Japan that he convened on behalf of the Friends World Committee for Consultation. As Yukio Irie notes in *A Zen Christian Pilgrimage: The Fruits of Ten Annual Colloquia in Japan 1967-1976* (which is dedicated to Douglas and Dorothy Steere), "We made the general theme of the first Colloquium twofold: 1) My Spiritual Journey; 2) A Believer's Social Responsibility Today."[20] Other references could be made, but these should suffice for demonstrating that the relation of prayer and social responsibility has been a central concern for Steere and that his experience gives him a unique perspective on this problem.

This Introduction has sought to present a problem for Christian spirituality which goes all the way back to the gospels, e.g., the conflict between Martha and Mary. It is a problem that has been addressed with varying degrees of adequacy throughout church history and, in the twentieth century, confronts us with a special urgency. Historically, the Quakers have provided one of the more satisfying answers to the problem and, in our day, Douglas Steere has articulated that answer in dialogue with modern theology, philosophy, and culture. It is an answer that deserves analysis and evaluation.

Several factors make a study of Steere's approach to the problem of relating prayer and social responsibility especially relevant for contemporary spirituality. Faced with the current interest in spirituality, many mainline Protestants fear a return to pietism while critical theologians, both Catholic and Protestant, are concerned to avoid subjectivism and "privatized" religion. With the resurgence of evangelical Christianity, the spirituality of Steere is especially apt in providing guidance for those seeking to avoid the pitfalls of a disengaged pietism or a restricted social vision.

This study will also contribute to a critical appraisal of Steere's spiritual theology and show him to be a key figure in contemporary spirituality. Some familiarity with Steere's person and work is valuable for complete understanding of twentieth century American spirituality. His contributions to ecumenism and interfaith encounter are significant and, although they will not be the focus of this book, his spiritual theology will be shown to provide a foundation for his ecumenical and interfaith writings.

Having introduced the problem, the author who engages the problem, and the benefits to be gained from studying his treatment of it, this study will proceed with a brief description of the tasks involved in each chapter.

The first chapter, "Steere in Context," seeks to situate Steere's approach to the relation of prayer and social responsibility in the context of his relation to the Religious Society of Friends, the times in which he has lived, and the intellectual and theological currents that influenced him. This background will also help in discerning how his thought has developed during his long career as a writer and lecturer.

The key sources for this biographical and intellectual sketch are 1.) Steere's writings, which often contain biographical information, 2.) Parker Palmer's biographical chapter on Steere and E. Glenn Hinson's essay in the *Christian Century* (1985), "Douglas V. Steere: Irradiator of the 'Beams of Love'," 3.) references to Steere in various publications, and 4.) personal conversations with Dr. Steere.

The second chapter, "Steere's Treatment of the Relation of Prayer and Social Responsibility," will examine Steere's writings in order to determine the key principles of his approach to the problem. As Steere's writing has extended over fifty years and has been addressed to many diverse audiences, this study will organize Steere's writing and teaching on this subject into five broad theses. Each thesis represents a theme that is developed repeatedly throughout Steere's long engagement with this problem. The theses are intended to provide a structure within which Steere's approach can be described and analyzed. The study will examine chronologically five key books and several pamphlets and articles to determine how each develops one or more of these theses. Each significant manuscript will be analyzed in the light of its historical, social, and personal context. The value of this method is that it will yield insights into how Steere's thought developed in relation to these key factors. In this chapter, the study will focus on text analysis rather than attempt to trace Steere's literary sources.

The theses that will organize this study are: 1.) Prayer (especially corporate prayer) deepens an awareness of creatureliness and evokes a consciousness of solidarity with all persons and all creation. Out of this perceived solidarity "seeds of concern" surface in the consciousness of the one who prays. 2.) Prayer nurtures an awareness of God's infinite concern for every person and fosters a willingness to participate in God's redemptive order. 3.) Prayer cleanses action, work, and service of their repetitive nature and restores their frame of meaning. 4.) Acts of social responsibility clarify and test the genuineness of prayer. 5.) Both prayer and social responsibility are incomplete in themselves. They are partially integrated alternation and fully integrated through simultaneity.

The first thesis deals primarily with awareness, the second with willingness, the third, fourth, and fifth with execution. The last three could perhaps be collapsed but have been separated for the sake of clarity.

So that there will be no misunderstanding of the terms employed in this study, it will be necessary to define the scope of two key terms. For the purposes of this study, the broad term "prayer" (unless otherwise qualified) will include intercession, adoration, petition, listening prayer, and contemplation. The term "social responsibility" will be understood as concrete expressions of care for some part of God's creation and it will include action, work, and service. These definitions are necessary because Steere approaches the problem from a great variety of perspectives, e.g., work and contemplation, prayer and action, inward and outward journey, etc.

Chapter Three, "Steere's Assimilation of von Hügel and Woolman," will analyze Steere's assimilation and incorporation of the thought of these two mentors. More specifically, the chapter will examine the role these authors play in the formation of the five theses that outline Steere's approach to the problem.

The fourth chapter, "Other Literary and Theological Sources," will broaden the search for Steere's sources, paying particular attention to the influence of Kierkegaard in Steere's existential realism. This chapter will also consider the question of Steere's dependence on these sources for his treatment of the relation of prayer and social responsibility.

Chapter Five is entitled "A Critical Evaluation of Steere's Spiritual Theology." It will consider the value of Steere's treatment in dialogue with the contemporary authors[21] who are making the greatest contribution to understanding this issue. Steere's treatment will also be analyzed in the light of traditional issues for spiritual theology, i.e., the role of ritual and liturgy in the formation of Christian community and Christian character, the issues of quietism and enthusiasm, and concerns about private revelation.

In the sixth chapter, "Steere's Contribution to Contemporary Spirituality," the critical perspective gained in Chapter Five will yield to a broader appraisal of Steere's leadership in ecumenical spirituality and his treatment of the relation of prayer and social responsibility. His approach to this issue will be examined to determine what it offers contemporary Christian spirituality as it seeks a more adequate understanding of this enigmatic relationship.

NOTES FOR THE INTRODUCTION

[1]Perhaps St. Symeon Stylite (389-459) can be regarded as one who completely divorced prayer and social responsibility. According to tradition, he remained on a pillar for thirty-seven years. Fundamentalists, until recently, have also divorced piety and social responsibility. On the other extreme are the advocates of religionless Christianity who follow only the "moral" teachings of Jesus.

[2]The term "evangelical piety" is used here to represent the broad range of Christian discipleship within the evangelical Christian community. Positively, it includes leaders like Jonathan Edwards and John Wesley, who were able to wed deep personal faith with rigorous theological understanding. Negatively, evangelical pietism is a reaction to a sterile theology and often replaces theology with feeling, e.g., Count von Zinzendorf. For evangelical attitudes toward social responsibility see footnote 4 & 8.

[3]The term "kataphatic" represents an orientation to prayer that emphasizes the use of imagination and images. It is at the opposite pole from "apophatic" prayer that advocates imageless, wordless, emptying prayer. Two other poles for analyzing prayer are the affective and speculative orientations in prayer. The affective emphasizes the heart and feelings; the speculative emphasizes the mind and intellect. See Urban Holmes, *A History of Christian Spirituality* (New York: The Seabury Press, 1981).

[4]The abolitionist movement is only one of several issues that engaged socially minded evangelicals of the nineteenth century. Donald W. Dayton has charted evangelical social concerns (including evangelical feminism) in his book *Discovering an Evangelical Heritage* (New York: Harper and Row, 1976).

[5]Walter Rauschenbusch and the first generation of the social gospel are an exception to this judgment. Rauschenbusch and his colleagues approached social issues from a deep, personal, Biblical faith.

[6]For an analysis of neo-orthodoxy's approach to subjectivity and objectivity see Emil Brunner's *The Divine-Human Encounter*, trans. Amandus W. Loos (Philadelphia: The Westminster Press, 1943). The thrust of Brunner's thesis is that neo-orthodoxy has attempted to move beyond the subjectivity of pietism and the objectivity of Orthodoxy to a fresh experience of Biblical faith.

[7]Besides Brunner's book mentioned above, see: Karl Barth, *Prayer*, 2nd ed., ed. Don Saliers, trans. Sara Terrien (Philadelphia: Westminster Press, 1985) and Dietrich Bonhoeffer, *Life Together* (New York: Harper and Row, 1952).

[8]This shift among evangelicals parallels an analogous shift toward abolitionism among nineteenth century evangelicals. Again, see Donald Dayton, footnote 4 above. For an analysis of the growing social activism among contemporary evangelicals see: Robert Booth Fowler, *A New Engagement: Evangelical Political Thought, 1966-1976* (Grand Rapids, Michigan: William B. Eerdmans Publishing Company, 1982) and Richard Quebedeaux, *The Young Evangelicals: Revolution in Orthodoxy* (New York: Harper and Row, 1974). Quebedeaux distinguishes between

separatist fundamentalism, open fundamentalism, establishment evangelicalism, and new evangelicalism. Fowler writes of mainstream (*Christianity Today*), moderate (Carl Henry), reform minded (Church of the Savior), and radical (the Sojourners community) evangelicals.

[9]John Cobb, "The Identity of Christian Spirituality and Global Consciousness," Unpublished paper written for the faculty of the School of Theology at Claremont, Ca., Fall 1975, p. 1.

[10]Ibid., p. 1.

[11]Ibid., p. 1.

[12]In addition the work of John Cobb, there are a number of authors who are addressing this issue today; specifically, William Willimon, Stanley Hauerwas, and Donald Saliers, Robert McAfee Brown, and Donal Dorr. The work of Willimon, Hauerwas, and Saliers, representing a fairly cohesive approach, will be included in the critical evaluation of Steere in Chapter Five. During the middle decades of this century, Thomas Merton and Steere appear to be the main American authors addressing this issue. The key work by Donal Dorr is *Spirituality and Justice* (Maryknoll, New York: Orbis Press, 1984). Robert McAfee Brown's key contribution is *Spirituality and Justice: Overcoming the Great Fallacy* (Philadelphia: The Westminster Press, 1988).

[13]Urban T. Holmes, *A History of Christian Spirituality* (New York: The Seabury Press, 1981), p. 6.

[14]Louis Bouyer, *Orthodox Spirituality and Protestant and Anglican Spirituality*, in *A History of Christian Spirituality III* (New York: The Seabury Press, 1969), p. 163.

[15]Ibid., p. 163.

[16]Elton D. Trueblood, *The People Called Quakers* (New York: Harpers, 1966), p. 222.

[17]Elizabeth Gray Vining, Preface to *Quaker Spirituality* ed. Douglas V. Steere, (New York: Paulist Press, 1984), p. x.

[18]Douglas V. Steere, *On Beginning from Within* (New York: Harper and Row Publishers, 1943), p. vii.

[19]Wendy M. Wright, "Review of *Together in Solitude*," *Theology Today*, October '83, 40:362-364.

[20]*A Zen-Christian Pilgrimage: The Fruits of Ten Annual Colloquia in Japan* (The Zen-Christian Colloquium, 1981), p. 6.

[21]See footnote 12 above.

CHAPTER ONE

STEERE IN CONTEXT

This biographical chapter will sketch the context in which Steere's spiritual theology has developed. The first section of the chapter will outline the formative factors in his intellectual and religious development. The second section will examine Steere's involvement in the execution of two Quaker concerns. Both sections will contribute to a contextual understanding of Steere's treatment of the relation of prayer and social responsibility.

Steere's Intellectual and Religious Development

Douglas Steere was born on August 31, 1901, in Harbor Beach, Michigan. When he was two years old, his family moved to Detroit where his father worked as a mail clerk for a railway. The family was not rooted deeply in a religious community, "But eventually the family began attending church, and during the years of Douglas' youth were involved with the Methodist, the Presbyterian, and the Evangelical and Reformed traditions."[1]

Steere left Detroit in 1918 to attend Michigan Agricultural College (now known as Michigan State University). He was influenced in this decision by an uncle "who was convinced that the future of our society lay in scientific farming."[2] Steere did well in his studies, but they did not satisfy his hunger for answers to the deeper questions of life. When he completed his degree, he borrowed $1,000 and left for Harvard to study philosophy.[3]

During his early semesters at Harvard, Steere felt overwhelmed by loneliness and inadequacy. The answers he had hoped to find at Harvard seemed more elusive than ever. In a recent conversation, Steere confided with me that during the depths of his despair "the river was beginning to look pretty good." In the midst of this struggle, Steere was invited to spend a weekend with a group from the newly-founded Oxford Movement. Although he never joined the group, he was influenced by the periods of meditation which the Movement called "Quiet Times."

This discipline grew in Douglas' own life into extended periods of "listening prayer," in an effort to come into direct, experiential contact with the Guide whose still, small voice was so easily lost in the thunder of philosophical systems.[4]

Supplied with this discipline, Steere was able to continue his studies and hope that, eventually, there would be some way of reconciling his spiritual life with his philosophical studies.

While at Harvard, Steere became acquainted, through classes or personal contacts, with some of the leading philosophers of the day, e.g., William Ernest Hocking, Alfred North Whitehead, and Clarence I. Lewis. Of these three, Clarence I. Lewis, with his brilliant insights in the field of ethics, influenced Steere most.

In the spring of 1925, Steere decided to take his doctoral comprehensive exams, even though he had some misgivings about his readiness; however, he passed his exams in psychology, history of philosophy, logic, and ethics. Later in the Spring he completed his course work and graduated with an M.A. in philosophy.

It was also in early 1925 that Steere began making plans to study at Oxford, having been accepted for an appointment as a Rhodes Scholar. It seems, however, that all the heady events of 1925 were eclipsed by a "blind date" with Dorothy Lou MacEachron. They were able to see each other only three times in 1925, but were engaged in 1927 when Steere returned after two years at Oxford. They were married in 1929.

During Steere's three years at Oxford, he was drawn gradually toward the Quaker community. His first contact was quite by accident. As a result of a minor back injury caused by rowing, Steere visited Dr. Henry T. Gillett, a Quaker physician who was later to write Rufus Jones about Steere. Dr. Gillett was a radiant Quaker and introduced Steere to Neave Brayshaw and other "weighty" English Friends. Although Steere found the Oxford Meeting dull and stuffy, he first experienced a "covered"[5] Quaker meeting at one of Canon Streeter's reading parties.

The Oxford years exposed Steere to a host of notable scholars. The Oxford rhythm of two eight week terms followed by a six-week reading period allowed Steere to travel frequently to the continent. Some of the notable English and continental scholars Steere met or heard lecture are: Evelyn Underhill, C. C. J. Webb, C. H. Dodd, John Macmurray, Rudolph Otto, Rudolph Bultmann, Friedrich Heiler, and Martin Heidegger. John Macmurray, who was lecturing at Balliol College, made an especially strong impression on Steere. Steere and Macmurray became good friends, meeting at long intervals and reading each others' books. Macmurray's personalism, probing the self to its ground of mystery, has deeply influenced Steere's spiritual theology. Steere was also attracted by Macmurray's passion for community and human solidarity.

Despite this contact with such an impressive host of living scholars, the ones who made the deepest impression on Steere were encountered through reading. During his time at Oxford he decided to write his Harvard dissertation on

Baron Friedrich von Hügel. In reading von Hügel, Steere was first introduced to Soren Kierkegaard, whom von Hügel described as a "passionate prophet of the transcendence of God." These two authors supplied the philosophical foundation for Steere's existential realism, a philosophical stance to which Steere has consistently adhered.

Existential realism does not represent a philosophical school that won Steere's intellectual allegiance; rather, it is a category that Steere created to express his philosophical stance. None of his professors at Harvard or Oxford advocated such a stance; it is Steere's own effort to unite the critical realism that he found so persuasive in the writings of von Hügel with Kierkegaard's existentialism, which he valued so highly for its usefulness in probing the depths of the subject. The development of this philosophical perspective will receive closer attention in Chapters Three and Four.

Steere returned to the United States in 1928 to teach philosophy at Haverford College. In 1929, after he and Dorothy MacEachron were married, she joined him at Haverford. Describing this period, Parker Palmer writes:

> By accepting a life and work at Haverford College, the Steeres clearly aligned themselves with the Quaker community and its concerns. In 1929, Douglas moved even closer to the Quaker circle by becoming a member of the group which envisioned and then established Pendle Hill. Both Douglas and Dorothy had been deeply impressed with the work of the American Friends Service Committee, and by 1930 Douglas had been made a member of its Board and chairperson of one of its sections.[6]

The Steeres' movement toward Quakerism was given added impetus by their congenial experience as attenders at Haverford Monthly Meeting; by their encounter with Henry T. Hodgkin, the first director of Pendle Hill, whom Douglas describes as "the greatest Christian I have ever had close communication with;" and by their shared reading of John Woolman's *Journal* in the Winter of 1932. The following Spring, Douglas and Dorothy joined the Society of Friends through Haverford Meeting, . . .[7]

Now officially "Quakers," the Steeres began their long and productive ministry as Friends.

As "convinced" Quakers the Steeres felt little sense of attachment to either the Hicksite or Orthodox[8] branches of Quakerism, which were the dominant branches of Quakerism around Philadelphia. Although the breach between these two branches was closing, the division still remained. In 1930, the Steeres joined with a small group that reopened Radnor Meeting. They remained members of Haverford Meeting until Radnor Meeting was properly organized in 1936 and, then, transferred their membership there. As the people meeting to reopen Radnor Meeting came from both the Hicksite and Orthodox branches, these Friends were determined to form a United Meeting. When the Meeting was approved in 1936, it opened as the Radnor *United* Meeting. The breach between these two branches of Quakerism was finally closed in the mid-fifties.

In his Introduction to *Quaker Spirituality*, Steere identifies the type of Quakerism into which he was introduced at Haverford.

> I am not a birthright Quaker but became a Friend "by convincement" some fifty years ago. I came, at that time, into the classical, unprogrammed, nonpastoral, silent-meeting-for-worship type of Quakerism that marked the first two centuries of its life.[9]

This type of Quakerism is to be distinguished from the pastoral (some would say "evangelical")[10] type of Quakerism that predominates in the mid-West and West. It is the classical (some would say "mystical") form of Quakerism that captured Steere's allegiance. His commitment to classical Quakerism is apparent in the selections he chose for the volume on Quaker spirituality.[11] Steere's Haverford College colleagues, Rufus Jones and Thomas Kelly, figure prominently in his selections. Both Jones and Kelly are considered Quaker mystics, but Steere does not consider himself a mystic; rather, like Evelyn Underhill, Steere prefers to say, "I have had my times of slowing down." Nevertheless, in the Society of Friends, Steere is considered a mystic.

Despite Steere's commitment to classical Quakerism, there is an evangelical dimension to his personal experience that should be noted. In *Work and Contemplation* he writes about the hunger for forgiveness and illustrates this hunger from his own experience.

> I dreamed one night recently that I had killed a man and the great despair came over me now of being cut off from ever again approaching God and my fellows in Him. Then as swiftly came the realization, "Now you must throw yourself on Jesus Christ. Now you are a sinner like all other murderers whom only his ransoming life can redeem." And the great evangelical experience took on fresh reality for me.[12]

As this experience came long after Steere's commitment to the Christian faith, this passage should not be interpreted as an expression of a "born again" experience, but it does indicate the evangelical aspect of Steere's spirituality.

Although politics never became a consuming passion for Steere, in the early 1930s he joined the Fellowship of Christian Socialists and, in 1932, he supported the candidacy of Norman Thomas. His efforts to insert the socialist alternative into the Republican-Democratic dialogue in the autumn of 1932 met with little success in the predominantly Republican Haverford community. His political activity since that time has been primarily private.

When Steere finished reading Woolman's *Journal* in the winter of 1932, the formative years of his intellectual and religious pilgrimage came to a close. With the exception of Romano Guardini, Steere had encountered the key authors who were to shape his career and writings, viz., Baron Friedrich von Hügel, Soren Kierkegaard, and John Woolman. His religious quest, though never finished, had found permanent roots in the Society of Friends.

Steere also became established in his professional life during the early thirties. He finished his doctoral dissertation in 1931 and received the Harvard Ph.D. in the same year. In 1933, Haverford College invited Steere to assume Rufus Jones' chair in the philosophy department. "To give him time and space for preparation, the College granted Douglas a sabbatical leave in 1933-34."[13]

Steere chose to spend his sabbatical year in Germany at the invitation of Dr. Maria Schluter-Hermkes, who offered to open to him the heart of German Catholic spirituality. Her husband was able to arrange for Steere to spend a month at the Benedictine monastery of Maria Laach. During the month at Maria Laach, Steere "found himself moving away from classical Protestantism (with its overemphasis on human depravity and its underemphasis upon God's passionate caring) but was drawn more deeply toward the mystical heart of Catholicism."[14] Steere's spiritual guide at Maria Laach was Pater Damasus Winzen, who was later to be become founder and prior of Mt. Saviour monastery in New York.

Following his month at Maria Laach, Steere spent two months in Tubingen studying with Karl Heim (a Lutheran theologian who was one of the earliest Protestant theologians to be influenced by Martin Buber's personalistic, encounter existentialism) and two and a half months in Berlin. While in Berlin, Steere attended the lectures of Nicholai Hartmann, came to know Romano Guardini, and became both a client and student of Fritz Kunkel. Dorothy Steere joined Douglas in Berlin and they were together for the remainder of the sabbatical year.

Steere had also determined to undertake the translation of one of Kierkegaard's works during the sabbatical year. When Steere asked Eduard Geismar, a leading Kierkegaard scholar, to suggest one of Kierkegaard's spiritual books for translation, Geismar unhesitatingly recommended *Purity of Heart*. This work of translation, along with travel and Quaker visitation, occupied the remainder of the sabbatical year.

During their time in Germany, the Steeres witnessed the rise of Fascism.

Everywhere Douglas and Dorothy went they found Jews and socialists and people in the labor movement coming to Quaker centers for consolation, advice and assistance.
    The work, of course, frequently placed Friends and their helpers under rigorous scrutiny from the political authorities. Viennese social workers who were working for the Quakers in distributing life-giving help to persecuted workers' families were regularly arrested and jailed for their efforts, and the Steeres themselves were detained briefly one day as a consequence of accompanying some of these Friends on their rounds."[15]

This involvement with the mission work of German Quakers marked the beginning of a life-time of traveling ministry for the Steeres. The contacts they established during the sabbatical year (in Germany, Denmark, and Norway) played a central role in their future traveling ministry.

This outline of Steere's life--through the 1934 sabbatical--has provided information about the formative intellectual and religious factors that shaped his life.   As Chapters Two, Three, and Four will analyze the development of his religious thought as it is expressed in his writings, it will not be necessary to devote more time to Steere's intellectual and religious development. Rather, the remainder of this chapter will be devoted to Steere's active life--his social leadership and ministry.

Two Key Concerns

Steere's scholarship, social leadership, and ministry have been an incarnation of his intellectual approach to the relation of prayer and social responsibility. He has carried out the "seeds of concern" that arise in prayer. His definitive concern has been to minister to the hungering souls of men and women. This concern finds expression in his writings, retreat work, lectures, and personal contacts. Its expression will be examined in the next chapter. There are other concerns, however, that cannot be adequately examined through his writings and they should not be overlooked. These concerns and their unfolding is part of the context in which Steere has expressed his spiritual theology.

It is hard to overestimate the role that the American Friends Service Committee and the Friends World Committee have played in the way in which Steere has expressed his key concerns. Steere acknowledges the influence of the AFSC, along with several other Quaker institutions and persons, in a paragraph he wrote for the *Friends Journal*. The *Friends Journal* asked several Quaker leaders to respond to the question, "To what degree does Quakerism influence your creativity?" Here is Steere's response.

I have no adequate instrument to clock the source of any creativity that I may have. As a convinced Friend who has had over 50 years in Quaker company, I have certainly, from the outset, been deeply influenced by the stimulus that both the American Friends Service Committee and its British counterpart have given me by their unflinching concerns for the needs of my fellows, and I have for a sizable piece of my life been drawn into shaping my life to have a small part in their outreach. Pendle Hill and the steady attendance at corporate silent meeting for worship in many parts of the world have renewed me again and again and laid on me fresh concerns to be carried out. In my own interior life, in my writing, and in my life as a teacher, these leadings have all had their part. My love for John Woolman, for Isaac Penington, for Rufus Jones, and for Henry Hodgkin has never dimmed and I am sure they are guests of my life that have quickened me again and again.[16]

Remembering that Steere became a member of the Board of Managers of the AFSC in 1930, it is not hard to imagine its formative influence in his approach to social concerns.

As was noted in the Introduction, Steere's first responsibility with the AFSC was to serve as chairman of the Work Camps Committee, which he did for ten years. Nevertheless, the concern that most shaped Steere's life from 1937-1948 is what he sometimes refers to as his "Finnish obsession." Here is Parker

Palmer's succinct outline of the execution of this concern.

That sabbatical trip to Germany in 1933-34 ended with a brief visit to Denmark and Norway in June of that year, marking the beginning of a social concern which was to occupy the Steeres throughout the war years and beyond. Although they were involved in Quaker relief work in Germany itself throughout World War II, Douglas developed a special concern for conditions in Scandinavia. So in the summer of 1937 he led a small "Quaker Embassy" to Norway [an embassy that was initially rejected by the AFSC] to meet with some of the cultural, religious, and political leaders of the Scandinavian countries.

Not only was that Embassy helpful in establishing the first Friends Meeting in Finland, but it also laid the groundwork for the post-war Quaker relief work so badly needed there. This work was initiated by Douglas himself under the sponsorship of the AFSC and in cooperation with the Finnish Christian Settlement Movement. When that work came to its conclusion in 1948, the seeds of friendship sown by those who participated in it came to a new fruition in the establishment in 1950 of a new international Folk High School called Viittakivi. Even today, Viittakivi continues to maintain a Quakerly presence for international harmony and understanding, and its ties with the Steeres remain close.[17]

What Parker Palmer does not mention is that, not only did Steere initiate Quaker relief work in Finland, Steere also played a key role in training the post-war relief workers. From 1943-45, he was director of the Graduate Reconstruction and Relief Training program at Haverford College.

The significance of Quaker post-war relief effort was recognized in 1947 by the award of the Nobel Peace Prize to the AFSC and its British counterpart. Henry J. Cadbury, chairman of the AFSC, accepted the award on behalf of the two groups. On November 1, 1947, *The New York Times* contained this summary of the Quaker effort.

Quakers will not fight or recognize war. But they brave death in battle and in disaster in every capacity but that of bearers of arms. Their ambulance corp, their relief workers, did the greatest work in the two world wars.[18]

Steere's work in training relief workers and in initiating the Finnish relief work was an important element in the Quaker relief effort.

The other key concern that has shaped Steere's life is his desire to foster mutual enrichment through ecumenical and interfaith encounter. His efforts in ecumenism have not been motivated by a desire to effect an institutional reunion of the divided Christian family. Neither has his work in interfaith understanding been oriented toward achieving theological agreement. Rather, in both cases, he has been extraordinarily successful in getting people together for spiritually enriching religious encounter. He has given his approach the title of "mutual irradiation." In such encounter, each religion seeks to

expose itself with great openness to the inward message of the other, as well as to share its own experience, and to trust that whatever is the truth in each experience will irradiate and deepen the experience of the other . . . mutual irradiation would try to provide the most congenial setting possible for releasing the deepest witness that the Buddhist or Muslim might make to his Christian companion, and that the Christian might make to his non-Christian friend.[19]

These words, written in 1968, reveal the essence of Steere's ecumenical and interfaith approach.

Steere's experience in ecumenical ventures predates his own efforts to establish ecumenical and interfaith gatherings. He served on the Federal Council of Churches' Commission of Theologians on Relations of the Church to War (1944-45) and the Commission on Atomic Warfare in Light of Christian Faith (1945-46). He also participated in the World Council of Churches' Commission on the Responsibility of Christian Churches for the Prevention of War in the Atomic Age (1956-60), which met several times in Geneva and once in Britain. Before Vatican II, Steere belonged to Una Sancta, the European movement that nurtured new relations between Protestants, Roman Catholics, and Eastern Orthodox.[20] He acted as the official Quaker observer at sessions two, three, and four of Vatican II where he worked "with peace-minded Roman Catholics to get the single line in Schema 13 acknowledging conscientious objection to war."[21]

Since 1962 Steere has been involved in initiating and organizing ecumenical and interfaith gatherings. In an effort to improve relations between Christians in the East and West, Steere "organized a group of 15 Americans and five European religious leaders who met their opposite numbers from Eastern Europe for an intimate conference in Karlsbad, Czechoslovakia."[22] During the Vatican II sessions, Steere met informally with Godfrey Diekmann and out of their conversations the Ecumenical Institute for Spirituality began to take form. In a recent telephone conversation, Dr. Diekmann told me that, during the third session of the Second Vatican Council, he and Steere were talking at a coffee bar when Steere expressed his view that the Council, while discussing theological, ecclesial, sacramental, and liturgical issues, was neglecting to discuss that which is closest to the heart--the spiritual life. Together they planned for the first meeting of the Ecumenical Institute for Spirituality. Diekmann referred affectionately to Steere as "Mr. Quaker" and spoke of him as "self-effacing and gentle."

The Ecumenical Institute for Spirituality began meeting annually in 1965 and Steere continues to be an active participant. Commenting on the Steeres' work in ecumenism, Parker Palmer writes:

Perhaps the strength and importance of the Quaker-Catholic connection which the Steeres have helped forge has not yet been fully appreciated. Today, as the American Bishops join with Friends and others in the anti-nuclear movement, I cannot help but credit the channels of conversation and prayer the Steeres have helped open between Catholics and Quakers through all these long years.[23]

The "channels of conversation and prayer" have not been limited to these formal efforts to encourage ecumenical understanding. Even more important are the spiritual friendships which the Steeres have cultivated over many years.

As early as 1960, Steere had a concern to gather Christians and Hindus together in India for what he called a Quaker Ashram, but it was never established. Even though the Quaker Ashram failed, Steere did not interpret the failure as a sign that his concern was misguided. Rather, in his Quaker understanding of the following out of a concern, an act of faithfulness that fails is just as important as one that succeeds. Every act leads to something else, and, as it turned out, his work on the Quaker Ashram prepared the way for a valuable Hindu-Christian encounter in 1967. This group of Hindu and Christian scholars met for a full week in the month of April at Ooctacamund in the South of India. The ecumenically chosen Christians included three Roman Catholics, one Syrian Orthodox, one Mar Thoma Bishop, four Protestants, and an Indian Quaker educator as Chairman. Two of the better known Christian participants were Bede Griffiths, an English Benedictine monk, and Father Klaus Klostermaier, a German Benedictine monk.[24]

In the case of Steere's concern for interfaith understanding, the Friends World Committee for Consultation served as the vehicle for the following out of his concern (just as the AFSC served as the vehicle for his Finnish concern).

No sooner did Vatican II end than Douglas turned his attention eastward to the need for deeper dialogue between Christians and the great religions of the East. Under the sponsorship of the Friends World Committee for Consultation (of which he was chairman from 1964 to 1970) Douglas spent April and May of 1966 traveling in Japan, meeting with Zen Buddhist and Christian leaders, and obtaining their endorsement for the first Zen-Christian Colloquium which was held in March 1967. During this same period he also arranged for a meeting of Hindus and Christians which was held in India in April of 1967. The Zen-Christian dialogues have continued annually to this day . . .[25]

Steere indicates that he has often been asked why the Quakers chose this small elite group, the Zen Buddhists, as their first partners in such an encounter. His response to this question reveals his own estimation of the Quaker role within the Christian community, as well as his reasons for seeking an encounter with Zen Buddhists.

Our choice could be justified on cultural grounds, because this group, although small in number, occupy [sic] a unique place in Japan, and are in many ways a living and highly articulate organ of the inward non-Western spiritual Japanese life. They are, as well, a group who may one day take a guiding role in re-kindling this spirit when the momentary [it does seem so "momentary" today] Japanese immersion in Western secularism has run its course. But sound as I believe these reasons for our choice to have been, it must also be confessed that Quakers found this a natural group to turn to, since for some time we have been in the most friendly relations with Zen Buddhists who as anti-liturgical, iconoclastic, unconventional witnesses to the spirit as opposed to the letter of the law have, in the Buddhist world, some marked similarities to Quakers in the Christian community.[26]

This answer discloses the affinity Steere felt for Zen Buddhism and indicates his conception of the Quaker posture within the Christian community.

William Johnston (professor at Sophia University) and Enomiya Lassalle, both members of the Society of Jesus, are two widely known scholars who participated in the Zen-Christian Colloquia. Evaluating Steere's leadership in the colloquia, Enomiya Lassalle writes:

> About twenty years after the war, when the spiritual turmoil had settled somewhat, Dr. Douglas Steere had the inspiration of forming a group of Christians and Zen-experts. Through great effort which included many private visits to both parties, he finally succeeded. At that time it was a most suitable way of promoting world peace. How indeed could world peace ever be established, unless peaceful relations were obtained between the world religions?
>
> The first gathering of this group made a deep impression which will never be forgotten by those who took part. It was a most estimable effort by Dr. Steere to promote better understanding and friendship between Japanese Zen and Christianity.[27]

This sketch of Steere's interfaith undertakings does not detail the enormous obstacles that had to be overcome to arrange for these gatherings. Nor does it mention the providential assistance that came to Steere in the most surprising ways. In Steere's understanding of the unfolding of a concern, the obstacles test and clarify the concern while the providential assistance makes the person carrying out the concern aware that he or she is not working alone.

Most important in the carrying out of all Steere's concerns has been his effort to focus on the personal. He is not only interested in providing food for the Finns, but also in establishing warm personal friendships with them. This is the key to Steere's peacemaking. For him, peace is "vital interaction."[28] His travels in relief work, in Quaker visitation, and in work for ecumenical and interfaith understanding are based on creating the bonds of friendship between peoples of other religions, races, and nations.

This biographical chapter would not be complete without a brief description of the Steeres' recent activities. I first met Douglas Steere in the fall of 1984, shortly before my dissertation committee approved my proposal for a dissertation on Steere's religious thought. Dr. Steere generously set aside the better part of a day for our conversations. We met in the morning at his college office and in the afternoon at his home on the Haverford campus. I remember being impressed by his *joi de vivre*, his humor, and his kindness. We continued to meet periodically while I was working on the dissertation. Since that time I have visited with the Steeres occasionally and exchanged letters regularly. My experience has confirmed what so many have said about the spiritual encouragement their friendship offers.

In my dissertation on Steere, which I was writing in 1985, I provided this brief account of his activities at the time.

At the age of eighty-four, Steere remains actively involved in the projects to which his life has been dedicated. During the academic year, the Steeres reside at a house on the campus of Haverford College (formerly the residence of Rufus Jones), where Steere is T. Wistar Brown Professor Emeritus of Philosophy. The Steeres spend a major portion of the summer months at their on home on Lake Michigan. Steere teaches as an adjunct professor in the Upper Room's Academy for Spiritual Formation in Nashville, Tennessee. He remains an active participant in the meetings of Ecumenical Institute for Spirituality. Tilden Edwards, one of the members of that institute, recently told me that, among the participants, Steere is still considered a "weighty" Friend, "a wonderful Christian gentleman--very balanced, very open." Steere continues to serve on the board of Pendle Hill, the Quaker center for religious and social studies. Both of the Steeres are in great demand as speakers and leaders of retreats. Steere continues his writing and has two works that are soon to be published by the Upper Room.[29]

Since that time the Steere's have moved to a lovely retirement center (The Quadrangle) just a few miles from the Haverford campus and quite close to their beloved Radnor Meeting. Although they have given up lecturing and leading retreats, they are quite active in the Radnor Meeting and in their retirement center.

Conclusion

This biographical sketch has charted Steere's intellectual and religious development along with his actions in following out two Quaker concerns. This knowledge will enrich an understanding of Steere's spiritual theology and the organizing theses. This biographical sketch also shows that his religious thought is not an intellectual abstraction, but rather a type of Quaker praxis arising out of his involvement with the American Friends Service Committee and the Friends World Committee for Consultation. The principles expressed in the organizing theses have guided Steere in a life of exemplary social responsibility.

NOTES FOR CHAPTER ONE

[1]Parker Palmer, "Douglas and Dorothy Steere: More than the Sum of the Parts" in *Living in the Light: Some Quaker Pioneers of the Twentieth Century*, ed. Leonard S. Kenworthy, (Kennett Square, Pa.: Friends General Conference and Quaker Publications, 1984), pp. 221-222.

[2]Ibid., p. 222.

[3]Ibid., p. 222.

[4]Ibid., p. 222.

[5]Here is Thomas Kelly's eloquent account of a "covered" or "gathered" meeting: See *Quaker Spirituality*, p. 312.

In the practice of group worship on the basis of silence come special times when the electric hush and solemnity and depth of power steals over the worshipers. A blanket of divine covering comes over the room, a stillness that can be felt is over all, and the worshipers are gathered into a unity and synthesis of life which is amazing indeed. A quickening Presence pervades us, breaking down some part of the special privacy and isolation of our individual lives and blending our spirits within a superindividual Life and Power. An objective, dynamic Presence enfolds us all, nourishes our souls, speaks glad, unutterable comfort within us, and quickens us in depths that had before been slumbering. The Burning Bush has been kindled in our midst, and we stand together on holy ground.

[6]Palmer, p. 226.

[7]Ibid., p. 226.

[8]Steere considers the division (1827) to be based primarily on personalities; however, the Hicksites are generally considered to be the more liberal, socially oriented camp while the Orthodox considered themselves more Biblically based and more in the true spirit of George Fox.

[9]Douglas V. Steere, Introduction to *Quaker Spirituality*, ed. Douglas V. Steere and preface by Elizabeth Gray Vining, (New York: Paulist Press, 1984), p. 3.

[10]For an analysis of "mystical" and "evangelical" Quakerism see Howard Brinton's, *Friends for 300 Years* (New York: Harpers, 1952).

[11]Review of *Quaker Spirituality* in *Quaker Religious Thought*, 21 (Summer 1985): 38-39.

[12]Douglas V. Steere, *Work and Contemplation* (New York: Harper and Brothers, 1957), p. 48.

[13]Palmer, p. 227.

[14]Ibid., p. 227.

[15]Ibid., p. 228.

[16]*Friends Journal*, 30 (November 15, 1984): 13.

[17]Palmer, p. 230. Other than Parker Palmer's account, Steere's travel letters, stored at the Quaker Collection at Haverford College, are the only available documentation of Steere's Finnish relief work.

[18]*New York Times*, November 1, 1947, p. 17, col. 7.

[19]Douglas V. Steere, *Mutual Irradiation: A Quaker View of Ecumenism* (Wallingford, Pa.: Pendle Hill Publications, 1971), p. 8.

[20]Ferner Nuhn, *Friends and the Ecumenical Movement* (Philadelphia, Pa.: Friends General Conference, 1970), p. 35.

[21]Ibid., p. 35.

[22]Ibid., p. 37.

[23]Palmer, p. 229.

[24]Steere, *Mutual Irradiation*, pp. 22-23.

[25]Palmer, pp. 229-230.

[26]Steere, *Mutual Irradiation*, p. 18.

[27]Enomiya Lassalle, "The Timeliness of the Zen-Christian Colloquium" in *A Zen-Christian Pilgrimage* (The Zen-Christian Colloquium, 1981), p. 54.

[28]Douglas V. Steere, "Development for What?" in *Development for What?*, ed. John H. Hallowell, Lilly Endowment Research Program in Christianity and Politics, (Durham, N. C.: Duke University Press, 1964), p. 224.

[29]John D. Copenhaver, Jr., *The Relation of Prayer and Social Responsibility in the Spiritual Theology of Douglas V. Steere* (Washington, D.C.: The Catholic University of America, 1986) Unpublished dissertation available in CUA library, p. 36.

CHAPTER TWO

STEERE'S TREATMENT OF PRAYER AND

SOCIAL RESPONSIBILITY

Chapter One examined the intellectual and religious factors in Steere's development. This chapter now turns to the treatment of prayer and social responsibility in his many writings. The five theses listed in the Introduction (and repeated here) serve as a device for organizing the investigation. They are: 1.) Prayer (especially corporate prayer) deepens an awareness of creatureliness and evokes a consciousness of solidarity with all persons and all creation. Out of this perceived solidarity "seeds of concern" surface in the consciousness of the one who prays. 2.) Prayer nurtures an awareness of God's infinite concern for every person and fosters a willingness to participate in God's redemptive order. 3.) Prayer cleanses action, work, and service of their repetitive nature and restores their frame of meaning. 4.) Acts of social responsibility clarify and test the genuineness of prayer. 5.) Both prayer and social responsibility are incomplete in themselves. They are partially integrated through alternation and fully integrated through simultaneity.

Five books and six articles will be examined chronologically as sources to determine how these themes are developed during the course of Steere's career. The selected books and articles, though only part of Steere's publications, are fully representative of his religious philosophy. In the process of this examination, the adequacy of the organizing theses will become clarified.

Prayer and Worship, which was published in 1938 by the Association Press, will be examined first. Although *The Open Life* (a pamphlet published by the Book Committee of the Religious Society of Friends in 1937) and *Toward the Practice of Prayer* (a pamphlet published by the Friends Book Store) preceded it, *Prayer and Worship* marks the beginning of Steere's career as a "popular" devotional writer. In the same year, Harper and Row published his translation of Kierkegaard's *Purity of Heart is to Will One Thing*.[1] This latter book, "with the authors incisive introduction to Kierkegaard's thought, established Douglas Steere as a significant religious scholar."[2] 1938, then, marks the beginning of Steere's serious publishing career--both as a popular devotional writer and as a significant religious scholar--and it is appropriate that this study begins here.

Prayer and Worship

Steere had been teaching at Haverford for ten years when *Prayer and Worship* was published and had occupied the T. Wistar Brown chair in philosophy (previously occupied by Rufus Jones) for four years. The Hazen Foundation asked Steere to write a book that shared what he considered important about prayer and worship with the new generation of college and university students. (Some of the other writers included in this Hazen series are: John C. Bennett, Georgia Harkness, Kenneth Scott Latourette, Henry P. Van Dusen, and Robert L. Calhoun.) Steere had hoped the book would be published under the title of *The Nurture of the Interior Life*, but the Hazen editors made him settle for *Prayer and Worship*. In the Foreword of the 1978 reprinting of the book, Steere allows that the book was written in a small woodshed in Bucks County, Pennsylvania, where he hid away on numerous weekends. It is dedicated to Rufus M. Jones, whom Steere describes as "the most generous of friends and colleagues" and one who "for a long generation quickened in people a sense of the nearness of God." *Prayer and Worship* has been translated into Swedish, German, and Chinese and over one hundred thousand copies were sold prior to 1978.

Prayer and Worship is important because many of the themes that dominate Steere's writings are introduced in it. The author begins by noting the younger generation's hostility to Christianity; not because of its teachings, but because it is not "Christian enough."[3] For some students, says Steere, the issue is the "apparently incurable mediocrity of soul that fills the Christian ranks."[4] In this statement Steere reveals the concern most central to his life work. He is deeply concerned with the scandal of mediocrity. Through a lifetime of teaching, he has tried to evoke and nurture great souls within the Christian community. He possesses a consuming hunger for sanctity and has sought to evoke that hunger in others.

In this particular book, Steere seeks to address the problem of growth in the religious life:

> Here is the problem of this book: How does a man become increasingly a Christian when he already is one? How does he begin from where he is and at least be in motion away from "not Christian enough"? In other words, this book is concerned with growth in the religious life.[5]

He notes that what distinguishes the life of Christian saints is not so much the dramatic circumstances of their entry into the religious life, but "the fact that over a period of years they grew out of what they were into what we know them to have become."[6]

Steere emphasizes that the saints are not a different species from other Christians; rather, they differ from ordinary Christians only in the intensity of their devotion and the transformation of the personality that is the result of their devotion. Steere acknowledges the contemporary repulsion for the word "devotion," but argues that it is the appropriate word for indicating a steady, habitual abandonment to the workings of divine grace. This emphasis on devotion also provides a clue to Steere's career: he already understands himself to be a devotional writer.

Another theme that Steere introduces in this book is the cultivation of the "interior life." Speaking of the saints he writes, "These men and women seem to be living from within outwards and to be inwardly awake and alive."[7] He believes that certain saints are remarkably astute psychologists; not because of intellectual curiosity, but because they combine the experience of the saint with the psychologist's gift of analysis.[8] He writes:

> The saint may not be the best theologian, as some have claimed, but he is not to be scorned if what we are seeking is to know the nature of the self, of its errors, of its evasions, of its cultivation; in short, if we are seeking out a much-needed psychology of the deeper reaches of life.[9]

Steere sees these saints as the great guides in the cultivation of the interior life and draws on them as a Biblical scholar draws on the scriptures.[10]

Steere is persuaded that it is the task of devotion to "quicken" the partially awakened Christian into a fervent and devout Christian. In this book Steere considers three "aids" in this transformation: private prayer, corporate worship, and devotional reading.

In the chapter entitled "The Practice of Private Prayer," Steere describes prayer as 1.) "a response to the ceaseless outpouring of love and concern with which God lays siege to every soul,"[11] 2.) "the soul's sincere desire,"[12] and 3.) "speech with God.[13] As Steere develops these descriptions, it becomes clear that each is somehow related to social responsibility. Specifically, all three pertain to the second thesis, which is "Prayer nurtures an awareness of God's infinite concern for every person and fosters a willingness to participate in God's redemptive order." Henceforth, this thesis will be referred to as the "willingness" thesis.

Steere first describes prayer as a response to the prior love of God. Prayer enables a person to sense the love that is at the heart of things.

> The prayer of devotion is a response, a reply, the only appropriate reply that a man or a woman could make who had been made aware of the love at the heart of things, the love that environed them, that rallied them, that wearied out evil and indifference by its patient joy. To sense that is for a person to long to love back through every relationship he touches.[14]

Prayer nurtures an awareness of God's love at the heart of all creation evoking a similar response (willingness) in the one who prays.

The definition of prayer as the "soul's sincere desire" is not Steere's definition; rather, he describes it as an impressive definition which "has appeared."[15] From this perspective, prayer is mostly unconscious. " . . . the fearful person prays by his acts of withdrawal, of cringing, of brooding, of distrust; and the person of faith prays by his or her openness, freedom, readiness to take risks, trust of the future."[16]   Even though Steere considers this a helpful definition, he seeks to go beyond it.

> There is a large measure of truth in this interpretation. For many forms of prayer do send down into the unconscious positive imagery, positive resolutions, positive incentives to action. And these forms of prayer would willingly recognize that these elements operate within the unconscious to aid, and to bring into fruition in the life of inward desire what is begun above the threshold of consciousness, what is intentionally and consciously sought after in prayer. Yet since this deep unconscious intention of the soul is able to be reached and affected by consciously directed intention, prayer in this sense becomes not merely the soul's sincere desire, but prayer is the process of intentionally turning the focus of the soul's sincere desire upon the active nature of the Divine Love and by every device within its power holding it there until it becomes engaged.[17]

Through perseverance in prayer a person becomes aware of the "active nature of the Divine Love" and, if sincere, clings to that awareness until it finds expression in his or her life. When this happens the person who prays becomes a participant in God's redemptive order.

The definition of prayer as "speech with God" is not Steere's either. He mentions it because it is a fairly common definition. He accepts its validity but considers deep prayer as more nearly "work with God." In prayer, there is a training of the will in order to bring it into conformity with the will and nature of the object of devotion. Steere uses the analogy of a Zen artist who must spend hours moving his body and brush in a synchronizing response to the curves of the mountain he would paint.

> The swift and agile acts of devotion that follow are only the setting down on the canvas of daily life what is felt into and moved into and yielded to in prayer.[18]

Although prayer often seems to be passive, it often conceals the most intense activity. Its real work is the transformation of the will. Unless the will is "tendered" and transformed to coincide with the will of God, the amazing New Testament promises about the power of prayer do not apply.[19]

> In the most real prayer of all there is wrought that refocusing of the life of the one who prays until he is brought to abide in the Divine love and the character of the Divine love abides in him. Then and then only does the promise of extending that transforming power indefinitely really hold.[20]

Private prayer is one of the key aids in bringing the human will into harmony with the divine and unless this coincidence occurs there is little to be expected from prayer.

From these definitions of prayer, it is clear that, for Steere, prayer and social responsibility are intrinsically related. Social responsibility is not something tacked on to prayer to give it legitimacy; rather, it is inherent in the nature of prayer.

Each definition addresses the issue of willingness and what prayer does to foster it.

After establishing this theological foundation for understanding prayer, Steere turns to the practice of prayer. He writes about the nature and value of solitude, spoken prayer, silent prayer, petition, intercession, and adoration. In all these forms of prayer there may come clear insights of things to be done, especially if prayer includes listening and sensitivity.[21]

> These insights are precious and are to be heeded if we are to live in response to that which we feel in prayer. When they involve some real readjustments that may be costly to effect, the Quakers have called these *concerns*. They lack a word for the tiny promptings, the gentle whispers that are equally as important and that may represent concerns in the forming.[22]

Prayer, if viewed in this perspective, may be considered "incipient action." Steere insists, however, that sensitivity to a concern is not sufficient; the concern must be carried out in "holy obedience." In this construction prayer leads to social responsibility and a partial integration occurs through the alternation of prayer and acts of social responsibility.

The fifth thesis states that, "Both prayer and action are incomplete in themselves. They are partially integrated through alternation and fully integrated through simultaneity." In the future I will refer to these two complementary approaches as the integration/alternation thesis and the integration/simultaneity thesis.

In *Prayer and Worship* the integration/simultaneity thesis is not developed; the emphasis is on the alternation of prayer and social responsibility. Steere fully recognizes the great gulf that exists between intention and fulfillment. He suggests that this very difficulty be faced during the time of prayer.

> Here in the silence, as that power gathers, it is well to face the difficulty one will meet in carrying out this concern. Here in the silence it is well to see the only semi-inflammable character of the bridge you mean to burn; to face the inertia, the resistances, the amused smiles of friends, the coldness and want of understanding on the part of many who resent having their attention called to social injustice in which they are involved--the strangling doubts of your own later hours . . .[23]

Nonetheless, the concern must be carried out, for "If we ignore these leadings, they poison future prayer."[24] Prayer loses its vitality when it ceases to be responsive.

> Holy obedience to the concerns that come, that persist, and that are in accord with co-operation with God's way of love is not only the active side of prayer, but is the only adequate preparation for future prayer.[25]

From the above it is clear that, for Steere, both prayer and social responsibility are incomplete in themselves. A relationship exists in which each is impoverished without the other. When prayer and social action alternate a healthy environment for prayer and action exists. There is, however, tension--this salutary relationship is not easily achieved or maintained.

The integration/alternation thesis also appears in Steere's treatment of solitude. He chides those who say that they are able to dispense with regular periods of solitude and prayer, and notes Jesus' practice of retirement for prayer. The common witness of the saints is that "there is a maintenance cost to the spiritual life."[26] Using a market analogy he notes that, "Imports must balance exports."[27]

In the chapter on "The Practice of Corporate Worship," Steere entitles a section "Creatureliness and Social Responsibility." This section illuminates the first thesis, i.e., Prayer (especially corporate prayer) deepens an awareness of creatureliness and evokes a consciousness of solidarity with all persons and all creation. Out of this perceived solidarity "seeds of concern" surface in the consciousness of the one who prays. (Henceforth, this thesis will be referred to as the "awareness" thesis.) As Steere's chapter is on corporate worship, the question arises whether corporate worship can be included under the category of prayer. For the purposes of this paper the answer will be yes--it is certainly so in Quaker worship. Although in most other churches formal prayer is only one part of worship, the whole worship experience is encompassed in an attitude of prayer.

In corporate worship a person draws near to God as "one of the great family of fellow creatures."[28] The worshiper approaches God in humility as he or she realizes that in the loving regard of God each person is of equal worth.[29]

> For in this sense of creatureliness, the springs of the only enduring center of equality between men are forever being renewed. Here is the heart of a social gospel that is eternal. Here each is visited with a sense that he/or she is . . . responsible for all and can never wrench lose from that responsibility.[30]

Although Steere does not use the word "solidarity," it is clear that in the shared experience of creatureliness the worshiper senses his or her solidarity with the other worshipers and out of this solidarity arises a conviction of responsibility for all.

In summary, *Prayer and Worship* makes an important contribution to understanding the organizing theses. Already it is possible to see an outline of Steere's approach to the problem. The elements of awareness, willingness, and execution have all been formulated in at least an introductory way. In the awareness thesis, the only element missing is the connection between creatureliness and "seeds of concern." The willingness thesis receives the most complete treatment of any of the theses and it appears fully developed at this early stage. The third and fourth theses are not addressed in this work. The integration/alternation aspect of the fifth thesis is introduced, but the integration/simultaneity aspect is not presented.

Lest it be interpreted that Steere developed the integration/simultaneity thesis later in his career, it should be noted that this thesis had already been articulated in his 1937 William Penn Lecture entitled *The Open Life*. As this thesis is more fully developed in later works, it will not be analyzed at this early stage.

On Beginning from Within

The next book written by Steere is composed of five essays delivered at Harvard University in 1942 and 1943 and published under the title of *On Beginning from Within*. The titles of the essays that form the chapters of this book are 1.) The Saint and Society, 2.) The Authority of the Saint, 3.) A New Set of Devotional Exercises, 4.) Devotion and Theology, and 5.) Death's Illumination of Life. In the preface Steere notes the occasion for each essay.

The final essay was given at Harvard University on April 14, 1942, as the Ingersoll Lecture. The first four essays were given at Harvard University in March and April, 1943, as the William Belden Noble Lectures. Parts of them were previously delivered at the Episcopal Theological Seminary in Virginia on the Reinicker Foundation, and at the Chicago Theological Seminary on the Alden Tuthill Lecture Foundation. For the encouragement of these occasions and for gracious hospitality I am indebted to Dean Willard Sperry, Dean Wallace Rollins, and President Albert Palmer.[31]

He also indicates that these essays are primarily concerned with the "intensification of the life of God in the individual hearts of men."[32]

In many ways this book builds on the foundation laid in *Prayer and Worship*. In spite of Steere's statement in the preface that these essays are concerned with "the intensification of the life of God in the individual hearts of men," the first essay is at least as concerned with society as it is with the interior life of the Christian. As *Prayer and Worship* dealt primarily with the disciplines that enable a Christian to move toward Christian maturity, it is appropriate that the essay entitled "The Saint and Society" shows how the person who has reached Christian maturity (the saint) affects society. Although the relation of the saint to society appears peripheral to this study, it is intimately related to the inward journey/outward journey[33] theme that will appear in works to be examined later. Steere's treatment of sainthood does not fit neatly into the organizing theses, but it is included because it addresses the question of efficacy in relating prayer and social responsibility. First, it is necessary to understand how Steere relates prayer and sainthood.

The three "aids" to Christian growth described in *Prayer and Worship* are private prayer, corporate worship, and devotional reading. The prayerful nature of corporate worship has already been mentioned and the same could be said about devotional reading. Each may be viewed as a means of commun-ion/communication with God. If persons become "Christian enough" by diligence with these aids, then saints are the heroic Christians whose devotion has been inflamed by them. Saints are first and foremost persons of prayer. The completeness of their abandonment to God is the outgrowth of their inner life of prayer. To say this another way, growth in prayer fosters growth in Christian character, occasionally producing a "saint."

For Steere, the saint is peculiarly effective in producing beneficial social change. The purpose of his essay, "The Saint and Society," is to analyze how the saint affects social life. As he begins this essay, Steere notes the current Protestant passion for a "new design for society" and dismisses the solutions of both socialism and capitalism as being "horizontal." In place of these solutions, Steere suggests that religion is the best vehicle for bringing about a more just and humane society. Specifically, it is the saints and prophets who are the agents of this change.

Although he does not want to deny the complexity of the forces at work upon society, Steere agrees with Plato that behind the outer appearance of society is "a man writ large."

There, behind society's outer facade of toughness, this analysis maintains that there is, and must always be, a center that is peculiarly vulnerable to the life of a man or a band of men who might exemplify society's deepest yearning and call out a response from it that would alone make any enduring structural changes possible.[34]

This center is hard for Steere to define but he finds that Rousseau's concept of the "general will" and the idea of a *consensus gentium* point in the right direction. This vulnerable center is "as intimately connected with the corporate institutions of society as the nerve center of inner consent is connected with the habit mechanisms of an individual person."[35] According to Steere, a habit is largely dependent on inner consent in order to continue; once consent is withdrawn the habit mechanism is in jeopardy. If habits and corporate institutions are to continue then they must be continually confirmed at this level of inner consent. The superficial social critic is impressed by the apparent solidity of society's facade, but behind it lies this vulnerable center where "one always finds a man, and a man's wants, and before it is plumbed a man's deepest wants."[36] It is to these "wants," these deepest human needs, that the saint appeals. This ability to discern the deepest needs of persons accounts for the saint's peculiar efficacy in bringing about social change. In his essay entitled "The Authority of the Saint," Steere writes, "For the universal Godman that speaks in the apostle has an invisible ally in the breast of every man, no matter how deeply concealed or repudiated it may be."[37] The saint (or apostle) has this vulnerable center for an ally in every person he or she meets.

Following this introduction, Steere begins an analysis of the nature of the saint and those characteristics that make the saint an effective instrument for social change. First of all, the "saint begins with himself and with what he must do, not with denunciations of society and its wrongs."[38] The saint is a radical in the sense that he or she has gone to the root of the problem and is "acutely aware that all the projected sins of society are present within him."[39] Here Steere distinguishes the saint from the revolutionary who is only interested in social change.

At this point the saint is to be sharply distinguished from many social, revolutionary leaders who see no connection whatever between their own personal lives and conduct and the "cause" to which they dedicate themselves with such abandon and who have faith that if you change the outer situation, personal change will occur of itself.[40]

The saint is concerned to begin from within and seeks personal transformation prior to social transformation; but, having begun in the "first person singular," the saint has no naïveté about the "world's natural goodness." Nor does the saint share the social revolutionary's naïveté that manipulation of the political or economic environment will make "all men good." The saint does not have these illusions because, "The saint knows sin for what it is because he knows it within himself."[41]

In this "beginning from within" Steere detects the point at which the "saint begins the Christian revolution."[42]

For the saint to begin relating society to the end, when the end was not in sight for his own life, would be absurd. Hence he begins with the relation of his own life to the end, and with the end deeply aroused within himself, he goes on to relate all that he touches to the true end, keeping the end always in sight.[43]

It is this focus on the end, the goal, that reveals the prophetic nature of the saint.

This witness to an order impinging upon ours but never realized here is a perpetual threat to society's idolatrous attempt to set itself up as the exclusive object of worship--the golden calf of its time. . . . So long as staunch, devoted Christian individuals remain, there is at work in society a powerful force to reassert the principle of order and to compel the state or any social institution to consider its relation to the true end of individual men.[44]

So, for Steere, the Christian social revolution begins with a personal revolution in the life of the Christian. This revolution begins by having the end "deeply aroused within himself."

The second trait that characterizes the saint is what Steere calls "joyous heroism." The saint "stops at nothing when his witness to his dearest love is at stake."[45] "To regard them [the saints] is to suffer a frontal attack on the safety factor with which most of us seek to surround our lives."[46] The joyful heroism of the saint challenges all who observe his or her life.

The saint is not a professor who puts to society a convincing set of arguments. He puts before men a life and an embarrassing invitation which they must decide to accept or reject.[47]

The saint's life calls those who observe it to new responses to life.

This joyful heroism is accompanied by "staying power" (the third trait of the saint). This tenacious perseverance grows out of the saints "singleness of vision" and "inner renewal."

The fourth trait of the saint is that the saint "cares not for humanity but for men. . . . Having begun with himself the saint never stops there."[48] Saints care for their fellows not abstractly but personally. Unlike secular social revolutionaries the saints are unwilling to sacrifice individuals in order to forward the cause. The "personalism" which characterizes this fourth trait is a major theme in Steere's writings and will be examined later in this study.

The fifth trait that Steere emphasizes is the saints' faith that group life is redeemable.

> . . . the saint cuts through the lines of the sacred and the profane, of the personal and the social, and regards all life as sacramental and deals with it as such. To treat group life as inevitably immoral, inaccessible to brotherhood, and unsacramental, and to accept an unbridgeable gulf between personal and group relationships after the fashion of our currently popular socio-theological pessimism, are for the saint acts of high treason.[49]

Although the saints know the power of group egotism and corporate sin, they also know they are not alone and that God has ways of dealing with corporate sin. The saints refuse to be intimidated by institutionalized evil.

After this interpretation of the nature of sainthood, Steere adds one caveat-- the saint is not infallible. He notes Augustine's harsh treatment of the Donatists, Bernard of Clairvaux's persecution of small heretical peasant sects in southern France, and William Penn's trust in a corrupt steward that led to Penn's spending a year in a debtor's prison. In spite of these shortcomings, the saint's vision has often cut through society's conventional wrappings to get at the heart of an issue.

The other essays in *On Beginning from Within* contain little that pertains to this study, but there are two revealing passages that should be considered. In his essay entitled "A New Set of Devotional Exercises," Steere concludes by persuading the reader to seek an integration of prayer and social responsibility. He describes the alternation thesis and, in spite of its value, states that "it tends to depict prayer and life as too mechanically detached from each other."[50] The real goal for the new devotional exercises is a full integration of prayer and work in "working collectedly." The term "simultaneity" does not appear in this essay, but is represented in Meister Eckhart's term, "working collectedly."

> This is the goal of these new spiritual exercises and the norm of the devotional life by which they are to be checked. The norm is not whether they make stiff Christian soldiers, or whether they produce feudal Christian liegemen, but whether they draw men and women in the thick of life to live as creative apostles, to work collectedly in His service.[51]

From this we see that, for Steere, the goal of the devotional life consists in drawing the life of devotion into service and service into an awareness of the presence of God.

The remaining passage to be considered comes from his Ingersoll lecture entitled "Death's Illumination of Life." This passage is related to the willingness thesis and argues that the saint's unselfish service is not based on drivenness, but on inner freedom. After a penetrating analysis of western society's concealment of death (an analysis that appears to anticipate some insights from Ernest Becker's *The Denial of Death*[52]), he concludes with a passage subtitled, "Life Is Lent to Be Spent." He presents the example of several Christian saints who have completely given themselves to the service of their fellows and asks some searching questions about their lives.

> We can, in concluding, hardly evade asking whether this disregard of death and of its consequences and this self-consuming concern for the redemption of others is, at bottom, any more than a preview of the successful attainment of western society's attempted concealment of death and of its frantic encouragement of all to forget their future destiny and to lose themselves here and now in exhausting social services for the benefit of others . . .[53]

Several pages later Steere answers his query with resounding affirmation of the saint's freedom based in the saint's death to death.

> Only a perverse or a blinded observer could attribute this fearlessness, this carelessness of themselves but devouring concern for others that mark these self-spending servants of men, to any socially induced anesthesia to the drastic character of death, or to the collective's encouragement of their devoting themselves to social services. They seem rather to be men and women who have died to death and to the fear of death as they have abandoned themselves to a power that vanquished death in the same breath that it called for an ever-present willingness to die . . .[54]

This theme (dying to death) and the phrase, "Lent to Be Spent," appear often in Steere's writing and discloses the willingness grasped in prayer to be spent in the service of others.

In spite of the way these essays illuminate the willingness and integration theses, their chief value is that they go beyond the boundaries of the organizing theses and reveal broader implications. Persistence in the discipline of prayer (which represents the life of devotion) provides the condition for growth in sanctity, occasionally resulting in saintliness. Spiritually grounded acts of social responsibility occasionally produce social change. In this perspective, 'prayer and social responsibility' exist in an analogical relation to the 'saint and society. '

prayer   ::   saint
social responsibility   ::   social change

This understanding enriches the study of prayer and social responsibility and reveals the broader implications of their relation.

Work and Contemplation

In 1950 Steere was invited to deliver the 1952 Rauschenbusch lectures at Colgate-Rochester Divinity School in Rochester, New York. As part of his preparation he spent part of May, 1950 at the Harvard Business School meeting with professors and getting acquainted with what the Harvard Business School had contributed to the management side of the modern process of industrial work. Steere delivered the lectures in the spring of 1952 (Harry Emerson Fosdick preached) and Harper and Brothers published them five years later under the title *Work and Contemplation.*[55] As such a study is not the usual business school fare, it is surprising that the Harvard Business School purchased 1500 copies of the book and sent them out to their master list of business executives.

These lectures are of utmost importance for this study because in them Steere focuses all his attention on the problem being considered here. The respect given the Rauschenbusch Lectures in the American religious community also suggests their importance. In these lectures, Steere's mature thought is set out in its most systematic manner.

Steere's Introduction sums up his involvement with the problem. After giving an account of his experience with work camps and relief work, he describes his abiding interest in the contemplative life.

> From the other side, I have long been deeply concerned with the life of contemplation and with its centrality in the life of man. At the outset of any study of this deepest reach of the human spirit there arises the question of the relation of contemplation to the will, to human action, to action that reaches out to implement charity in this inwardly quickened concern for others. To understand the full reaches of contemplation in a man and to distinguish contemplation as life-flight, from contemplation as life-extending, as life-intensifying, is to be compelled to return to the nature of action, of work, and the way in which contemplation and work are inwardly related.[56]

This quotation gives the general scope of Steere's concern in this study. The goal is "to plow the ground in which one day a truly Christian philosophy of work could be planted."[57]

Later in the Introduction, Steere outlines his argument as it is developed in each chapter.

> The first of these essays [The Nature of Work] explores the nature of human work and concludes with the emergence of a frame of meaning as a necessary if not a sufficient condition of responsible work. The second essay [The Nature of Contemplation] examines the character and process of contemplation by which each level of awareness of the frame is brought into focus. The third essay [The Eclipse of Man in Modern Industrial

Work] traces a century of mounting criticism of the liquidation of the frame of meaning from industrial work and suggests some clues to measure a reversal of this process. The fourth essay [Manual Work and the Intentional Community] confirms these clues by showing the renewal and the kindling of responsibility in men and women in intentional (frame conscious) communities and situations where work is done in adherence to these principles. The fifth essay [Work and Contemplation] returns to an examination of contemplation but in terms now of what work does to clarify and embody it. This completes the circle of mutuality of work and contemplation and lays down their united presence and operation as a condition of any culture that will not be subject to eventual repudiation by the amphibian nature of man.[58]

This outline presents the broader context from which the concepts related to the organizing theses will be drawn.

In beginning this study, Steere seeks to ground his philosophy of work in a particular anthropological understanding. For Steere, the human person is "an amphibian animal with a mingling of *homo faber* and *homo contemplativus.*"[59] Human nature is truncated when one or the other is ignored. They are and should be intimately related. This intimate relation is seen in Steere's definition of work. "For human work is the intentional focusing of sufficiently disciplined and directed energy upon the dream, or the design, . . . to effect its realization in some tangible medium."[60] The dream or design is known through contemplation.

It is because man is a contemplative being that he cannot bear a condition of meaninglessness, or irresponsibility, without it rotting him out. Because he cannot shake off the contemplative bent that queries, that integrates, that searches for the underlying significance of what he is involved in, work, as such, no matter how secure the post, how handsome the pay rate, how contracted the hours, is never enough.[61]

Based on this understanding of humanity, Steere constructs his philosophy of work and contemplation.

With these presuppositions exposed, it becomes clear that Steere's anthropology provides the foundation for his treatment of the relation of prayer and social responsibility. Their inseparability is rooted in human nature. The possibility of their integration is grounded in the unity of the human person. This anthropological foundation undergirds every concept related to the organizing theses.

Steere's analysis of contemplation especially illuminates the first thesis. The first part of the first thesis (i.e., prayer deepens an awareness of creatureliness) is one of the assumptions Steere recognizes as being implicit in his acceptance of the Thomistic definition of contemplation (i.e., contemplation is a simple, unimpeded and penetrating gaze on truth); he writes:

One of these assumptions is that in contemplation we are confronted by a given with which we are not identical and from which we are in some way separated. This is the realistic cleft between the contemplator and what he contemplates, and all the sweep of contemplation whether it be of the physical world or the social scene or in friendship or love or in the most profound act of worship, witnesses to this cleft.[62]

It is in the experience of the "irreducible residue of mysterious otherness"[63] that the contemplator senses his or her creatureliness in a feeling of awe and reverence. Although the contemplator overcomes some of this otherness in contemplation, identity with the contemplated is never realized. "For identity, no matter how much it may appear to be approached at the deepest levels of contemplation, is never attained."[64]   Contemplation, in its deepest religious dimension, makes the contemplator fully aware of his or her creaturehood.

In these essays, Steere connects the awareness of creatureliness with the consciousness of solidarity with all persons and all creation. If contemplation leads to adoration and an awareness of creatureliness, it also draws one into a consciousness of solidarity with all creation. In contemplation, the human person is drawn to relate things. The first power of contemplation is the "apprehension of unity."[65]

It is, then, the genius of contemplation at its basic level to apprehend unity, to relate, to pierce through the surface separations of experience to uncover the frame, and to see how its segments are joined.[66]

Steere does not use the term "solidarity," but the apprehension of unity indicates a consciousness of fundamental relatedness to all creatures.

Although contemplation enables the contemplator to "apprehend unity," this unity is not an undifferentiated unity. The second power of contemplation is to recognize different levels of reality, each having its own integrity. There are the "levels" of the physical universe, of aesthetics, of ethics, and of the spirit.[67] Contemplation apprehends that these levels of reality impinge upon each other, but recognizes that they have their own integrity.[68]

The third power of contemplation goes beyond the apprehension of unity and the apprehension of the integrity of different depth levels of reality. The third power of contemplation is to respond appropriately to God. This third power goes beyond the first thesis. It is related to the second thesis, especially the "willingness to participate in God's redemptive order." The "ability to respond appropriately to God" and "the willingness to participate in God's redemptive order" are virtually synonymous. As willingness plays such a central role in these essays, it will receive special attention.

As was noted in *Prayer and Worship*, Steere has already conceived of prayer as "response to God." He develops this theme further in *Work and Contemplation*. He writes, "Yet unless it [prayer] is a pure act of rote, the fragile human arms of prayer are always focused on God and are willing to yield, or at least not closed to being made willing."[69]   Prayer is not genuine unless the one praying is willing to be made willing. Genuine prayer is characterized by attentiveness and obedience, and in its higher ranges these two are closely related.

In contemplation, however, attentiveness and obedience may never be separated from each other, for as though in some ascending scale, the higher the level of reality contemplated, the more sweeping the demand for obedience of the whole man until in religious contemplation, attentiveness seems almost to have been merged with obedience.[70]

In religious contemplation, the spectator gives way to the participant because the whole person is involved in it. In religious contemplation, as opposed to secular contemplation (which encourages detachment and disinterested observation), the will, the intellect, and the emotions are all involved. There is an "abandonment of detachment" in the highest levels of contemplation.[71]

As it involves the whole person, genuine prayer will eventually plunge the one who prays into a crisis situation. Steere illustrates this "crisis" with the following story.

The British painter Turner was once asked to help a friend find a proper place in a room to hang a painting. It was tried in many places but none seemed to fit. Turner remarked that it was useless to try to fit such a painting into such a room. The room needed to be rebuilt to fit the painting.[72]

Just so, the one who persists in prayer is brought into a situation "where the presence of the living God will irradiate him and leave him no alternative but to rebuild the room, or to break off the contemplation."[73] The depth of this crisis is witnessed to in the lives of the many "masters of prayer" who have experienced an "inner conspiracy of jamming static" after making a well-intentioned beginning in contemplation. This "jamming static" is caused by the "undue adhesions of the world"--the unburned boats, the unfaced fears, the secret wills-to-be-defeated.[74] These are the times when the living God is "burning up sheath after sheath of the claimful surface self, the 'lump' that covers the real self, and the pain of the cauterization of the highly uninflammable material that envelops the soul."[75]

The costliness of this "inward journey," this persistence in prayer, is a theme that appears frequently in Steere's writing and is related to the second thesis. The first part of the second thesis states that prayer nurtures an awareness of God's infinite concern. It is because God is "engaged in an unfathomably costly process of cosmic redemption"[76] that any genuine human response will also be costly. To participate in God's redemptive order is to share in God's "unfathomably costly" engagement. Indeed, to be fully involved in God's redemptive order is death to the surface self.

When he turns to mystical prayer, Steere describes it as having an especially salutary effect upon will. In mystical prayer, God is simultaneously effecting a purgation and restoration of the soul.[77] The restorative effect of mystical prayer upon the will is described in this way.

In the mystic's contemplation, we have only an intense focus of what happens to all men in genuine prayer as they pass from the voluntary self-guided willful acts of attentiveness over to that attention which is involuntary, when the living God stirs the will in secret and leaves them inwardly tendered and refreshed and renewed. Here participation has outstripped knowledge.[78]

This type of encounter with the living God leaves the mystic at God's disposal, expendable in God's service.[79] The role of purgation and restoration are also expressed in terms of dethronement and re-enthronement. All secondary "areas" of contemplation (e.g., aesthetics and ethics) are dethroned. Their claims to absolute priority are set aside and the highest reality is re-enthroned.

The simultaneous re-enthronement of the highest reality that man can contemplate has an unexpected effect. Now he finds that only what he gives up, he possesses, but is no longer possessed by. For only as this re-enthronement of the living God strips the auxiliary functions of this life of their claims for absolute priority, only then do these functions disclose to him their true nature.[80]

In this re-enthronement of the highest reality, all the other areas of contemplation find their proper place and the human will is correctly aligned.

Having examined the theme of re-enthronement in *Work and Contemplation*, this study moves from the second thesis to the third, viz., Prayer cleanses action, work, and service of their repetitive nature and restores their frame of meaning. (Henceforth, the third thesis will be referred to as the "cleansing thesis.") Although this thesis does not find its most complete treatment in these essays, it is introduced in an abridged form.

One of the central themes of these essays is that contemplation reveals the frame of meaning for work. Perhaps another way of saying this is that contemplation reveals and makes conscious the worldview in which work finds its meaning. When work is robbed of this undergirding vision, it becomes dull and meaningless. Or, as Steere puts it, "work without contemplation is bitter and blind."[81] It is blind because the end toward which the work is directed is obscured. Even when the worker has excellent pay, contracted work hours, and job security, the work is still deadening without a frame of meaning.

It [work] is seen, however, to be destructive of both the fiber and the nervous stability of man unless its frame of meaning is explicit enough to be drawn upon in the clarifying insight that comes within the toil of work itself.[82]

Contemplation enables the worker to keep the end in view and this perspective gives work its direction and meaning. ". . . when contemplation does permeate intense activity, it does not leave it as it was. For it tests it, sorts it out, alters it, frames it, and in turn the frame bears up or carries that which it has consented to and approved."[83] Steere describes this constant attentiveness to the end as carrying the "whole active life in the gaze of contemplation."[84]

If "work without contemplation is bitter and blind," it is also true that "contemplation without work is callow and empty."[85]   The latter affirmation is related to the fourth thesis, viz., Acts of social responsibility clarify and test the genuineness of prayer. (Henceforth, the fourth thesis will be referred to as the "clarification thesis.") This thesis is carefully developed in these essays; however, it is stated in a slightly different way. In these essays it could be stated best as, "Work clarifies and incarnates contemplation."

The final essay in *Work and Contemplation* is addressed precisely to this thesis. As he begins this essay Steere writes:

> In this final chapter, there must be a reckoning with the role of deed, of work as a means of clarifying, of disclosing, of giving form, as all creation must, to the frame which contemplation bares. For if it is true as has been declared, that all human work cries out for meaning, for a frame for what contemplation alone can supply, . . . is it any less true that this frame is only grasped as it enters into work, into the deed, into creation, and that work and contemplation require each other?[86]

Contemplation bares the frame of meaning, but that frame of meaning is nebulous until it is grasped and expressed through work or action or service.

As he develops his argument for the necessity of contemplation expressing itself in action, he asks the question, "Is contemplation alone self-vindicating?"[87] After noting that both Thomas Aquinas and the *Cloud of Unknowing* considered the beatific vision such a complete fulfillment of "man's deepest desire" that it needed no other justification, Steere makes his own case for mutual interdependence based on "the character and relation of the Creator, the creature, and the creation."[88]   In Steere's approach these three are all "bound inseparably together in a great drama of redemption."[89]   The physical order is not only "a rigorously disciplined order that continually monitors and tests his [man's] work,"[90] but "its own destiny is in some mysterious way linked to this creature, man."[91] This inseparable bond of creatureliness gives some hint of the connection between work and contemplation.

This clue gives a setting to the cosmic role of human work that has wide-ranging implications. For if man is in the midst of physical creation not as an alien, imprisoned there to work out his own salvation in fear and trembling, but rather as one who answers to God not only for himself and for his fellows but also for the plant, the animal, and mineral kingdom with which he has been entrusted, he enters into a fresh and positive relation with them. Now there can be no salvation alone. There can be no kicking and slashing at creation that clings to man in order that he may get some swift Gnostic form of salvation and go to the Father alone. Now he must manifest his own redemption in work, in the redemption of the created order, in the habit patterns of his own body . . .[92]

This is not a restatement of the Protestant work ethic, in which Steere finds an inadequate theology of nature. He considers his approach a "bolder" one because work is no longer merely the "backdrop for man's ascetic exercise," but a joint effort with the Creator to implement the divine vision. Work is no longer the way in which the elect express their salvation; rather, work itself has redemptive value.

> For if man's redemption involves his relations with his fellows and with whole physical creation, the action, work, the mobilizing of the will to implement the vision, and the insertion of these mobilized powers into the matrix of the created world of fellow men and the whole physical creation, all assume a very positive role. For they . . . release both in the workman and in the creation a free road for the redemptive power to operate.[93]

From the preceding it is clear that, for Steere, contemplation must find expression in work. A little later he writes, "In this earthly life it is this indispensable engagement of contemplation with action, with deeds, with work, that clarifies and confirms what the very contemplation contains."[94] Drawing from the gospels he asserts that Mary, Martha's contemplative sister, does not know "what she has received [in contemplation] until it engages with the creation in which she stands."[95] As always, Steere supports his argument with numerous other examples and illustrations. It will prove helpful to examine two of the illustrations that are especially revealing in understanding how work clarifies contemplation.

The first illustration is drawn from another passage in the gospels. The disciples have not been able to exorcise a young man possessed by a demon. They return to Jesus discouraged. For Steere, this "failure" in their ministry, their work, helped clarify what was yet lacking in their contemplation.

> Here in the work of healing we have the insertion of contemplation into the resistances of creation, and we have the simultaneous revealing of the contemplation itself as still too callow, still too empty. It believed it had grasped the root of the way to heal, but clearly it had not. Greater abandonment to God, greater caring for the one to be healed, greater identification with the creation, greater faith in the redemptive healing power that is available, all are needed by the workman. What a clarification of the original contemplation, what an illumination of what is still wanting, the work brings to bear on contemplation in this instance![96]

In this particular example, the healing ministry is described as the insertion of contemplation into the resistances of creation. Here contemplation is directly related to work and when contemplation is inadequate, so is the work. This failure teaches them what is lacking in their contemplation.

In another revealing illustration, the relation between the work and contemplation are not so close and yet the work still offers clarification to contemplation. In his experience with Quaker work camps, Steere saw many workers arrive with high hopes and preconceived blueprints for an ideal Christian community. After eight weeks at a work camp one girl confessed to Steere, "You know, living and working with this group has taught me that I personally am not fitted yet, even to live in the community I thought I meant to bring to pass--let alone press it on others."[97] The manual labor of the work camps tested the genuineness of the each worker's commitment to his or her vision of a better world.

In these work camps where day after day a full eight hours of hard manual labor is accomplished, there is a dawning upon those unused to manual labor of just what work does to test the validity of ideals and purposes that seem so real in contemplation. When at the beginning of the second hour of a scorching afternoon the back seems about to give out and every stroke of the hoe in the mortar mixing box seems a pillory of pain, there is a dim realization of what the redemption of creation is about and a slight intimation of what it means to be mixed into the travailing stuff of a world that must be changed. . . . Visions remain, but they shake down. The unconscious fear that always haunts us about visions that have not been worked upon begins to disappear and these young workers emerge from the camp humbler and quieter, but far more dangerous contemplators. Contemplation is no longer for them a disembodied indulgence. Now it is connected with creation and is bent on reshaping it.[98]

Here work has tested the contemplative vision and has perhaps altered it as the worker became more acquainted with the stuff of creation and the tools available. The connection between the vision and the labor has been clarified and the necessity for embodying the vision has been established.

In this book, the first part of the fifth thesis (Both prayer and social responsibility are incomplete in themselves.) has been introduced forcefully into the clarification thesis. Steere's approach to this issue is grounded in his theology of cosmic redemption. If the very being of God is engaged in an unfathomably costly process of cosmic redemption, then the one who contemplates God must also be engaged in this process. When engagement is lacking then something is lacking in the contemplation. Steere contends that any Christian philosophy of work that neglects "pressing the responsibility of the vision to interpenetrate creation"[99] will rob contemplation of the self-clarification that work gives it. For Steere, work and contemplation are inseparable. It is out of this inseparability that the integration thesis arises.

Although Steere never uses the term "integration" to describe how he relates prayer and social responsibility, it is the most appropriate term to describe his approach. Several other terms have been carefully considered but were found to be inadequate or misleading. If integration is understood in the common meaning that it is given in Webster's New World Dictionary (i.e., integrate: 1.) to make whole or complete by adding or bringing together parts, 2.) to put or bring together into a whole, unify), then integration is the appropriate word. A key quote to support this thesis is found in Steere's response to his rhetorical question, "Is contemplation alone self-vindicating?" "Now this claim that links these two integral human movements of work and contemplation as interdependent, inseparable, and mutually clarifying must be prepared to face a good deal of evidence to the contrary."[100] He describes these two human movements as "integral." This is as close as Steere comes to describing his treatment as an integration; however, it is sufficient to indicate that he considers these two movements to be integrally related. Any two movements which are made "inseparable" must be integrally related.

What, then, is the nature of this integration? The nature of the integration envisioned by Steere is one in which prayer and social responsibility are interdependent, inseparable, and mutually clarifying. Although the idea of mutual enrichment might be included within the concept of mutual clarification, it is appropriate to add, "mutually enriching." These various elements have already been seen in the treatment of the cleansing and clarification theses. As he closes these essays, Steere is concerned to show how such an integration can be accomplished.

A partial integration of work and contemplation may be achieved through alternating work and contemplation; they are both present, but they do not penetrate one another. Work and contemplation are both engaged in, but not at the same time. In work, the frame of meaning is forgotten and energy is gradually expended until there is little meaning in or energy for the work. Contemplation and worship help restore the frame of meaning and energize the worker for a return to labor. In this approach, a partial integration is achieved because both work and contemplation are necessary and form a healthy rhythm. In spite of this positive correlation, Steere is swift to recommend a more complete integration.

The integration that Steere advocates is one in which work and contemplation are inseparable and interpenetrate each other. As has already been shown, Steere's theology of contemplation is an incarnational contemplation. Contemplation must enter into work and it must draw work up into itself.[101] ". . . if it [contemplation] must mingle and involve itself with work, then the sharp line of separation that the alternation principle places between the activity of work and the activity of contemplation begins to vanish."[102] In certain types of work, especially works of charity, the "frame of meaning emerges with great clarity and throws over the work a very special aura . . ."[103] With such an attitude, "Work almost ceases to be work when done in such a cause, and the line between work and prayer becomes razor thin."[104] When work and contemplation become so intimately related that they simultaneously interpenetrate one another, then the result is a consciousness of "working collectedly," which is higher than both work and contemplation.[105]

This concept of "working collectedly" is intimately connected to the idea of "unceasing prayer." This connection is revealed earlier in Steere's essay on contemplation.

> This order [the uppermost reach of contemplation] does not draw men out of their surroundings but seems rather to draw them into the very redemptive process that is forever laid like a great poultice over the world. And at its highest reach of all, it does this by dissolving away the customary line between action or work and contemplation. For there is a point where, blasphemous as it may sound, the contemplator is always at prayer and where he is free to carry his action into the contemplation and the contemplation into the action.[106]

The contemplator who is always at prayer is the one who knows how to pray without ceasing. For Steere, this unceasing prayer is an "abiding disposition" rather than conscious, discursive or repetitive prayer.[107]

The concept of "working collectedly" goes beyond the alternation thesis and is the heart of the simultaneity thesis. Steere has written that the line which separates work and contemplation becomes "razor thin" in certain types of work and when contemplation and work mingle the line "begins to vanish." In the highest reach of contemplation, it "dissolves away the customary line." Here is a complete integration. It appears so complete that it might be confused with a merging of work and contemplation. This is not, in fact, the case; rather work and contemplation thoroughly interpenetrate one another to create the condition of "working collectedly." Here is Steere's description of this integration.

Here is a principle that is beyond alternation. For here the contemplation in the midst of work is self-renewing. Here each buoys up the other. Here contemplation has entered work and work has helped to clarify and embody the contemplation. In the moments when this takes place, the worker feels himself vastly alive in the very work itself, for now the work is drawn into the frame and the frame into the work, with the worker standing at the nodal point, powerless yet in the presence of bottomless power. Now alternation, which is a common enough condition, gives way to patches of simultaneity where the worker finds himself "working collectedly," where he is at one with his work.[108]

It appears that alternation, when practiced over a period of time, will occasionally give way to simultaneity. Evidently, there is a giftedness to this experience because Steere uses the reflexive mood "the worker finds himself 'working collectedly.'"

The integration that Steere achieves in these essays is remarkable. Here work and contemplation stand in a relationship which is interdependent, inseparable, interpenetrating, mutually clarifying, and mutually enriching. The highest reaches of both work and contemplation are found in "working collectedly."

In his closing paragraphs, Steere returns to the contemporary work place and warns that if society rejects the human need for integrating work and contemplation then he expects "a far more terrible alternation than any that was earlier referred to, namely, an alternation in which the church is left to care for what are called the 'emotional needs,' for a work-less contemplation; and the factory for a contemplation-less work."[109] He calls on those who have felt the thrust of the redemptive process to go on "decoding" our systems of work and worship, stripping them of their pretensions, and showing what they do to human faces.

If human faces can only come alive and begin to feel responsibly connected with what they are and what they do, and what they are in what they do, in a setting where work and contemplation are fused, then they must tirelessly and imaginatively press this fact on church and industry alike by both precept and example. For in the swiftly-changing character of both church and industry, the enduring feature and the one by which both will finally be judged is whether together they are furnishing a setting where the amphibian man is able to come alive and to grow into his responsible destiny.[110]

This closing emphasis on anthropology ties his essays together and shows that Steere's ultimate purpose is the fulfillment of human nature and destiny. The personalism expressed in these closing sentences is characteristic of all his writings and a clue to his vocation.

On Listening to Another

Steere prepared his Swarthmore lecture in the summer of 1954 at his home in Mackinaw, Michigan. He and his wife, Dorothy, spent the summer there preparing for the year ahead. Although the Swarthmore lecture was not delivered until May of 1955, the British Quaker Committee wanted the manuscript by the year's end so that it could be printed for the Yearly Meeting. It was also during this summer that Douglas and Dorothy Steere co-authored *Friends Work in Africa,*[111] a book written for the Friends World Committee.

The Swarthmore Lecture was published in England under the title *Where Words Come From* and in the United States under the title *On Listening to Another.*[112] The original title is derived from a passage in John Woolman's *Journal*[113] in which Woolman describes his experience in a religious meeting held among Native Americans along the Susquehanna River in Pennsylvania. When Woolman stood and prayed, the interpreter who rose to translate his words into their language was asked (by his chief) to sit down and allow the prayer to go untranslated. "After the meeting, the Indian chief, Papunehang approached Woolman and through an interpreter said of the prayer whose English words he had not understood, 'I love to feel where words come from.'"[114] In this special art of listening to "where words come from," Steere has found an analogue for Quaker worship and the unfolding of Quaker "concerns." In the Introduction he writes:

> The lecture is devoted to an examination of what is involved in listening and being listened to. It seeks a fresh approach to an interpretation of the genius of Quaker worship and to its articulation in vocal ministry and in practical concerns in terms of the process of listening.[115]

Until the publication of his long introduction to *Quaker Spirituality*[116] in 1984, this lecture remained Steere's most complete treatment of Quaker spirituality. It is considered a spiritual classic by many and has been included in the final volume of the Doubleday Devotional Classics.

The themes which are developed in these lectures touch most closely upon the awareness and willingness theses. As these lectures are addressed to a Quaker audience, Steere addresses these themes within the context of Quaker thought and practice. Because of this approach, these two theses have a different flavor than they had in the Rauschenbusch lectures.

Steere uses an incisive analysis of the art of listening to introduce his treatment of the nature of Christian worship. He begins his treatment of Christian worship with a brief summary of a traditional order of formal worship. The formal elements of the order of worship are considered to be "outward invitations to inward states of soul, to inward stages of experience, which if they laid hold of the worshipper as they are intended to do would bring him into the presence of the Listener and renew and refresh his life."[117] In a revealing passage that follows this treatment of formal worship, Steere outlines his own agenda for the inward order of Quaker worship.

> In laying them [the outward forms of worship] aside as Quakers do in their silent waiting worship, there is a responsibility whose magnitude it is scarcely possible to exaggerate that is placed squarely upon the Quaker worshipper himself. Here indeed is a service of worship that demands that every believer be his own priest. For in the Quaker meeting for worship, the member must still his body, still his mind, must attend to the presence of God, must thank and adore him for being what he is, must feel the incongruities in his own life that are out of keeping with such a presence, must long for their removal and for forgiveness, must be inwardly absolved, must become conscious of persons and situations in special need and draw them into this presence, must wait in utter stillness before God, and if some even deeper insight into his own condition should be discovered to him by any vocal ministry that may occur in the meeting or by the unhurried stay in the presence of the Divine Listener, he must be ready to yield to what is required of him.
> It is sobering to reflect that unless the Quaker worshipper who has laid aside these outward aids used by his fellow Christians has learned their interior equivalent and has grasped the gentle art of guiding his own spirit through such an hour of worship, . . . this silent waiting worship can disintegrate for him into a boring state of deadness, into a situation of vegetative stagnation, or what is more likely, can be replaced by a period of strictly mental effort on a variety of themes that is not to be distinguished from intellectual application in any secular setting.[118]

This lengthy quote summarizes Steere's agenda for Quaker worship; however, it cannot stand alone because there is a further dimension of Quaker worship which goes beyond this careful inward ordering. There is a dimension of Quaker worship which corresponds to what spiritual theologians have called infused contemplation, when the worshipper ceases ordering the worship and is caught up in the object of worship.

> The dilemma which anyone seeking to explain Quaker worship faces is that only when this inner ordering has dropped into the background as we are swept up into the presence of the Listener himself, only when what was willfully and consciously begun, has been crowded out of consciousness by something to which it led, can the real significance of the preparation become apparent, and yet by that time this inner ordering seems like trivial scaffolding compared with what has now been discovered.[119]

It is within this understanding of Quaker worship that Steere turns to expand upon the various "steps in the practice of Quaker corporate worship."[120]

Not all of the steps in the practice of Quaker corporate worship are related to the two theses that this essay addresses, but they should be listed in order that the broader scheme may be understood. As Steere leads the reader through these steps, he describes: 1.) quieting the body or, as Steere puts it, "get Brother Ass, the body, properly tethered and out of the way,"[121] 2.) dealing with distractions, 3.) the role of adoration, 4.) intercession, 5.) vocal ministry, and 6.) the unfolding of concerns. The steps of adoration, intercession, and the unfolding of concerns are the ones which shed the most light on the first and second theses.

The first part of the awareness thesis states that "Prayer (especially corporate prayer) deepens an awareness of creatureliness." Both adoration and intercession play a central role in deepening an awareness of creatureliness. After quieting the body and dealing with distractions, the first step in worship (following Steere's outline) is that of adoration. Adoration fosters an awareness of the transcendence, the otherness, of God. It is this consciousness of God's awesome transcendence that deepens an awareness of creatureliness.

> If in a friend or in one we love there is always a final solitude, a final depth that we forever approach but never penetrate, is it surprising that in the living God, we find an abyss of being that in adoration brings us into a mingled sense of awe and of glad creatureliness? How good to be the creatures of such a creator, the branches of such a vine, the friends of such a Friend.[122]

This "glad creatureliness" is the fruit of adoration, the first movement in worship.

Intercession also plays an important part in deepening the awareness of creatureliness. In a section entitled "Corporate Worship and the Redemptive Community," the effect of intercession upon the awareness of creatureliness is clarified. From Steere's perspective, when Quakers gather for worship, they gather not as group of individuals concerned with their own "separate reveries" but as a "company of worshippers."[123] "They know something of the needs of their fellow worshippers; they know something of the sufferings and needs of the world. . . . This realization and these needs are gently brought into the worship in the form of intercession."[124] In this common neediness, the worshipper's awareness of creatureliness is deepened. The ability, however, to intercede for these needs is dependent upon some earlier preparations and inner commitments.

> But if I do not know my fellow members, if I do not call on them, if I am not concerned for them, if my mind and my personal resources are not at the disposal of both near and distant situations of need at other times, this leading of the spirit to bring before the presence of God these needs has neither sincerity nor deep intent behind it.[125]

This understanding presents some problems because the reasoning appears circular. If one is to offer genuine intercession, then one must come to worship ready to expend oneself in the service of others; and yet, worship and prayer are the very means of creating such an expendability. This problem is resolved if it is remembered that persistence in prayer exposes this lack of sincerity and creates a crisis in the life of the worshipper that must be resolved before any progress in prayer can be made.

When Steere turns to "Quaker Worship and the Unfolding of Concerns," the relation of creatureliness to social concerns becomes apparent. The awareness of creatureliness nurtures a consciousness of solidarity with all persons and all creation. Solidarity implies more than mere awareness. It anticipates the second thesis (the willingness thesis) in that it indicates a decision to stand with, to support the needy creature. It is out of this perceived solidarity that a concern may arise.

> This tendering of the heart and being drawn into a fresh sensitiveness to the needs of other, this malleable willingness to be used in meeting that need, is the condition in which what Friends have called a 'concern' may arise.[126]

Although the term solidarity does not appear in this passage, the idea is represented in the phrases "sensitiveness to the needs of others" and "willingness to be used in meeting that need."

Before examining the way in which this lecture informs the second thesis, it is important to understand what Steere means by a "concern." According to Steere, the word is used too lightly today. "In its truest form, a concern refers to a costly inner leading to some act that in the course of its fulfillment may take over the life of the one it engages."[127] The way in which a concern unfolds may vary a great deal.

> Occasionally the concern has put its finger on a specific thing to be done and on the initial steps in carrying it out. . . . More often the concern has laid hold of the person in terms of a deep inner distress over the wrongness of some situation or a yearning to minister to some condition of need without more than the first minute step being clear to him as to how to deal with it. . . . If the first step that is laid upon him is not undertaken, the later ones are not disclosed.[128]

The importance of this first step plays an important part in all Steere's writings. The first step may seem trivial, but in "God's eyes there are no 'little' things."[129] It may be as simple as a letter or a visit, but "everything matters" and "everything leads to something further."[130] With this understanding of a "concern," this study can turn to the second thesis.

As was mentioned earlier, the theme of solidarity anticipates the second thesis, but it cannot replace it, for the second thesis is more theological. In the second thesis, willingness is rooted in an awareness of God's infinite concern for every person. This awareness of God's infinite concern is implicit in the most profound understanding of a "concern."

> At this level, it can be said that in a genuine concern, a person has been drawn into the living inward linkage of man and God, man and man, and of man and creation. For to be brought into a condition of awareness of the compassion of the living Listener is to have disclosed to the worshipper a realization of the redemptive order of love that girdles our world for its healing.[131]

This is a new kind of solidarity, a solidarity with God's infinite concern for all creation. Here willingness precedes the unfolding of a concern because the very unfolding process is aborted when willingness is absent.

Steere's conception and articulation of God's "infinite concern" is grounded in an incarnational theology. The very willingness to participate in God's redemptive order is inspired by remembering the incarnation of God's love.

For one who has listened to another person with a bowed mind and tendered heart, how much is vindicated, is inwardly confirmed and made alive by the gospel story of the Listener entering human flesh and blood and caring so deeply as to consent to have it stripped from him again in order to arouse men to his infinite caring. . . . For to listen, there can be no bottom to the caring for the other. Yet we know that this caring is not a verbal affair. It must be sealed by some unmistakable material evidence of vulnerability on the part of the Listener.[132]

This quote gives us a feeling for the christological base of Steere's spiritual theology. It is the nature of God, revealed in Jesus Christ, that inspires Christians to service and makes them willing to be spent in caring for their fellows. They participate in God's redemptive order because, in prayer, they have been united with God's infinite concern for every person.

Although the first and second theses find the most complete treatment in this lecture, Steere concludes with a brief summation of what action does for prayer; or, rather, in this context, what action does to the concerns that arise in prayer. As the fourth thesis affirms, action clarifies prayer. In the case of a "major concern," the first act is to share the concern with the Quaker community. In the context of communal discernment, the concern may be reshaped and refined. Sometimes this corporate scrutiny can be chastening to the person who shares a concern, but it serves to clarify what was received in prayer.

For a genuine concern is marked both by its persistence and, strangely enough, by its flexibility and openness about the means by which it is carried out. . . . This openness to continual correction has had the practical effect of revealing to many who followed a concern how brittle and fragile was the thread of their commitment when they undertook it and how far the Divine Listener had used this concern to draw them on into his redemptive action and to cleanse and clarify them, a process that worship had only begun.[133]

The clarification that comes in the process of following a concern serves to draw the one who follows it into a more costly and more complete commitment to incarnating God's infinite concern for all creation.

As the focus of this lecture is upon Quaker worship rather than the practice of prayer, it does not give as much attention to action as the previous works. Using the art of listening as an analogue for Quaker worship, Steere has made an original and enlightening analysis of worship in the Society of Friends. The first two theses are included within the fabric of Quaker worship. The last three theses deal more with what happens to prayer once it is taken out of the place of worship and into the world of action. These themes within Quaker worship will receive a more complete treatment when Steere's introduction to *Quaker Spirituality* is analyzed.

Dimensions of Prayer

The final book to be analyzed in the light of the organizing theses is *Dimensions of Prayer*.[134] The Woman's Division of Christian Service of the Board of Missions of The Methodist Church asked Steere to write the book and published it in 1962 and reprinted it in 1977 and 1984.

The purpose and scope of this book are remarkably similar to that of *Prayer and Worship*. Steere assumes that his readers are not looking for an apologetics of the Christian faith, but for a workbook on prayer. He also assumes that his readers are committed Christians seeking to deepen their life of prayer. Although he does not write about "becoming Christian enough," he does refer to Kierkegaard's effort "to become a Christian . . . when one is a Christian of a sort."[135] Private prayer is considered the best instrument for making this transition to authentic Christian living and it is this instrument which Steere sets out to explore. As much of this book covers familiar ground, a complete analysis of each point related to the organizing theses will not be necessary.

Early in this book Steere emphasizes that "a redeeming order is already at work."[136] Although this concept has been implicit in much that he wrote before, it receives a new twist. Steere conceives of the redemptive process as a second creation. He writes:

> The redemptive process is already going on. It sprang out of the heart of the Creator of nature; it is a kind of second creation. It is directed to free souls who, in spite of belonging to God and owing all to God, are yet free to reject and repulse his costly advances. There is a company of the redeemed, a communion of faithful souls, both living and dead, who join with Christ and the Father in laying siege to the heart of the world. The cross is the symbol of this second creation, of this redemptive love.[137]

This conception of a redemptive process already at work supports all that follows. The person who prays is drawn into this redemptive process and swept along in the current of God's infinite concern for every person.

Steere's treatment of intercessory prayer is intimately related to his conception of the redemptive process. In intercessory prayer a person is joining forces with the God who is laying siege to every soul. Part of the efficacy of intercessory prayer rests in the fact that all souls are interconnected.

> Notwithstanding our ultimate aloneness, our individuality, evident in the final core of freedom and responsibility in each of us, we are all bound up in the "bundle of the living." (1 Samuel 25:29, R.S.V.) And even at the

most individual and most free and responsible pinnacle of our being, we are open to being helped and brothered by other souls. . . . Yet it would seem that souls are not only interconnected, but that they are interconnected in God, as though the many wicks of our lamps draw their oil from the same full cruse in which they are all immersed.[138]

This interconnectedness is of utmost importance to Steere. Because of this interconnectedness, there is no salvation alone. The goal of redemption is not the salvation of individual souls, but the redemption of all creation--it is a cosmic redemption. The power of prayer to deepen a consciousness of creatureliness, part of the first thesis, in turn evokes a consciousness of solidarity, which is expressed as "interconnectedness" in Steere's treatment of intercessory prayer. This interconnectedness provides the climate in which the "seeds of concern" can flourish. Steere's approach to ecumenism and interfaith encounter is also grounded in his conception of the interconnectedness of all souls in God and will be examined later in this study.

The last chapter of the book is entitled "The Dialogue of Prayer and Action," and there are several passages in it that illuminate the first three theses. In this chapter Steere takes the unfolding of concerns out of the context of Quaker worship and puts it in the context of private prayer. It may be remembered that in Steere's first book, *Prayer and Worship*, he stated that Quakers lack a word for the "tiny promptings . . . that may represent concerns in the forming."[139] In this book he coins a phrase to describe these tiny promptings, i.e., "seeds of concern." His treatment of concerns in this chapter reaffirms the second part of the awareness thesis; that is, that "seeds of concern" arise out of a perception of solidarity with all persons. He states that, "In prayer, the seeds of concern have a way of appearing. Often enough, a concern begins in a feeling of being personally liable, personally responsible, for someone or some event."[140] Here solidarity is expressed in terms of personal liability and responsibility.

In his treatment of contemplation Steere describes how prayer fosters a willingness to participate in God's redemptive order. In a brief paragraph he outlines his understanding of what contemplation does for willingness.

Contemplation is not a state of coma, or of religious reverie. If it is genuine prayer, we find our inward life quickened. We sense new directions, or our attention is refocused on neglected ones. We find ourselves being mobilized and our inward resources regrouped in response to the new assignment. We find, in short, that we have been re-enlisted in the redemptive order, that, in these ranks, our former reservations are brushed to one side and a new level of expendability emerges.[141]

In this outline, three effects of genuine prayer upon willingness are evident. The "quickening of the inward life" may be understood as spiritual refreshment. The "new directions" or refocusing on "neglected" directions may be conceived of as new or renewed vision. And, finally, in the "regrouping of resources" there is a mobilization for participation in the redemptive order.

Another concept related to the second thesis is that prayer leads to ethical intensification. Such an ethical intensification leads to a painful dissatisfaction with injustice and creates the condition for an active engagement in righting the wrong. Steere writes that, "There is an ethical sharpening in real Christian prayer which is highly dangerous to any complacency with the order of things as they are."[142] This ethical intensification comes about as the result of the power of prayer to nurture an awareness of God's infinite concern for every person, "for to come into the field force of God's infinite caring is to feel inwardly the terrible pull of the unlimited liability for another which the New Testament ethic lays upon us."[143] This ethical intensification appears to be involved in what was earlier described as gaining a renewed vision. In prayer, a Christian gains a renewed vision of God's infinite love and caring, inspiring the Christian to share in God's redemptive work.

Within the context of Quaker spirituality, communal discernment regarding "major" concerns serves as a means of refining and reshaping a concern. As he is writing here for Methodist readers, Steere has to make some adjustments. Here he speaks of submitting concerns that "might involve a considerable change" to "rational scrutiny."[144] This rational scrutiny may involve taking the concern to "wise and trusted people." It may also become clear when a person is engaged in following out a concern that it must be readjusted. In the process of submitting the concern to rational scrutiny, the concern arising in prayer is entering into action. The action serves to clarify what is perceived in prayer (fourth thesis). Steere describes the clarification which action brings to prayer in this way:

> As has already been said, no battery of tests can ever guarantee that a concern which comes in prayer may not be a mistaken one. Yet, if we are willing to have it questioned and are able to keep our faith in the living network into which our life has been drawn, then if we take the wrong fork at any point, and its wrongness becomes clear, perhaps painfully clear to us, there is always the next fork of the road where we may be drawn back in the right direction.[145]

The original bidding that came in prayer is clarified as it enters into action and, over time, the concern finds clearer direction.

The first part of the fifth thesis holds that prayer and social responsibility are incomplete in themselves. The necessity for both is expressed, in this book, in the nature of the "seeds of concern." Steere writes that, "Seeds, not fruit, are given in prayer, but they are given for planting."[146] For this reason prayer alone is insufficient. The seeds of concern rot unless they are planted in the soil of action.

This concludes the treatment of what this book offers to an understanding of the organizing theses, but there are several points pertaining to the efficacy of spiritually rooted social concerns that should be considered.

For example, Steere sheds light on the way acts of social responsibility that arise out of the life of prayer are different from those which have no grounding in it. Although Steere does not focus directly upon this question, he does offer an explanation of the difference. He writes:

There is a further feature of the following out of these concerns that rise in prayer. There is a sense in which the power of prayer indwells them even when they have passed from intention into action. It is not alone as in a truly personal act where it can be said that its goodness comes from the act of being all of one piece: what I am is what I do. Now it is not only what I am, but it is what God is, that threads into this act and gives it the power to open the life around it. It is this which makes it more than a sundered, separate event, that in fact makes it rather a facet of a living current which the prayer and the faithfulness in following out the prayer has unleashed in the situation.[147]

The concern that arises in prayer and is faithfully carried out draws on the very power of the One who inspired the concern. The concern is not merely a personal one which depends upon the personal integrity of the actor, but a divine concern which carries with it the power of the divine redemptive activity. The person who faithfully carries out a concern is unleashing the power of the God's infinite concern.

There is another factor which gives spiritually rooted social concerns special efficacy. The one who prays has a persistence and patience in carrying out a concern which is grounded in a knowledge that he or she is a co-worker with God. "The man who prays is made able to bear slow motion, the pace of a hen. He is given a dogged persistence, grounded in an assurance that he does not work alone."[148] This "staying power" on the part of the one who prays often wears down the resistances of those who oppose the redemptive process.

This concludes the treatment of the relation of prayer and social responsibility in the books that Steere has written. This analysis will now turn to the key articles and pamphlets that pertain to this subject. These articles cover the period from 1960 to 1984 and, thus, fill in much of the gap from the writing of *Dimensions of Prayer* to the present.

"Foreword to an Anatomy of Worship"

Between the last book considered, *Dimensions of Prayer* (1962), and the first article, "Foreword to an Anatomy of Worship"[149] (1960), there is an overlap of two years. Although this breaks the chronological sequence in which the works are being considered, it has the value of putting the articles in the context of a more complete understanding of Steere's spiritual theology. The articles play an important role in this study as they are often more revealing than the books in showing how Steere has related his spiritual theology to current events, i.e., third world development, the ecumenical movement, interfaith encounter, civil rights, and the Vietnam war. His approach to each of these issues is rooted in the spiritual theology already examined.

"Foreword to an Anatomy of Worship" appeared in the March, 1960 issue of *Pastoral Psychology*. Among the articles being considered, it offers the least insight into Steere's engagement with current social issues; however, it shows the philosophical framework underlying Steere's theology of worship. Just as Steere used listening as an analogue for the attitude of worship in *On Listening to Another*, here he uses anatomy as an analogue for the structure of worship. In this article Steere contrasts two approaches to worship that seem as opposed to each other as the "geocentric and heliocentric"[150] theories of the heavens; nevertheless, they must be reconciled. These two theories provide a fresh perspective on the organizing theses.

The first theory of worship suggests that worship is a response to a Challenger. It emphasizes the Otherness of God and a descending christology. Worship, even at its best, is an inadequate response to the "shower of costing love that has been spilled out upon man by a God whose ground of holiness our worship hovers before but never plumbs."[151] Such an approach to worship is difficult to evaluate because it is directed beyond human categories. In describing this problem, Steere writes:

> When we begin to ask how we may judge between the adequacy of a liturgical service, or a silent Quaker meeting for worship or a free church "sermon-centered" gathering, it is with great difficulty that this school of worship can sort them out. For all three services when they are genuine aim to take man beyond himself, to open his cabined life to another dimension, to reawaken him to what is really going on, to compel him to pay attention.[152]

Steere names this "school" of worship the "God-centered" approach. He contrasts it with the "worshiper-centered" school, which is much easier to evaluate.

The worshiper-centered school puts the accent on the human person and what happens to him or her in the worship experience. By a study of psychology or anthropology, the various acts of worship can be seen as revealing the "human needs and aspirations and projections of the worshiper."[153] The adequacy of the worship experience can be determined by judging whether it meets these human needs. For the "proper question is not 'Is the worship a suitable response to that which provokes it?' but rather, 'What does worship do for the worshiper?'"[154]

The questions above indicate the radical opposition of these two approaches to worship. Their judgment of each other can be harsh.

> To ask what worship does to the worshiper is to the first approach not only to ask an irrelevant question but to leave us open to a blasphemous cheapening of worship by looking upon it as a mere therapeutic device, perhaps a kind of tranquilizing drug to produce a state of peace of mind or peace of soul in the worshiper. To refer the quality of the worship, on the other hand, to its appropriateness to the Holy Presence to which it is responding would to the second approach be an attempt to place the norm of judgment outside human apprehension . . .[155]

These judgments upon each other indicate the fundamental difference of these two approaches.

Steere suggests (with tongue in cheek) that, rather than trying to solve the dilemma presented by these perspectives, it would be much easier merely to label the God-centered approach as the "objective or realist theory of worship and the second [the worshiper-centered] as the subjective or anthropological."[156] Along with these titles, it might be understood that each had it own particular value. For it would affirm that "adoration in worship required the first approach and that repentance and ethical concern was best dealt with by the second."[157] In this way these two approaches could be safely compartmentalized, and the issue could be set aside.

Although Steere can see no way to reconcile these two approaches, he is unwilling to have them compartmentalized and have the wholeness of Christian worship fragmented. As violently opposed as they appear, "both contribute their insight and must both claim our loyalty."[158] The first approach has correctly "described the field of force in which a challenge and a Challenger stand, and have made clear that to worship is to enter this magnetic field."[159] On the other hand, the genius of the second approach is that it "probes what is or what is not taking place in the worshiper upon the occasion of worship."[160] Steere argues for a holistic approach to worship which incorporates both aspects of worship.

Having argued for an understanding of worship that includes both approaches, Steere suggests some criteria for measuring the adequacy of worship which draws upon each of them. The criteria come in the form of Quaker queries. These queries are important for this study in two ways: first, they reveal Steere's most fundamental views on the nature of worship and, second, they sharpen an understanding of the first two theses.

The first set of queries is related to the deepening of an awareness of creatureliness (first thesis).

The first query might be: Does the service give a sense of the greatness and majesty and mystery of God? Does it help produce a feeling of awe and wonder before the God of the universe?[161]

Later he queries whether the service provides "an occasion for the worshiper to feel the raising up of concerns in his heart of specific things to be done?"[162] These queries encompass the meaning of the first thesis and show how fundamental it is in Steere's spiritual theology.

The second set of queries is related to the second thesis and the linkage to the first thesis is suggested by Steere.

Closely linked to this might be the query: Does the service arouse in the worshiper the fact of cosmic caring, that the God of the infinite universe is infinitely concerned for the soul of every man and woman and child? Does it give the worshiper a sense of God's act in Jesus Christ and of the costliness of this redemptive passion that has poured itself out toward him?[163]

These queries show that worship must nurture an awareness of God's infinite concern for every person (first part of the second thesis). In turn, this awareness should lead to a willingness to participate in the redemptive order. This concern is expressed in later queries.

> Does the service give the worshiper a sense that he is not alone but that as a Christian he is a member of a great community made up of the living and the dead, of the faithful, the martyrs, the saints, the grateful-hearted followers in every generation who are a part of a redemptive community that God is using to redeem the world? . . .
> Does the service of worship not only give a corporate sense of involvement in the redemption of all, but does it single out each worshiper and give him a sense of coming under the burning gaze of God? . . .
> Does the service of worship lay on the worshiper the burden of the world's suffering and heighten the worshiper's personal responsibility to become a link in the chain of the Divine causation? Does it draw him into the great fellowship of intercession?[164]

As these queries show, Steere not only emphasizes the need for a deep awareness of corporateness but also for a deepened sense of personal responsibility. These enrich one another and increase the willingness of the worshiper to be spent in the service of God.

These two approaches to worship refine the meaning of the first two theses in another way. The first part of both the first and second theses may be considered "God-centered." The awareness of creatureliness (first thesis) is deepened because, in prayer, one is confronted with the otherness of the Creator. An awareness of God's infinite concern (second thesis) is nurtured in prayer because the one praying is mindful of God's grace manifested in Jesus Christ. The first part of each thesis is God-centered and corresponds with what Steere earlier characterized as an objectivist or realist approach. The second part of the first two theses may be considered as "worshiper-centered." In each thesis the worshiper or "pray-er" makes a response to the givenness of God expressed in the first part. In the first thesis the response comes as the worshiper opens him or herself to the unfolding of concerns. The response in the second thesis is expressed as a "willingness to participate in God's redemptive order." The second part of each thesis is "worshiper-centered" and corresponds with what Steere calls the subjective (existentialist) approach. With this understanding it becomes clear that Steere's approach to worship and the relation of prayer and social responsibility is expressed in the context of his philosophical stance as an existential realist.

In this article Steere has sought to be sensitive to the claims of both approaches to worship. These two "schools" need each other. Although Steere never seeks to define the relationship of these two approaches, his analysis suggests that the worshiper-centered aspect of worship is an outgrowth of the God-centered approach. The existential response grows out of a realist foundation. As helpful as this may be for understanding the first two theses, Steere's real concern in this article is not to define the relationship of these "schools," but to advocate an approach to worship that incorporates the God-centered and the worshiper-centered aspects of worship.

"Development for What?"

Of all the articles being considered in this study, "Development for What?"[165] is most directly concerned with a current social issue. The article appeared in a book of the same title in 1964. In the foreword, the book's editor, John H. Hallowell, describes the issue that the book seeks to address:

> The emergence of new nations in Africa and Asia has presented the older nations of the Western world with a formidable challenge, for we in the West are now called upon not only to lend assistance but to justify the kind of assistance we deem most appropriate. The more involved we become with the problems of the new nations the less assurance we feel that we know with certainty the direction which "development" should take, . . . [166]

Eight authors address the issue from a variety of disciplines, i.e., economics, political science, sociology, history, and theology. Steere approaches the issue from a philosophical perspective. In introducing Steere's article, Hallowell writes:

> His essay has provided the title for our symposium and the questions he raises, though not easy to answer, are not intended, as he says, to discourage us from helping other peoples in their self-development but to suggest that we approach the problems with humility, with as much concern to learn as to teach, with as much eagerness to receive as to give.[167]

There is little reference to religion in Steere's article but it is revealing to find that, even addressing a political audience, the first two theses inform his argument.

Steere's personalism is apparent in his approach. He analyzes the human objectives of development and suggests that the neglect of the human objectives of development exposes the superficiality of the current effort. He writes:

> I have often wondered if one of the principal reasons why the study of the human objectives of development is so neglected by the writers of the developed countries is perhaps the fact that to carry it out with any thoroughness would inevitably involve us in an agonizing reappraisal of our own human goals, of our own value system, and of our own inward development or the lack of it. All of this can be so comfortably avoided if we can assume that our Western pattern of affluent life is what the developing countries are yearning for and that our technological apparatus will assure them of this if we put it into their hands.[168]

Steere argues that part of the responsibility of the giver of aid is to consider the human objectives in its giving. If the human objectives were seriously considered it might transform the development process.

> For at least until now, the giving countries are not giving in costly enough measure to even begin to take on the proportions adequate to the task, . . . nor are they really deeply involved in the issue of a major mobilization of their resources for this task. And it is doubtful that we can ever become genuinely engaged and committed until we are profoundly convinced that

what is being undertaken can be justified in terms of an achievable human goal that we inwardly approve of, and that it is a human goal which the recipients of this development program also accept.[169]

The inward searching to which Steere is calling the giving nations bears a striking resemblance to his proposal for personal growth (development). It is as if the nations are a group of individuals involved in interpersonal relations. The nation as well as the person must "begin from within" to realize solidarity with all peoples and to regroup and mobilize resources for an appropriate response to those in need. The similarities of his approach to the individual's social responsibility and the nation's social responsibility become even more apparent in the presuppositions that guide his presentation.

Steere outlines five presuppositions that guide his discussion of the human objectives of development. The first presupposition is related to the solidarity theme in the first thesis (i.e., that the awareness of creatureliness evokes a consciousness of solidarity). Under the section title, "We Are Already Involved with Each Other," Steere describes the economic and cultural interpenetration which already exists and cannot be reversed. This interpenetration is a given for Steere and it is the proper place to start. Although very modestly stated here, the givenness of interpenetration is a another way of speaking of solidarity. The identification of interpenetration with solidarity has been noted in the treatment of earlier works and lends credibility to claim that they are connected in this article.

The second section is entitled "Able But Unwilling?" and, obviously enough, pertains to the willingness thesis. In this section Steere claims that for the first time in human history the technological tools are available for meeting the "elemental human requirements of food, shelter, medical care, and education if these technological tools are adequately used."[170] After exposing how far short this possibility is from being fulfilled, he writes that:

> In the present situation, it is the spiritual problem of willingness, not the economic problem of ability, to help the developing nations which is the real issue. . . . Able but still largely unwilling is the only honest verdict that could be rendered in regard to our present token contribution of men and women or material to this cause of assisting a massive break-through on the part of the developing nations.[171]

If this "spiritual" problem is analyzed in the light of the first two theses it shows that the people of the giving nations have not become fully conscious of their "solidarity with all persons and all creation" nor have they cultivated "an awareness of God's infinite concern for every person." They have not given themselves to the discipline of prayer that could make them "willing to participate in God's redemptive order." This demonstrates that the solidarity with all people, evoked in prayer and contemplation, has a payoff in rendering one aware of social responsibility, while the same contemplative movement renders one "willing" to be active in addressing specific social needs.

The other three presuppositions that guide Steere's treatment of the human objectives in development are not related to the organizing theses.

The main value of this article is that it discloses how Steere applies the fundamentals of his spiritual theology to a particular social issue. The spiritual theology outlined in the first two theses informs his approach to the concrete social issues that he confronts.

"Common Frontiers in Catholic and Non-Catholic Spirituality"

In the foreword to the Steere's Pendle Hill pamphlet entitled *Mutual Irradiation* (1971), the editor observed that Steere has had a concern for "mutual irradiation" for almost two decades. According to the editor this concern had its beginnings in the Steeres' visit to Japan and India (1954) where they "opened themselves to Hinduism and Zen Buddhism, seeking to discern the message of each, and its relevance to the Christian life of the spirit."[172]   During his visit to Japan, Steere delivered a lecture entitled "The Quaker Message: Unique or Universal," which constituted the core of his later lecture entitled "Mutual Irradiation." Mutual irradiation is not limited to interfaith encounter; it also guided Steere's approach to ecumenism.

The next three articles to be considered reflect Steere's profound engagement with ecumenical and interfaith interpenetration.

During the 1960s Steere was involved in three sessions of Vatican II, the first intimate Zen-Christian Colloquium in Japan and a similar Hindu-Christian Colloquium in India, the Anglican Lambeth Conference in 1968, and the founding (with Godfrey Diekmann) of the Ecumenical Institute for Spirituality. These articles, all of which are informed by his experience of religious interpenetration, will reveal the way in which Steere's foundational spiritual theology--revealed in the first two theses--underlies his approach to ecumenical and interfaith encounter.

The first meeting of the Ecumenical Institute of Spirituality took place at St. John's Abbey at Collegeville, Minnesota in August, 1965. The participants included: Barnabas Ahern, Joseph Caulfield, John Coburn, Gordon Cosby, Horton Davies, Godfrey Diekmann, Bernard Haring, Thomas Hopko, Thomas Kilduff, Robert Lechner, Jean LeClerq, Richard Luecke, Boniface Luyckx, Michael Marx, J. O. Nelson, Elmer O'Brien, Robert Raines, D. H. Salman, D. V. Steere, and Keith Watkins. Steere and Coburn chose the Protestant participants and Godfrey Diekmann chose the Roman Catholics. At this gathering Steere presented a paper entitled "Common Frontiers in Catholic and Non-Catholic Spirituality."[173]   It was published along with the six other papers delivered in *Worship*. In 1965, in response to demand for more copies, these papers were issued in paperback form under the title *Protestants and Catholics on the Spiritual Life*.

In this essay the elements that are most valuable for this study come under the headings of "Individual Responsibility" and "Personal Involvement in Responsibility for our Fellows." Steere begins his treatment of individual responsibility by reflecting on his meeting with Abbot Herwegen of the Maria Laach monastery. Steere had recently arrived at Maria Laach in order to spend a month sharing the Benedictine life and asked Abbot Herwegen for a guide who could lay out a spiritual retreat for him. The Abbot responded that he had come to the wrong place; he should have gone to the Jesuits who believed in individual spiritual journeys. The Benedictines, the Abbot pointed out, "had no hope of salvation by their own prayers or inner yieldings. If they were saved at all, it was as a member of the Benedictine family and all quite unself-consciously as the result of the family's *Opus Dei*."[174] Steere considered the Abbott's amusing response a marvelous introduction to the flavor of Benedictinism, but suspected that each monk has an individual responsibility to give himself more completely to God and wondered if this responsibility could really be transferred to the "family." Steere adds that he is confident that the best contemporary Benedictine thought would confirm the need for individual responsibility.

Steere turns to the Quaker tradition as one that fosters the "individual's unmediated accountability to the indwelling Christ for following out the guidance"[175] that comes to him or her. For Steere, the fostering of individual responsibility to God is the ultimate task of ascetic theology; he writes:

> For if our ultimate task is to nurture the response which individual human beings make to the infinite donation of redemptive grace that draws at their lives, can it do this unless it finally succeeds in quickening this ultimate seed of accountability in the breast of the Christian? . . . If, in ascetic theology's guidance in the use of spiritual direction, confession, private and public prayer, fasting, devotional reading, or the service of the poor and the afflicted, it should happen that we dry up or diminish a man's inner responsibility to God in Christ or to his following the direct guidance of the Holy Spirit, and instead increase his dependence on the outward apparatus that we may provide, far from favoring him, we may have permanently crippled and deformed the very center or seed in him that God has bid us to arouse and encourage.[176]

This nurturing of the individual's response to the "infinite donation of redemptive grace" and the following of the "direct guidance of the Holy Spirit" are other ways of expressing what is meant in the second thesis by "a willingness to participate in God's redemptive order." Each is a way of responding to God.

Similar guidance occurs in Steere's treatment of "Personal Involvement in Responsibility for our Fellows." He mentions those who have been deeply involved (often to the point of being jailed for acts of civil disobedience) in the civil rights struggle, in support of Cesar Chavez's farm workers, and in peace and anti-nuclear vigils; and he notes how their involvement served to deepen their spiritual lives.

> Many Catholics and Protestants have found the nearest they have ever come to sensing what is really meant by abandonment to God has come in such experiences, and they know them as authentic means of kindling the life of God in their souls.[177]

Here acts of social responsibility have served to deepen their relationship with God. Although this does not fit the exact form of the fourth thesis (i.e., Acts of social responsibility clarify and test the genuineness of prayer.), it is closely related because it demonstrates that acts of social responsibility enrich the spiritual life. Indeed, the "kindling of the life of God in their souls" may have resulted from the clarification and testing that comes in acts of social responsibility.

The other "common frontiers" that Steere considers in this article are spiritual direction and the cultivation of the practice of private prayer, but there is little in them that illuminates the organizing theses. The main value of this article is that it reveals Steere's characteristic Quaker emphasis on the "individual's unmediated accountability to the indwelling Christ." Steere wants to guard against any method or system of spirituality that usurps the individual's direct responsibility to God.

The Hardest Journey

In March of 1968 Steere delivered the West Coast Quaker Lecture at Whittier College in Whittier, California. The lecture was jointly sponsored by the college and the California and Pacific Yearly Meetings of the Religious Society of Friends. This lecture, published in pamphlet form by Pendle Hill under the title *The Hardest Journey*,[178] is important for this study because it expresses the relation of prayer and social responsibility from the perspective of the inward and outward journey.

The hardest journey is the journey inward, the journey toward God. Many people experience the great difficulty of this journey and Steere notes that many Protestants and Roman Catholics in Britain and the United States have turned to Quakers for insights on the inward journey. He finds it humbling to be viewed as "seasoned veterans in the inward life when we ourselves know all too well our poverty and mediocrity in this area."[179] He sees, however, these queries as challenges to be better custodians of the Quaker heritage. This is the burden of his lecture--to help Quakers appropriate their tradition of inner openness to God.

As he begins to develop his subject, Steere turns to his recent experiences in ecumenical and interfaith encounter for what they have done to challenge and illuminate his understanding of the inward journey. He speaks first of how the encounter with Zen Buddhism challenged the Quaker participants. The encounter raised some deep questions. "Do we know at first hand how true subjectivity, awareness, attention, compassion, unlimited liability for our fellows, and a return to the infinitely compassionate ground of our being can take place?"[180] In the second part of the lecture he offers his own answer to this query and, though put in terms of the inward and outward journey, it follows the same pattern of Quaker spirituality as that outlined in *On Listening to Another*.

Steere's experience at Vatican II provides the theme for the next section of his lecture--it is entitled "The Epoch of the Holy Spirit." He introduces this theme by summarizing the debate between Cardinal Ruffini and Cardinal Suenens over the role of charisms in the Church. Steere was pleased that the Council favored

Suenens and reminds the audience that the witness of the Society of Friends has always been that the apostolic period of Christian witness has never stopped. He goes on to describe the role of the Holy Spirit in Quaker spirituality.

> For Friends who know no outward sacraments, this tendering action of the Holy Spirit is the baptism; it is the communion; it is the hallower of all facets of life. It is the revealer of injustice and the dissolver of men's dikes of reservation to the costly correction of those wrongs; it is the great magnet to draw men here and now from their enmities, their violence, their wars-- into the peaceable kingdom, and to soften their hard hearts to each other, restoring brotherliness and liability for each other; it is the reconciler, the enabler, the ever-present power of the inward Christ that was not only promised by the historical Jesus but that has been experienced and lived in here and now by how many millions of apostles.
> The starkly elemental Quaker meetings for worship, for business, and the Quaker faith in the following of inward concerns in a trust that if they are in right ordering, way will open for their fulfillment, are built on an experience of the continual operation of this Pentecostal Spirit.[181]

The power of the Holy Spirit to "draw men . . . into the peaceable kingdom," to dissolve "dikes of reservations," to enable response--all these indicate the role of the Holy Spirit in fostering a willingness to participate in God's redemptive order. The Holy Spirit is also described as being the ever-present power of the inward Christ. If this conception is paraphrased in the context of Steere's other writings it could be rendered: The Holy Spirit causes (through its tendering action) the "seeds of concern" to arise in the consciousness of the one who prays. The Holy Spirit also guides the unfolding and empowers the carrying out of these concerns.

Reflecting on the "fiercely activistic" engagement of many Protestant clergy and theologians, Steere suggests that the Quaker community (with its inwardly directed concerns) may have some important insights to share with the larger Christian community. In this time of activism (an activism which Steere suggests may be referred to by future historians as the "Jericho-Roadism of the late 60s") some may want to ask the Friends "how you keep from going over the cliff into the heresy of sheer activism."[182] Steere's answer is, of course, the inward journey and the necessity of beginning from within.

In his treatment of the inward journey, Steere returns to many of the familiar themes that have already been analyzed; however, his conception of concerns as a link between the inward and outward journey merits further consideration. Toward the end of the lecture he states:

> Now there has been little in this exploration of the journey inward about the seeds of concerns that, like the unused life in us, have a way of appearing when we are still enough to hear God speak. These concerns are the bridge over which the inward journey often moves outwards. When these seeds are sown in us they are not potted plants, and much is still needed to give them what they require to grow to full stature. . . . It is a wonderful thing when inward and outward journey are in living connection

for then we get a real sense of what it means to live in the Providence of God and to have a first-hand experience of Joachim of Fiore's 'Epoch of the Holy Spirit.'[183]

Concerns provide a "bridge," a "living connection" between the inward and outward journey and, for the purposes of this study, between prayer and social responsibility. This is where the "spiritually-rooted social concerns" come from. This presentation basically parallels the thought of the first thesis.

At the conclusion of this lecture Steere suggests that on occasion the inward and outward journey may "coalesce."[184] The condition for such a coalescence is a pervasive "mood of creatureliness." The inward journey may evoke such an profound awareness of solidarity with all creation that it quite naturally expresses itself in costly acts of caring for God's creatures. There is no mention here of alternation or simultaneity, rather the inward and outward journey appear more as two stages in the contemplative process. The mood of creatureliness that is nurtured by the inward journey carries over into the acting out of concerns. This conception represents an integration at the level of the first thesis. The inward journey is integrally connected to the outward journey through concerns.

"The Life of Prayer as the Ground for Unity"

With the exception of *Mutual Irradiation*, "The Life of Prayer as the Ground for Unity"[185] most clearly discloses Steere's approach to ecumenism. Steere delivered the paper "in 1969 at an International Workshop on Ecumenism organized by Catholics in Philadelphia and honored with the presence of Cardinal Willebrans."[186] It was published in *Worship* in 1971 and in *Together in Solitude* in 1982. This article, more than any other, shows that Steere's approach to ecumenism is grounded in the spiritual theology outlined in the organizing theses.

Steere sums up the purpose of his paper in this way:

> This radical medicine of prayer and contemplation, with its steady drawing and its tendering, its lifting up and its putting down, its singling out and its bringing into focus the ever new decisions with which we are confronted, is a medicine that we must help each other to supply.
> The plea for it, which it is the sole purpose of this paper to advance, may give us some clue as to how the ecumenical movement might be fed if, at this point, it could be persuaded to open itself to this inward side of its common life.[187]

This opening of the "inward side of its common life" characterizes Steere's approach to ecumenism. Whether it is social action or ecumenical encounter, Steere seeks to begin from within. The opening of the inward side creates the climate in which one can be penetrated by another's faith, as well as share one's own. This opening is extremely costly and goes beyond dialogue. It suggests vulnerability on the part of all who are engaged in the encounter. Steere has chosen the expression "mutual irradiation" for this kind of encounter.[188]

Although Steere seldom makes reference to the Quaker christology that permeates his approach, it should not be overlooked. His approach is consistent with the central Quaker conviction that there is a Light in every person and this Light is Christ. Although Quakers are not interested in proof-texting from the Bible, the Biblical basis for this conviction is found in John's gospel: "The true light, which enlightens everyone, was coming into the world." (John 1:9 NRSV) This opening of the deepest dimension of the inward life (the Light within) to one another is the sharing of the inward Christ and results in mutual irradiation. In contemplation, people come closer to the Light. As they come closer to the central Light of Christ, they come closer to one another. It is this common movement toward the inward Light of Christ and the sharing of this Light that characterizes Steere's spiritually grounded approach to ecumenism. If this christological presupposition is forgotten, Steere's approach may appear to lack a theological foundation.

Steere puts little emphasis upon institutional restructuring for the sake of ecumenism. Rather, he emphasizes what each tradition can offer the other for deepening its spiritual life and fostering its social responsibility; he writes:

> I believe that the ecumenical movement will be weighed in the gospel balance by the fruits it produces, and that in the end these fruits will have less to do than many surmise with the institutional restructuring that may or may not accompany its development. The real test will be whether it can help to turn us around, can help to deepen our personal and corporate prayer, can increase in us the universal love for our fellow creatures that the gospel ethic interprets in terms of an unlimited liability for one another, and can give us the courage and imagination to go about its implementation in the world.[189]

Although this passage is intended to offer criteria for measuring the true value of the ecumenical movement, it reveals a great deal about Steere's approach to ecumenism. The emphasis is on creating the climate for growth in sanctity rather than on ever larger and more inclusive institutions. The movement toward unity should come out of a "universal love for our fellow creatures" that is deepened in the personal and corporate life of prayer. This "universal love for our fellow creatures" corresponds to the "awareness of creatureliness" in the first thesis, and the phrase "unlimited liability for one another" is synonymous with the "consciousness of solidarity" that grows out of the awareness of creatureliness. This establishes that Steere's approach to ecumenism proceeds from his spiritual theology; specifically, from that outlined in the first thesis. From this perspective, the life of prayer is the ground for unity.

As the life of prayer is considered the ground for unity, Steere quite naturally follows the presentation of his approach to ecumenism by sharing his own insights into the life of prayer. The next two sections are entitled "Action Clarifies Prayer" and "Prayer Cleanses Action and Restores Its Frame." Both sections return to the familiar themes outlined in the organizing theses; however, in this article there are added insights into Steere's development of these themes.

In the section "Action Clarifies Prayer," Steere acknowledges that some "cleft" between prayer and action must be maintained. "To point out some cleft between the decking of the head in adoration and the washing of the feet [a reference to Walter Hilton's criticism of those who adorn Christ's head in prayer but neglect his feet], between the vision of prayer and the deed of commitment, is essential."[190] Nonetheless, Steere argues that this cleft can occasionally be bridged; he writes, "prayer does not always stop on the vision side of the cleft; and . . . action, the fruits, have always been a test of Christian prayer."[191] This crossing of the cleft is another way of expressing the integration/simultaneity thesis. As was seen in *The Hardest Journey* the bridge for crossing this cleft is found in the concerns that arise in prayer. Action is the means by which the vision of prayer is tested. Action clarifies the original bidding that came in prayer.[192]

The section entitled "Prayer Cleanses Action and Restores Its Frame" contains the most complete development of the cleansing thesis in all of his works. In considering this passage it is important to remember that it was written at the peak of the social activism of the 60s. Following his treatment of how action clarifies prayer, he continues:

> But to think that acts alone, even apparently selfless acts are enough to win justice for the deprived is again to fall into the cleft from the other side. For acts require vision or they themselves become loveless and bitter and lifeless. . . .
> Many may come into the life of prayer and worship today through disillusionment with action alone, just as the counter culture contemplatives are staggering their way by all kinds of routes to something that will transcend the highly disciplined industrial society, which seems to them to be harnessed to values which they, like the earlier Franciscans in their society, find not worth the effort. Others may be won to it by experiences of decisive action, by moments when they are swept beyond themselves. And still others may be drawn to pause when they find that at last they belong to mankind by having identified themselves with groups which until now they have never even faintly understood.[193]

Steere's development of the cleansing thesis here parallels that in *Work and Contemplation*. In the latter he asserts that "work without contemplation is bitter and blind,"[194] and in this article he writes that acts without the vision of prayer become "loveless and bitter and lifeless." Although acts alone are insufficient, in some cases they may make the actor crave for the frame of meaning that is revealed in prayer and worship. Specifically, Steere mentions three avenues by which people are often led through action into the life of prayer: disillusionment with action alone, moments of transcendence experienced in the midst of action, and action in solidarity with the oppressed, which fosters an awareness of creatureliness.

Steere asserts that the cleansing power of prayer is especially necessary for those who are committed to the path of nonviolence.

> For those determined to take the nonviolent approach both to help the deprived find their way to put a floor under their poverty and to lessen the

disparity in income, health, longevity, and educational opportunities, prayer becomes an even more indispensable agency toward the recovering of the strength and love for both the deprived and for those cast in the role of the depriver. For without this center of renewal there can be little hope of resisting the temptations to drop back into the violent way, and to help to build up the walls of hatred and contempt that the future will inherit for its destruction. Not by accident did Jesus resist those temptations in the desert and their repetition almost every day of his life.[195]

Prayer is portrayed here as a "center of renewal" that fosters a universal love that, while favoring the deprived, encompasses even those viewed as oppressors.

One of the greatest values of prayer, as it is developed in Steere's spiritual theology, is that it punctuates the automatic nature of much human activity. It serves as a tool for dishabituation. Activity without prayer leads to immersion in visionless activity. Steere describes the danger of such an immersion:

This means that if we sleep on in overactivity or underattention and smother these biddings in favor of the universe's repetitive mechanisms--the customary expectations which we have of each other, the rigidities of our relationships, the hopelessness and despair of any lasting or significant changes that sabotage positive measures for their unlimbering--then God's whole strategy may have to be altered.[196]

There may be new biddings that come in prayer or alterations to previous concerns, that if ignored, may hinder the redemptive process. As the third thesis states it, prayer cleanses action of its repetitive nature and restores its frame of meaning.

The examination of this article has established that Steere's approach to ecumenism is rooted in the spiritual theology outlined in the first thesis. It has also yielded additional insights into the cleansing thesis and has explained how Steere's spiritual theology informed his response to the social activism of the late 1960s.

Introduction to *Quaker Spirituality*

The final work to be considered is Steere's Introduction to *Quaker Spirituality*. Assuming that his readers have little acquaintance with the subject, Steere reviews the history of the Society of Friends and summarizes the distinctive traits of its spirituality. He also responds to the most common critiques of Quaker worship and practice, a response that will be carefully examined in a later chapter. The value, however, of the Introduction for this chapter is the way it informs the first thesis. The treatment of corporate worship and the unfolding of concerns enrich what has already been learned about them.

Steere seldom writes about private prayer without also indicating the importance of corporate worship. In this Introduction he describes some of the specific benefits inherent in corporate worship.

The individualism and pride and possessiveness that often creep into private prayer is dissolved away as we meet together in worship. The inward Christ makes the individual worshiper feel all afresh that he is just one ordinary sheep in God's vast fold, and often sweeps his heart with an overwhelming sense of creatureliness.[197]

Although an awareness of creatureliness may be sensed in private prayer, corporate worship confronts the worshiper with the reality of the larger human community and draws him or her beyond a purely individual perspective. Such a confrontation enables the worshiper to transcend the individualism, pride, and possessiveness to which private prayer is particularly vulnerable. As worship deepens, an even more profound identification with others may emerge.

In corporate worship, the inward Christ seems to gather the worshipping community and again and again to draw each person from his separate solitariness into a solidarity with all who breathe.[198]

The awareness of creatureliness, which is especially nurtured in corporate worship, evokes a consciousness of solidarity. The sense of solidarity is made more concrete by the presence of other worshipers. Without corporate worship, private prayer can easily replace solidarity with a vague sense of unity, diluting the consciousness of social responsibility.

The consciousness of solidarity is the penultimate dynamic of Quaker worship; the ultimate dynamic is the unfolding of concerns which arise out of the perceived solidarity. The worshiper moves from the "sin of self-absorption into personal commitment to new levels of life. It leads to the ever-repeated discovery that Christ's gift is most often linked to a task . . . that calls for prompt fulfillment."[199]   The task is, of course, made conscious through the seeds of concern.

In this Introduction Steere makes a thorough analysis of the unfolding of concerns. The description of concerns follows the pattern of previous works, but his examination of the execution of concerns discloses the structure of Quaker discernment.

How such guidance [the divine guidance sensed in worship] is to be regarded and how it is to be followed raises the whole question of discernment. In what ways may individual Friends be helped to test the authenticity of a concern and how may they be assisted in coming to clearness about their own gifts in connection with what this may demand of them?

Here again the strong corporate side of Quakerism, which is so little understood outside the Society of Friends itself, has been able to furnish spiritual assistance that has so often proved invaluable to the one who is seeking to follow the inward Guide.

The traditional procedure is to call together a small committee of clearness. The committee meets with the person and listens to his concern, putting searching questions as to the nature of the concern, the fitness of the person in carrying it out, and what may be the Meeting's final financial obligation, should financial assistance be needed. In putting the questions and in the worshipful silence they have together to ask for divine wisdom, new facets of the concern may come to light to help the person in the clarification of the guidance that has come to him. The Quaker meeting for business has also been a place where concerns can be brought, especially if the Meeting itself might be involved in sponsoring the person, as in the case of a concern to travel in the ministry and in being willing to issue a minute to commend him or her for the task.[200]

Both the "committee of clearness" and the business meeting provide opportunities for communal discernment. In the process a person's concern may be tempered or redirected, but, conversely, a person's concern may also cause transformations in the community. Steere emphasizes this reciprocal relationship in his treatment.

Even the community that is to encourage and support the concern may have to go through painful change before its members are ready to unite with it. It would be hard to exaggerate the patience, the humility, the purging, the costly transformation that may have to take place before clarity is reached as to the form in which the concern is meant to be realized, but equally in the person and in the community before they are suitable instruments to assist in its realization.[201]

The process of discernment clears the vision and prepares the heart of the individual and the community.

Two other factors affecting the disposition of a concern are providence and detachment from results. Steere stresses the "amazing and almost overwhelming instances . . . of obstacles being removed; of unheard-of support in the way of persons, of money and services; . . . that give confirmation to the fact that we are not working alone."[202] The redemptive order already at work speeds the concern to its fulfillment and confirms the original bidding. On the other hand, "Quakers know all too well the danger of falling victim to the 'results' disease, and of the temptation to reject leadings where the results are not assured or where they appear highly doubtful."[203] When concerns apparently fail or fall short of fulfillment, they are interpreted through the Cross. Apparent failures may be the channel by which the redemptive process progresses. Steere affirms that "love's way will some day weary out the obstacles."[204] Paradoxically, the execution of a Quaker concern is accompanied by confidence in providence and detachment from results.

Steere's Introduction to *Quaker Spirituality* has provided a fitting conclusion to this analysis of his treatment of the relation of prayer and social responsibility. It shows that the first thesis fits hand in glove with his interpretation of Quaker spirituality. It has also provided important insights into how concerns (the bridge between the inward and outward journey) are developed when they pass beyond the protective environment of corporate worship. If, indeed, it is best to "begin from within," then it is appropriate to end on the threshold of the outward journey.

Summary

Before summarizing Steere's treatment of relation of prayer and social responsibility, there is one point that requires some clarification. Although this analysis has emphasized Steere's concern to "begin from within," it would be misleading to think that Steere always insists on beginning from within. Steere met his match on the issue of beginning from within during his conversations with Zen Buddhists. This encounter shows that, for Steere, the imperative of Christian love sometimes transcends the importance of beginning from within. In describing this conversation, Steere writes:

> When we were told of a Zen master who rebuked a novice for helping a man push his cart, we blinked. Quakers, too, believe that a clean act must come from the inside out like a rose-bud unfolding, and not the way we make a box. We, too, believe in the turning inward to find the true ground for any valid concern. But we have experienced often that "the mountain" [a reference to Zen meditation] where we meet another's need, may open the way to the inward "mountains," and we found ourselves much less sure than our guests, the Zen masters, that "going into the mountain," as they know it, necessarily comes first.[205]

This quote indicates the role that action and service may serve in opening the deeper reaches of meditation and shows that they do not always have to proceed from the interior life.

In describing Steere's career, E. Glenn Hinson has written, "Steere has fought in an active setting for what Thomas Merton contended for in a monastery, namely, how contemplation can inform and enrich action."[206] This helpful estimation of Steere's work is interesting but incomplete. Steere has also endeavored to describe what action does to test and clarify prayer. The full scope of Steere's treatment is summarized in the organizing theses.

From the analysis of Steere's treatment presented in this chapter, it is possible to see how each of the five organizing theses arises from Steere's writings and to see the far-ranging potential they have for uniting the dynamics of contemplation and social responsibility. Each one of the theses arises from a perspective on human spirituality which refuses to bifurcate prayer and justice.

The first thesis is "Prayer (especially corporate prayer) deepens an awareness of creatureliness and evokes a consciousness of solidarity with all persons and all creation. Out of this perceived solidarity 'seeds of concern' surface in the consciousness of the one who prays." This thesis arose out of Steere's concern to relate worship to an active life of service. It serves as an outline of his understanding of Quaker worship and guides his approach to ecumenical encounter.

The second thesis (Prayer nurtures an awareness of God's infinite concern for every person and fosters a willingness to participate in God's redemptive order.) originated in Steere's desire to reveal how prayer can transform the human will and make a person an effective agent of the divine will. It is especially important in Steere's treatment of the upper reaches of contemplation and in the training of the saint.

The third thesis is "Prayer cleanses action, work, and service of their repetitive nature and restores their frame of meaning." It expresses Steere's concern for an understanding of the relation of work and contemplation that is true to the "amphibian" nature of the human person. This thesis plays an important role in his critique of modern industrial work and in his plea for a restoration of the contemplative dimension of work.

The fourth thesis (Acts of social responsibility clarify and test the genuineness of prayer.) is rooted in Steere's theology of the active nature of divine love. Just as God's love must find expression, prayer must find some way to embody the divine love encountered in prayer. The thought expressed in this thesis serves as a tool for criticizing any form of disembodied prayer.

The fifth thesis is "Both prayer and social responsibility are incomplete in themselves. They are partially integrated through alternation and fully integrated through simultaneity." This thesis emerges from the same anthropology which informed the third thesis. It outlines two ways in which the "amphibian" nature of the human person may find fulfillment. Simultaneity, as it yields to a "collected life," represents the ultimate fulfillment of human nature and destiny.

This concludes the analysis of Steere's treatment of the relation of prayer and social responsibility. The analysis has demonstrated that the organizing theses are drawn from Steere's spiritual theology and that they accurately reflect Steere's method of relating prayer and social responsibility. This study has also established that the most appropriate term for characterizing the relation of prayer and social responsibility achieved in Steere's writings is "integration." Each of the theses contributes to this integration. A critical perspective on Steere's integration will be reserved for Chapter Five.

In Chapters Three and Four, the sources for Steere's method of relating prayer and social responsibility will be examined. Chapter Three will analyze the powerful influence of von Hügel and Woolman in Steere's integration. Chapter Four will examine the other theological and literary sources in Steere's treatment of this problem.

NOTES FOR CHAPTER TWO

[1] Soren Kierkegaard, *Purity of Heart Is to Will One Thing*, trans. with intro. essay by Douglas V. Steere, (New York: Harper and Row, 1938).

[2] Parker Palmer, "Douglas and Dorothy Steere: More than the Sum of the Parts" in *Living in the Light: Some Quaker Pioneers of the Twentieth Century*, ed. Leonard S. Kenwothy, (Kennett Square, Pa.: Friends General Conference and Quaker Publications, 1984), p. 228.

[3] Douglas V. Steere, *Prayer and Worship* (Richmond, Indiana: Friends United Press, 1978), p. 1.

[4] Ibid., p. 3.

[5] Ibid., p. 3.

[6] Ibid., p. 3.

[7] Ibid., p. 6.

[8] Ibid., p. 8.

[9] Ibid., p. 6.

[10] Ibid., p. 8.

[11] Ibid., p. 13.

[12] Ibid., p. 15.

[13] Ibid., p. 17.

[14] Ibid., p. 14. In *Dimensions of Prayer*, Steere attributes similar definitions to Harry Emerson Fosdick and P. T. Forsyth, who define prayer as "dominant desire" and "ruling passion." See *Dimensions of Prayer*, pp. 66-67.

[15] Ibid., p. 16.

[16] Ibid., pp. 15-16.

[17] Ibid., p. 16.

[18] Ibid., p. 18.

[19] Ibid., p. 18.

[20] Ibid., p. 18.

[21]Ibid., p. 41.

[22]Ibid., p. 42.

[23]Ibid., p. 43.

[24]Ibid., p. 43.

[25]Ibid., pp. 43-44.

[26]Ibid., pp. 21-22.

[27]Ibid., p. 21.

[28]Ibid., p. 51.

[29]Ibid., p. 51.

[30]Ibid., p. 52

[31]Douglas V. Steere, *On Beginning from Within* (New York: Harper and Brothers Publishers, 1943), p. vii.

[32]Ibid., p. vii.

[33]The inward journey/outward journey theme is most clearly developed in Steere's pamphlet *The Hardest Journey*, which will be examined later in this chapter. The inward journey represents the journey toward God and toward self- understanding. The outward journey represents the journey toward others, toward an engagement with the social order.

[34]Ibid., p. 5.

[35]Ibi.d, p. 6.

[36]Ibid., p. 8.

[37]Ibid., p. 38.

[38]Ibid., p. 11.

[39]Ibid., pp. 11-12.

[40]Ibid., p. 12.

[41]Ibid., p. 12.

[42]Ibid., p. 12.

[43]Ibid., p. 12.

[44]Ibid., p. 30.

[45]Ibid., p. 14.

[46]Ibid., p. 15.

[47]Ibid., p. 17.

[48]Ibid., p. 21.

[49]Ibid., p. 22, 23.

[50]Ibid., p. 85.

[51]Ibid., p. 86.

[52]Ernest Becker, *The Denial of Death* (New York: The Free Press, 1973).

[53]Steere, *On Beginning from Within*, pp. 144-145.

[54]Ibid., p. 148.

[55]Douglas V. Steere, *Work and Contemplation* (New York: Harper and Brothers, 1957).

[56]Ibid., p. viii.

[57]Ibid., p. 2.

[58]Ibid., p. x.

[59]Ibid., p. 1.

[60]Ibid., p. 8.

[61]Ibid., p. 21.

[62]Ibid., p. 27.

[63]Ibid., p. 28.

[64]Ibid., p. 28.

[65]Ibid., p. 35.

[66]Ibid., p. 37.

[67]Ibid., pp. 38, 39, 40.

[68]Ibid., p. 39.

[69]Ibid., p. 42.

[70]Ibid., p. 42.

[71]Ibid., p. 43.

[72]Ibid., p. 44.

[73]Ibid., p. 44.

[74]Ibid., p. 45.

[75]Ibid., p. 46.

[76]Ibid., p. 128.

[77]Ibid., p. 50.

[78]Ibid., p. 51.

[79]Ibid., p. 52.

[80]Ibid., p. 53.

[81]Ibid., p. 22.

[82]Ibid., p. 22.

[83]Ibid., p. 34.

[84]Ibid., p. 34.

[85]Ibid., p. 22.

[86]Ibid., p. 118.

[87]Ibid., p. 120.

[88]Ibid., p. 123.

[89]Ibid., p. 124.

[90]Ibid., p. 124.

[91]Ibid., p. 124.

[92]Ibid., p. 125.

[93]Ibid., p. 127.

[94]Ibid., p. 128.

[95]Ibid., p. 128.

[96]Ibid., p. 132.

[97]Ibid., p. 138.

[98]Ibid., p. 138.

[99]Ibid., p. 120.

[100]Ibid., p. 120.

[101]Ibid., p. 142.

[102]Ibid., pp. 142-143.

[103]Ibid., p. 109.

[104]Ibid., p. 109.

[105]Ibid., p. 143.

[106]Ibid., p. 56.

[107]Ibid., p. 56.

[108]Ibid., pp. 143-144.

[109]Ibid., p. 145.

[110]Ibid., p. 145.

[111]Douglas and Dorothy Steere, *Friends Work in Africa* (London: Friends World Committee for Consultation, 1954).

[112]Douglas B. Steere, *On Listening to Another* (New York: Harpers and Brothers, 1955).

[113]*The Journal and Major Essays of John Woolman*, ed. Phillips P. Moulton, (New York: The Oxford University Press, 1971).

[114]Steere, *On Listening to Another*, p. i.

[115]Ibid., p. i.

[116]*Quaker Spirituality*, edited with introductory essay by Douglas V. Steere, (New York: The Paulist Press, 1984).

[117]Steere, *On Listening to Another*, p. 33.

[118]Ibid., pp. 33-34.

[119]Ibid., p. 36.

[120]Ibid., p. 39.

[121]Ibid., p. 39.

[122]Ibid., pp. 42-43.

[123]Ibid., p. 43.

[124]Ibid., p. 43.

[125]Ibid., p. 43.

[126]Ibid., p. 68.

[127]Ibid., p. 68.

[128]Ibid., p. 69.

[129]Ibid., p. 70.

[130]Ibid., p. 70.

[131]Ibid., p. 68.

[132]Ibid., p. 20.

[133]Ibid., p. 71.

[134]Douglas V. Steere, *Dimensions of Prayer* (Woman's Division of Christian Service, Board of Missions: The Methodist Church, 1962).

[135]Ibid., p. 2.

[136]Ibid., p. 14.

[137]Ibid., p. 15.

[138]Ibid., pp. 80, 82.

[139]Steere, *Prayer and Worship*, p. 42.

[140]Steere, *Dimensions of Prayer*, p. 97.

[141]Ibid., p. 95.

[142]Ibid., p. 106.

[143]Ibid., p. 106.

[144]Ibid., p. 100.

[145]Ibid., pp. 100-101.

[146]Ibid., p. 97.

[147]Ibid., p. 99.

[148]Ibid., p. 105.

[149]Douglas V. Steere, "Foreword to an Anatomy of Worship," in *Pastoral Psychology*, 11:10-15, March 1960.

[150]Ibid., p. 12.

[151]Ibid., p. 11.

[152]Ibid., p. 11.

[153]Ibid., p. 11.

[154]Ibid., p. 11.

[155]Ibid., p. 11.

[156]Ibid., p. 12.

[157]Ibid., p. 12.

[158]Ibid., p. 12.

[159]Ibid., p. 12.

[160]Ibid., p. 13.

[161]Ibid., p. 14.

[162]Ibid., p. 15.

[163]Ibid., p. 14.

[164]Ibid,, pp. 14-15.

[165]John H. Hallowell (ed), *Development for What?* (Durham, North Carolina: Lilly Endowment Research Program in Christianity and Politics by the Duke University Press, 1964).

[166]Ibid., p. v.

[167]Ibid., p. ix.

[168]Douglas V. Steere, "Development for What?" in *Development for What?*, Edited by John H. Hallowell, (Durham, North Carolina: Lilly Endowment Research Program in Christianity and Politics by the Duke University Press, 1964) pp. 214-215.

[169]Ibid., p. 216.

[170]Ibid., p. 216.

[171]Ibid., p. 218.

[172]Douglas V. Steere, *Mutual Irradiation: A Quaker View of Ecumenism* (Wallingford, Pa.: Pendle Hill Publications), p. back of front cover.

[173]Douglas V. Steere, "Common Frontiers in Catholic and Non-Catholic Spirituality" in *Together in Solitude*, (New York: Crossroad, 1982).

[174]Ibid., p. 7.

[175]Ibid., p. 9.

[176]Ibid., p. 9.

[177]Ibid., p. 16.

[178]Douglas V. Steere, *The Hardest Journey* (Wallingford, Pa: Pendle Hill Publications, 1968).

[179]Ibid., p. 1.

[180]Ibid., p. 3.

[181]Ibid., p. 4.

[182]Ibid., p. 8.

[183]Ibid., pp. 18-19.

[184]Ibid., p. 20.

[185]Douglas V. Steere, "The Life of Prayer as the Ground of Unity" in *Together in Solitude* (New York: Crossroad, 1982).

[186]Ibid., p. viii.

[187]Ibid., pp. 20-21.

[188]In *Mutual Irradiation*, Steere outlines four postures for interfaith encounter: annihilation of the other religion, syncretism or merging, hygenic co-existence, and mutual

irradiation. He defines mutual irradiation this way:

The fourth is a relationship of what I would call "mutual irradiation" in which each is willing to expose itself with great openness to the inward message of the other, as well as to share its own experience, and to trust that whatever is the truth in each experience will irradiate and deepen the experience of the other. . . . mutual irradiation would try to provide the most congenial setting possible for releasing the deepest witness that the Buddhist or Hindu or Muslim might make to his Christian companion, and that the Christian might share with his non-Christian friend.

The fact of mutual irradiation is an existential one that goes beyond mere description and has to be experienced to be penetrated. It is not likely to leave any of the participants as they were when they started. (p. 8).

[189]Steere, *Together in Solitude*, pp. 21-22.

[190]Ibid., p. 22.

[191]Ibid., p. 22.

[192]Ibid., p. 22.

[193]Ibid., pp. 23-24.

[194]Steere, *Work and Contemplation*, p. 120.

[195]Steere, *Together in Solitude*, p. 24.

[196]Ibid., p. 26.

[197]*Quaker Spirituality*, Edited with introductory essay by Douglas V. Steere, (New York: The Paulist Press, 1984), p. 29.

[198]Ibid., p. 29.

[199]Ibid., p. 29.

[200]Ibid., pp. 42-43.

[201]Ibid., p. 46.

[202]Ibid., p. 46.

[203]Ibid., p. 47.

[204]Ibid., p. 47.

[205]Steere, *Mutual Irradiation*, pp. 19-20.

[206]E. Glenn Hinson, "Douglas V. Steere: Irradiator of the Beams of Love," in *The Christian Century*, April 24, 1985, p. 418.

CHAPTER THREE

STEERE'S ASSIMILATION OF VON HÜGEL AND WOOLMAN

The writings of von Hügel and Woolman have exerted a powerful influence on Steere. He became acquainted with their writings early in his career and their work has been a guiding force in his life and thought. It is not surprising, then, to find that they are key sources in his approach to the problem of relating prayer and social responsibility. In this chapter Steere's writings will be examined to determine how he has incorporated the thought of these two mentors in his treatment of the problem. As Steere began reading von Hügel over five years before he started reading Woolman's *Journal*, it is appropriate to begin this study with an examination of Steere's assimilation of the spiritual theology of von Hügel.

Von Hügel: Source of Steere's Existential Realism

Steere began reading von Hügel during his tenure as a Rhodes Scholar at Oxford (1925-26). The writings of von Hügel deeply impressed Steere and he decided to write his doctoral dissertation on "Critical Realism in the Religious Philosophy of Baron Friedrich von Hügel." Von Hügel became a philosophical, theological, and spiritual mentor for Steere. Nevertheless, the depth and pervasiveness of von Hügel's influence on Steere is not always apparent. The *full* weight of von Hügel's influence is only observed after a careful analysis of both authors' writings. For an analysis of von Hügel's spiritual theology, this study will examine the studies of Albert A. Cock, John J. Heaney, Joseph P. Whalen, and Douglas V. Steere.

Some brief comments concerning von Hügel's life are necessary to set the historical stage for his writings. Although von Hügel (1852-1925) lived most of his adult life in England, he moved frequently throughout continental Europe during his youth and became fluent in French, German, Italian, and, of course, English. Steere describes von Hügel's singular lifestyle.

Living his adult life in England, Baron Friedrich von Hügel was that vanishing phenomenon in the Anglo-Saxon world of letters, a *privat-Gelehrte*, a scholar who was not dependent upon a professional university post or an ecclesiastical or public station for his living, but gave himself with abandon to the fields of choice.[1]

Baron Friedrich never attended any school or university. I have never come across any comment of his own on how he believed this to have affected him.[2]

Von Hügel's frail health and deafness also contributed to his life of retirement. The studies that most captivated von Hügel's interest were those pertaining to the spiritual life. Joseph Whalen summarizes the primary sources for von Hügel's self-education.

Von Hügel's central preoccupation with spirituality gives his large erudition a strongly pastoral direction and character. The massive study of Greek and scholastic philosophy, of Kant, Hegel, Feuerbach, and his own contemporaries, seems always subordinate to early and wide reading in the Fathers, the German and Spanish mystics, and especially in French school spirituality: Bossuet, Fenelon, Grou. He speaks of fifty years' close acquaintance with Augustine's *Confessions* and of almost daily reading of the Gospels and the *Imitation of Christ*.[3]

In spite of his vast erudition, it was von Hügel's personal relationship with two spiritual directors (Father Raymond Hocking and Abbé Huvelin) that most affected his spiritual life.

In his public life von Hügel is best known as an influential leader in the modernist movement. Whalen notes that:

While escaping censure, von Hügel played a leading role, perhaps more as catalyst than as a seminal thinker or innovator, in the 'modernist' movement. . . . We may remark here, however, that his writings consistently, increasingly, and finally even polemically, show a marked insistence on two essential positions whose violation he, von Hügel himself, came to regard as 'modernism' in the heretical sense: in exegesis he argues the necessity of sheer historical 'happenedness' as the basis of Catholic creed and dogma; and in philosophy and theology he grounds all possibility of religion in the 'fact' of God as ontologically absolute, distinct, prevenient Personal Spirit, and this independent of and prior to each man's, and all humanity's experience of this fact.[4]

The positive element of the modernist movement, in von Hügel's thought, was the effort to articulate the faith in a manner consistent with the best in contemporary thought. In this sense, modernism was more of an attitude than a movement. Von Hügel defines this view of modernism as:

A permanent, never quite finished, always sooner or later, more or less, rebeginning set of attempts to express the old faith and its permanent truths and helps--to interpret it according to what appears the best and the most abiding elements of philosophy and the scholarship and science of the later and latest times.[5]

Even though this approach appears moderate in tone, Steere notes that

> on the central modernist demand of the right of unrestricted scientific historical criticism, von Hügel never gave in and had he been in priest's orders and hence been forced to sign the anti-modernist oath in 1910, it is difficult to see how he could have remained within the church.[6]

John J. Heaney, whose work presents an exhaustive analysis of Von Hügel's role in the Modernist crisis, contends that at the

> roots of Modernism lay a triple thesis: a denial of the supernatural as an object of knowledge . . . , an exclusive immanence of the divine and of revelation . . . which reduced the Church to a simple social civilizing phenomenon; and a total emancipation of scientific research from Church dogma which would allow the continued assertion of faith in dogma with its contradiction on the historical level . . . [7]

In examining each Modernist thesis in relation to von Hügel's theology, Heaney concludes that von Hügel's thought "shared in only one of the ideas [the thesis concerning the emancipation of scientific research from Church dogma] officially condemned in the Modernist crisis."[8] Even on this point von Hügel expressed this view only as a private opinion--never in his published works.[9]

In turning from the historical context of von Hügel's writings to the content of his spiritual theology, it may be helpful to examine Cock's summary of von Hügel's major contributions.

> Here in the Baron von Hügel's work what permanent values are enshrined? I take them to be seven:--First, the threefold analysis of the constituents of any world religion . . . Second, the delineation of the specific genius of Catholicism set in relation to a delicate appreciation of other religious systems, . . . Third, the steady maintenance of the note of Joy, or Bliss as ultimate in the Divine Nature with a full recognition of the Cross, of suffering as the law of approach from the finite individual to infinite person in God; . . . Fourth, a rare realization that in affirmation there is life, in blank negation there is death . . . Fifth, the justest estimate of the obligations of both the married and celibate states; . . . Sixth, a never failing appreciation of the distinction of origins and validity . . . Seventh, a profound appreciation of the reality of marginal consciousness, the dim as well as the clear, is real.[10]

These seven "values" are central concerns for von Hügel and outline the scope of his spiritual theology. Nevertheless, one of the contributions which has made the most profound impression upon Steere is von Hügel's articulation of a critical realism. Cock notes that von Hügel's stance as a critical realist is stated best in the preface to the second edition of *The Mystical Element of Religion* (1923). In it von Hügel writes:

> By now I perceive with entire clarity that though religion cannot even be conceived as extant at all without a human subject humanely apprehending

the Object of Religion, the reality of the Object (in itself the Subject of all subjects) and its presence independently of all our apprehension of it--that its Givenness is the central characteristic of all religion worthy of the name. The Otherness, the Prevenience of God, the One-sided Relation between God and man, these constitute the deepest measure and touchstone of all religion.[11]

This realistic emphasis is mirrored in Whalen's summary of von Hügel's definition of religion. "If religion for von Hügel is the 'deepest of all experiences of the deepest of all facts', it is therefore, in itself, twofold: it is the fact of God, and it is man's experience of that fact."[12] Cock suggests that one of von Hügel's ruling intuitions "is the givenness of God"[13] and that the experience of this givenness consists, in von Hügel's words, in "the vivid continuous sense . . . [of] God the Spirit upholding our poor little spirits."[14] Cock also notes that von Hügel has written that "there is found to exist the sense of a 'more-than-merely-subjective'."[15]

By virtue of both his writings and his personality, von Hügel had enormous influence on Anglo-Saxon theology during the first half of this century. "Of his greatest work, *The Mystical Element of Religion,* William Temple wrote: 'It is quite arguable that this is the most important theological work written in the English language during the last half-century.'"[16] Two years after von Hügel's death, a writer for *The Times Literary Supplement* estimated von Hügel's importance in this way.

Were we asked to name the Roman Catholic thinkers who have in modern times left an enduring mark on the religious mind of England, we should mention Newman and we should mention von Hügel, but no third without doubts and reservations.[17]

It is also worth noting that in 1920 von Hügel received the honorary Doctor of Divinity from the University of Oxford, the first Roman Catholic to be so honored since the Reformation.[18]

These tributes are sufficient to indicate that von Hügel was an outstanding scholar and religious writer. But Michael de la Bedoyere, one of von Hügel's most important biographers, locates von Hügel's greatest contribution in another area--his role as a "unique personal explorer and guide into the deepest things of the spirit."[19] This is an assessment with which Whalen and Steere concur.[20] The impact of von Hügel's personality may be felt in these words of Evelyn Underhill: "He is the most wonderful personality I have ever known--so saintly, so truthful, sane, and tolerant. I feel very safe and happy sitting in his shadow, and he has been most awfully kind to me."[21] Besides Evelyn Underhill, some of the scholars who have been deeply influenced by von Hügel are: Professors Norman Kemp Smith, George Tyrrell, A. E. Taylor, Archbishop Soderbloom, Clement Webb, Canon Lilley, Claude Montefiore and, among contemporary Americans, Douglas V. Steere and Morton Kelsey.

John J. Heaney offers a very different interpretation of von Hügel's significance. While recognizing the vast breadth of von Hügel's scholarship (including the fields of Biblical studies, Church history, geology, philosophy, mysticism, and theology) and the force of von Hügel's personality, Heaney contends that "Friedrich von Hügel is of rare importance because of his standing as a symbol of the Catholic struggling with the problem of authority and liberty."[22] Of the interpreter's of von Hügel being consulted in this study, Heaney alone situates von Hügel's most enduring contribution in his struggle with the problem of authority. Along these lines, Heaney faults Steere's book on von Hügel for neglecting to bring out "the concrete issues with which von Hügel was involved during the Modernist crisis. It was on these very tensions that his devotion fed."[23]

With this brief introduction to von Hügel's religious realism and the central themes his spiritual theology, this study will turn to an examination of how Steere has assimilated von Hügel's thought on the relation of prayer and social responsibility.

In beginning this examination of Steere's assimilation of von Hügel's thought on the relation of prayer and social responsibility, it will be helpful to mention the deficiencies that both Cock and Whalen note in von Hügel's social vision. Cock writes that "it cannot be said that he was seized by social questions in such a way as to make his religious philosophy bear pertinently and practically on the call to be up and doing for the social service of our day."[24] Whalen does not want to minimize the great social value of von Hügel's spiritual theology, but he is critical of the neglect of any substantive application.

A far more serious limitation in this spirituality--and one needing far-reaching supplementation--concerns the narrowness of von Hügel's social and political consciousness. Here we have the experience, or lack of it, of a man little larger than his own time and personal situations. For in the face of social questions above all, von Hügel is a baron, a Victorian, and a victim of the isolation caused by his deafness. Now it ought to be clear from our study of his writings that von Hügel enjoys a strongly developed conviction at once about experience, about thought and life--about secularity and religion--as only *socially* appropriated gifts and achievements. Further, this conviction about man's essential sociality is not casual, but is central to von Hügel's incarnationalism and one of its greatest strengths. And our criticism here must not be allowed to slight that accomplishment. But if this powerful understanding of the individual personality as *gift* as well as condition of community is noteworthy (and it is), and if the ecclesial, communitarian sources and goals of fully Christian personal piety are impressively clear (and they are), nevertheless the social and liturgical *expression* and *actuation* of that personality and piety find only brief and thin consideration in von Hügel's writings.[25]

The limitations of von Hügel's social vision and his failure to develop the social implications of his spiritual theology are, in some ways, "supplemented" by Steere's spiritual theology. Certainly, Steere has little to offer by way of liturgical expression, but he has given serious attention to the social expression and actuation of a Hügelian spirituality.

In his doctoral dissertation Steere discusses the social limitations of von Hügel's thought. Steere's critique (1931) already reveals the thrust of that his own spiritual theology will take.

> [Von Hügel] gives little or no evidence of any intimate acquaintance with the social or group aspect of mysticism which played so important a part in the religious life of 14th and 15th century Germany and the Low Countries, and in 17th century England. He has also neglected those mystics who, being deeply touched by the Reformation and with its new emphasis on the capacities of human personality, have found their mystical quest expressible in terms of the language of their day. The former omission has made him oblivious to the mystical group as an instrument for social reform and for good works in general.[26]

Even at this early point in his career, Steere is seeking to link religious experience with social change. His reference to 17th century England shows that he already sees the Quaker community as expressing this linkage.

Steere's most extended treatments of von Hügel's spirituality are found in his essay on von Hügel's *Selected Letters* in *Doors into Life* and in his book entitled *Spiritual Counsels and Letters of Baron Friedrich von Hügel*.[27] John J. Heaney, who reviewed Steere's book on von Hügel in the *Heythrop Journal*, writes that:

> This work is a perceptive collection which covers the full range of von Hügel's specifically spiritual thought and counsel. . . . The editor's introductory essay, despite the Victorian flavor of the paragraph headings, is a fine synthesis of the Baron's approach, especially his direction of Evelyn Underhill.[28]

Both this book and Steere's essay in *Doors into Life* will be consulted to pinpoint Steere's assimilation of von Hügel's thought in his treatment of the relation of prayer and social responsibility.

The powerful influence of von Hügel pervades Steere's treatment of the relation of prayer and social responsibility. Aspects of von Hügel's thought can be discovered in each of the organizing theses; however, it is in the first thesis that the hints of existential realism are to be found. The first part of the first thesis, which is: "Prayer (especially corporate prayer) deepens an awareness of creatureliness" is deeply rooted in the critical realism which Steere found so persuasive in von Hügel. The "awareness of creatureliness" is grounded in the givenness, the Otherness, the reality of God. In his essay on von Hügel in *Doors into Life*, Steere writes:

> Von Hügel, especially during the latter part of his life, emphasized the givenness, the prevenience the ever-present reality, the over-againstness of God. . . . There is no reducing this transcendence, this priority of God to any subjectively exhaustible terms.[29]

In von Hügel's insistence on the givenness of God, Steere asserts that von Hügel

recovered for the Anglo-Saxon religious world the dimension of transcendence in the Christian faith and thus did much to correct a current strain of subjectively-tilted psychologism in liberal religion.[30]

This emphasis on the transcendence of God evokes the human response of adoration. Noting the relation of adoration and critical realism in von Hügel's spiritual theology, Steere writes:

> His insistence in personal counsel, for example, that religion is adoration, and that any approach to religion that ignores the adoration of God is 'like a triangle with one side left out' gives the clue to a major factor in his rejection of idealism in favor of realism, of an admission that there is a vast givenness in God which we encounter, which we apprehend but never fully comprehend, which penetrates us, which stirs our organs to response, and yet which always preserves its abyss of mystery in the very course of quickening our souls--what is this but a description of a kind of stance by which the soul is poised and directed toward the Object of adoration?[31]

Adoration is the creaturely response to the reality, the Otherness of God. This supports the assertion that the "awareness of creatureliness" is grounded in Steere's assimilation of von Hügel's critical realism.

The solidarity that arises out of the awareness of creatureliness is only possible because, although God is Other, God is an immensely penetrating reality. Von Hügel writes that "the joy of religion resides, surely, in the knowledge, the love, the adoration of One truly distinct from, whilst immensely penetrative of, ourselves."[32] This openness of the human person to the reality of God includes an openness to all reality. Therefore, there is interaction, an interpenetration, perhaps even a "mutual irradiation," with the whole created order. This conception is supported by Whalen's insight that, although von Hügel is opposed to subjectivism, he makes a "ringing affirmation of subjectivity, of man's involvement with a reality that is *organic*, of the 'interaction of any one thing with everything else.'"[33] Here is the theological basis for the solidarity that is evoked by the awareness of creatureliness.

Although the existentialist aspect of Steere's existential realism is less clearly derived from von Hügel's spiritual theology, Steere finds von Hügel's approach congenial with an existentialist perspective. In a letter to a former student (dated March 18, 1981), Steere writes:

> Dying in 1925, von Hügel nevertheless felt after and sensed the outlines of the fact that we first of all dimly grasp the whole, we dimly grasp the Given, and that out of this, quite derivatively, we get the more discreet images.
> Here von Hügel was feeling for what Gabriel Marcel (with whom I have a close affinity) with all the stimulus of the rediscovered existentialism of our times (that von Hügel was denied) was reaching for in his *Mystery of Being*.[34]

In von Hügel's emphasis on the subject's response to the Given, Steere discerns a sort of pre-existentialist existentialism. Whalen refers to this emphasis (on the response of the subject) in his treatment of von Hügel's thought on the production of personality; he writes, "Man as *individual* and as becoming is the *project* [of religion]; as *personality*, he is the on-going, always increasing *achievement* of the conscious, subjective appropriation . . . of the fact of God."[35] This focus on the subject becomes more evident in the second thesis.

The historical and institutional element of religion is emphasized when Steere examines von Hügel's treatment of the human response to the given. The human response is bound up in willingness, which is the subject of the second thesis, "Prayer nurtures an awareness of God's infinite concern for every person and fosters a willingness to participate in God's redemptive order." Describing von Hügel's emphasis on what the institutional element of religion does for the will, Steere writes:

> The only appropriate response of a man to the divine initiative is a whole response--one that will call for his whole nature which means the habit life of his will, the thrust of his intellect, and the total response of his emotions. . . . The first of these features, the habit-life of the will, von Hügel connects with the institutional or historical side of religion . . . We are not self-made. We are born into a family. We receive our language, our primitive expectations and obligations, our very heroes from the nurture of the group. We are compelled to draw on the deposits of others in this precious bank every day of our lives. Therefore, there must be a bank to carry over to us the gifts of the spiritual insights of the ages past. . . . Von Hügel knew his own and his fellows weaknesses and faced them with his characteristic frankness. We are creatures of short memories.[36]

The connection of memory with the will makes the institutional aspect of religion a necessity. The institutional element of religion serves as a reminder of Christian identity and vocation. In another place Steere writes:

> In the full awareness of the shortness of man's memory, he must make sure that there is no neglect of the historical and institutional element that serves as a constant reminder of man's calling and of his redemption, and which in the course of kindling in him an unlimited liability for others, enlists him as member of the great company of the living and the dead who are involved in the redemption of the cosmos.[37]

Without this cloud of witnesses there is little likelihood of the individual being enlisted in the redemptive order. Here is a full appreciation for the importance of the community in the formation of individual Christian volition.

In turning to the other three theses, Steere's assimilation of von Hügel's thought must be interpolated, as Steere does not specifically cite von Hügel as a source when dealing with the issues involved in these theses. Nevertheless, as Steere is an astute reader of von Hügel, it is safe to assume that Steere has assimilated von Hügel's thought on these issues. For von Hügel's thought pertaining to these theses, this study will rely on Whalen's analysis.

The thought expressed in the third thesis, which is that "Prayer cleanses action, work, and service of its repetitive nature and restores its frame of meaning." is mirrored in von Hügel's statement that "without recollection, external action rapidly becomes soul dispersive."[38]   Here "soul dispersive" is roughly synonymous with a dissolution of the "frame of meaning." The corollary truth would be that action with recollection leads to soul integration (or a restoration of the frame of meaning).

The fourth thesis, which suggests that "Acts of social responsibility clarify and test the genuineness of prayer." is expressed in von Hügel's social test for the genuineness of prayer. Whalen writes:

> The second, and social, test of the genuineness of prayer is 'if, in coming away from it, you find yourself humbler, sweeter, more patient, more ready to suffer, more loving (in effect even more than in affection) towards God and man'. Therefore, if prayer is itself a preoccupation with God and a disoccupation with self, it is, in its intended result, not a disoccupation with the world, but rather the 'loving of God, Christ, and others'. Indeed, healthy prayer leads beyond itself, into the world of men and projects . . .[39]

In another place Whalen writes:

> . . . any notion, whether of a God preoccupied wholly with himself, or of a human contemplation of him which does not move *beyond* him to active love and concern for our fellow-men, has 'no place in an incarnational religion'.[40]

Here prayer is not deemed genuine unless it leads beyond itself to service, action in the world. This incarnational emphasis is apparent in both Steere's thought and action.

The first part of the fifth thesis sums up the third and fourth thesis. It states that "Both prayer and social responsibility are incomplete in themselves." Von Hügel sums up the incompleteness in a noteworthy sentence.

> '. . . Without . . . contact with the material and the opposition of external action, recollection gradually grows empty; and without recollection, external action rapidly becomes soul-dispersive.'[41]

The second part of the fifth thesis, which states that "they (prayer and social responsibility) are partially integrated through alternation and fully integrated through simultaneity," deals with several key issues in von Hügel's thought. Von Hügel is unwilling to collapse prayer and action; rather he seeks a creative tension in which a disciplined life of prayer informs and transforms the active life. Nevertheless, the goal is a life in which prayer enters into action. Whalen provides a perceptive summary of von Hügel's thought on this crucial issue.

> But von Hügel's emphasis here on the spirit of prayer, and his own penchant for prayer as a state, in no wise supports that *interpretation* of Ignation 'contemplation in action' where the *tension* of work *and* prayer--

and the time and the habits such definite, regular prayer requires--disappears from view. Von Hügel's man is never a one-ness, and he is an *accomplished* harmony only rarely, at his best, and at moments. Von Hügel's man is a durational multiplicity *aimed* at harmony; he is an ongoing, unending rhythm and tension, always in *process* of overcoming and resolving itself in the dynamic, utter fullness, the perfect coming-to-self in the other which is personality as found in God alone. Only as perennial action *and* prayer does man move *towards* the goal of his becoming: his harmony as *fully* personal being, as prayer-in-action.[42]

Von Hügel recognizes the necessity of alternation, of perennial prayer *and* action, but the ultimate goal is a harmony, a full integration, of prayer-in-action. This prayer-in-action bears a striking resemblance to the what Steere describes as working collectedly. When the Christian is able to be conscious of God as the ultimate end of human destiny and yet also be conscious of human responsibility for the world, then the conditions for simultaneity emerge. Von Hügel writes that when such conditions exist

> . . . there may result the deepening of the humane ends by Christian ethics, and the humanising of the Christian end--so that life, within the humane ends, may simultaneously, be service to God; and the service of God may simultaneously, transfigure the world.[43]

In this understanding a true simultaneity emerges. The life of action, of social responsibility, becomes the service of God and the service of God transforms the world. Although Steere does not mention von Hügel in his development of the concept of simultaneity, the similarities of his conception with that of von Hügel indicate von Hügel's seminal influence.

Beside von Hügel's influence in the organizing theses, two other themes in Steere's writings--the amphibian nature of the human person and the costliness of the spiritual journey--figure prominently in von Hügel's spiritual theology. It may be remembered that the "amphibian" nature of the human person was a major element in the anthropology that grounded Steere's study of the relation of work and contemplation. Whalen notes von Hügel's affirmation of the amphibian nature of the human person and writes, "Man is 'incurably amphibious', and von Hügel is bent on probing the total environment and resources the better to argue and provide for the complexity and greatness of man's destiny."[44] The costliness of the spiritual journey is also a theme sounded in von Hügel's spiritual theology; he writes:

> I believe that not to be aware of the costliness, to unspiritualized man, of the change from his self-centeredness, from *anthropocentrism* to *theocentrism*, means not only a want of awakeness to the central demand of religion, but an ignorance or oblivion of the poorer, the perverse, tendencies of the human heart.[45]

The costliness of true holiness is a theme that appears frequently in the writings of both Steere and von Hügel.

This analysis of Steere's assimilation of von Hügel's spiritual theology, as it pertains to this study, has demonstrated the critical significance of von Hügel's thought on Steere's treatment of the problem. Yet, the influence of von Hügel on Steere is not merely intellectual; his influence inspired, or at least confirmed, Steere's vocational direction. Steere's assessment of von Hügel's greatest contribution offers insight into Steere's own career.

[W]hen we come at last to assess the significance of the contribution of this religious giant, I believe that it will be as a guide and an encourager of souls that he will be chiefly remembered.[46]

Yet the bent of mind of von Hügel never leaves out of sight for a moment the object of his quest: namely to minister to the hungering souls of men.[47]

These observations on von Hügel's contribution are remarkably revealing of Steere's ministry.

As was mentioned earlier, the full weight of von Hügel's influence on Steere's spiritual theology can only be realized after a careful analysis of each author's writings. Nevertheless. when Steere lists the sources for his spiritual theology in the Introduction to *Together in Solitude*, von Hügel is the first non-Quaker mentioned. The weight of von Hügel's influence may also be felt in a letter I received from Steere in August of 1984. Steere wrote that it is possible to "see the thrust of my contribution in the way of presenting a Quaker approach that is profoundly influenced by Roman Catholic thought in one of the boldest thinkers in the first quarter of this century: in old Baron von Hügel."

Despite von Hügel's enormous influence, there is another dimension of Steere's spirituality that can only be understood within the context of his deep roots in Quaker spirituality, especially the spirituality of John Woolman. It is to Woolman's influence that this study now turns.

Woolman: Steere's Quaker Guide

Steere began teaching at Haverford College in 1928 and immediately established close ties with the Quaker community. When he married Dorothy MacEachron in 1929, she shared his interest in Quaker religious life. In 1929 he met with the group of Quakers who were responsible for envisioning and establishing Pendle Hill, a Quaker Center for study and contemplation. He became a member of the Board of the AFSC in 1930. Nevertheless, it wasn't until after the Steeres read Woolman's *Journal* in the winter of 1932 that they decided to join the Religious Society of Friends. The beauty and purity of Woolman's life made a deep impression on the Steeres and hastened their formal commitment to the Quakers.

In the Introduction to *Together in Solitude* Steere mentions some of the people who have had the most profound influence upon him.[48] He notes that his Quaker guides have been Isaac Penington and John Woolman; however, it is the influence of Woolman that is so visible in all of Steere's work. There are references to Woolman in each of the books examined and in several of the articles. Besides being Steere's Quaker guide, Woolman serves as Steere's model for a "collected life" (or sainthood) and for the carrying out of a concern.

Steere acknowledged his great debt to Woolman (and four other authors) in the Introduction to *Doors into Life: Through Five Devotional Classics* (1948); he writes:

> This little book is in the nature of an attempt to make a token interest payment on a debt. The debt is a very personal one. For the five devotional books which are the focus of attention here have been doors into life for me, and the personalities behind them have exerted a continual drawing power.[49]

The continual drawing power of Woolman is evidenced in references to him scattered throughout fifty years of writing and lecturing.

Steere's admiration for Woolman's *Journal* is apparent in the first paragraph of his essay in *Doors into Life*.

> John Woolman's *Journal* is an eighteenth-century autobiography of singular power. In all its homespun modesty, it reveals the heroic example of a spiritually guided and centered life that was poured out in self-spending service to a dispossessed group, the Negroes, whose condition of slavery mocked the Christian profession of the time. I would not hesitate to call the moving life which this unusual diary records, the life of an American saint.[50]

This is the highest commendation Steere can make of a person or a book.

Steere is not alone in his respect for the *Journal*. It was held in great esteem by Samuel Taylor Coleridge, who wrote, "I should almost despair of the man who could peruse the life of John Woolman without an amelioration of heart."[51] Charles Lamb, who received a copy of the *Journal* from the poet Charles Lloyd, was deeply moved by it and later remarked that it was the only American book he had read twice.[52] Phillips P. Moulton, editor of the most authoritative version of the *Journal*, writes that "As a personal revelation, the *Journal* rightly takes its place in American literature alongside such classics as Franklin's *Autobiography*, Thoreau's *Walden*, and Whitman's *Democratic Vistas*."[53] And, of course, the *Journal* was selected to be included in the Harvard Classics.

Steere's essay on Woolman's *Journal* in *Doors into Life* was originally prepared as one of his Carew Lectures at Hartford Theological Seminary in February of 1945. This essay provides the greatest insight into Steere's assimilation of Woolman's ideas. Although Steere frequently refers to Woolman in other works, this is the only one that gives sustained attention to the way in which Woolman was grasped and transformed by a concern. Phillips P. Moulton, the distinguished editor of the *Journal*, listed Steere's essay among his secondary sources and described it as "exceptionally valuable."[54]

Of the five devotional books examined in *Doors into Life*, Woolman's *Journal* is most clearly concerned with the problem of relating prayer and social responsibility. In describing the *Journal* Steere notes that:

> John Woolman's *Journal* unites the life of prayer and worship and social concern and is a never-ending renewer of the faith that Jesus meant us to take literally the words of the Lord's Prayer: "Thy kingdom come, thy will be done *on earth* as it is in heaven" . . .[55]

This quote gives an indication of how Steere's effort to unite prayer and social concerns parallels the spirituality found in the *Journal*.

In his essay on Woolman, Steere begins by providing a brief biographical sketch of the author and his times.

> He was born in 1720 and became a part of a third-generation Quaker community near Burlington, New Jersey. The founder of the Quakers, George Fox, had only begun his preaching in England seventy years before and William Penn, the Quaker statesman, had died in 1718 only two years before this date. Benjamin Franklin was fourteen years old at the time of Woolman's birth, and George Washington was born twelve years after Woolman.[56]

Steere is careful to note that:

> He had a good schooling and had ample access to books both in his own home and in the well-stocked, if somewhat carefully chosen, libraries of the Quaker families in his neighborhood, so that there is no evidence to support the view of Woolman as a poor ignorant boy who received his culture wholly from within.[57]

Although opportunities presented themselves for profitable business ventures, Woolman chose a small business as a tailor and orchardist to support himself and his family. This small business, combined with a simple lifestyle, allowed him to devote much of his energy to the concern that was his real vocation.

Early in his life Woolman felt an uneasiness about slaveholding that gradually developed into a concern that consumed his life. Steere notes that "The owning of Negro slaves in New Jersey at this period was common and little more was thought of it than would be thought of owning and deriving dividends from shares of stock in a business corporation today."[58] The practice of slaveowning was common among the Quakers of his day; but, by a life-time of loving confrontation, Woolman (along with his associates) all but cleared the Quaker membership of owning slaves.

This brief biographical sketch drawn from Steere's essay will suffice as the background for his analysis of Woolman's spiritually-centered social concern. To guard against those who would abstract Woolman's social vision and action from its religious roots, Steere begins his analysis by examining the religious culture that produced such a sensitive soul. Quaker corporate worship is seen as the key element in his religious development.

> There is no possible way of understanding the life of Woolman without a
> sympathetic grasp of the central place in his life which this openness to God
> in the silence of the corporate meeting for worship played.[59]

It is in the soil of such worship that the seeds of a concern could form in
Woolman's life.

The unfolding of a concern in Woolman's life (as it is presented by Steere)
follows the outline of the first thesis, "Prayer (especially corporate prayer) deepens
an awareness of creatureliness and evokes a consciousness of solidarity with all
persons and all creation. Out of this perceived solidarity 'seeds of concern' surface
in the consciousness of the one who prays." Steere emphasizes the importance of
the religious community, of corporate worship and prayer in Woolman's formation.

> [A] saint can only come from an established religious community. For only
> where there are others who have lived or are living such a life of abandon,
> is there the encouragement, the expectation, the nurture that prunes away
> individualistic excess and yet helps give the setting for continual renewal.
> A man or a woman must have this if at one and the same time they are to go
> beyond the customary compromises and mediocrity of the ordinary life and
> yet retain such touch with the heart of the common life as to reveal it to itself
> for what it might become and to appeal to this common life as a saint has the
> power of doing. Without such a community or tradition the one who feels
> called to this deeper devotion may hesitate, falter, or stop short, or he may
> develop willful eccentricities or grievances which may end by making him
> only a queer enemy of the people and cut him off from the true life of full
> devotion.[60]

A little later Steere adds that Woolman was "encouraged, sensitized, and shaped"[61]
by the Quaker community.

It was out of this community and its corporate worship and prayer that
Woolman's awareness of creatureliness was deepened and his consciousness of
solidarity with all persons and all creation was evoked. Woolman recalled in his
Journal that, even at the age of nineteen, "my heart was tender and often contrite,
and universal love to my fellow creatures increased in me."[62] This creature feeling
extended to the whole created order. Steere quotes two important passages from
the *Journal* that illustrate that Woolman's care embraced the animal kingdom.

> As the mind was moved by an inward principle to love God as an
> invisible being, so by the same principle it was moved to love Him in all
> His manifestations in the visible world; that as by His breath the flame of
> life was kindled in all animal sensible creatures, to say we love God as
> unseen and at the same time to practice cruelty toward the least creature
> moving by His life, or by the life derived from Him was a contradiction in
> His life.[63]

I believe where the love of God is verily perfected, and the true spirit of government watchfully attended to, a tenderness towards all creatures made subject to us will be experienced, and a care felt in us that we do not lessen the sweetness of life in the animal creation which the great Creator intends for them under our government.[64]

This "tenderness toward all creatures" is synonymous with the solidarity of the first thesis. This tenderness (or solidarity), evoked by corporate worship and prayer, prepared Woolman to respond when he observed his fellow creatures being abused.

With this understanding of Woolman's spiritual formation and religious commitment, Steere proceeds to describe Woolman's outward journey as an abolitionist and sensitizer of Quaker consciences. In a section entitled "The Growth of a 'Concern,'" Steere provides a helpful summary of the first stages of Woolman's concern.

John Woolman's uneasiness and concern against slave-holding developed slowly out of the root of this inward love for his fellow creatures. The steps are most instructive to follow. His employer owned a woman slave and one day told him to prepare a bill of sale for a customer who had bought the slave. Woolman's concern was not yet fully clear. He was an employee and his master had ordered it done, and the customer was an elderly member of the Society of Friends. He made out the bill "so through weakness I gave way and wrote it," but he told his employer and the buyer of the slave that he believed that slave-keeping was a practice inconsistent with the Christian religion. On the second occasion, Woolman was better prepared and when asked by a customer to draw up papers for the transfer of a slave, Woolman declined, admitting that many Quakers kept slaves but that he felt the practice to be wrong. The *Journal* records: "I spoke to him in good will and he told me that keeping of slaves was not altogether agreeable to his mind; but that the slave girl being a gift made to his wife he had accepted her." When the occasion arose again, John Woolman with much inward trembling confessed his scruples and refused the request of an elderly Friend. Woolman reports in his *Journal*, however, that "a few days after he came again and directed their freedom, and I then wrote his will."[65]

This account of the beginning stages of Woolman's concern shows how a concern about an injustice becomes more focused as the subject acts within the social milieu that produced the injustice. In this case, the concern did not arise full blown from Woolman's experience of prayer and worship. Rather, the broad concern for the felicity of all creatures came directly out of the experience of worship, but the more particular concern about slave-holding developed through interaction in the social realm.

Steere recognizes the importance of social interaction in a section entitled "Personal Exposure Broadens the Concern." Here it becomes clearer that only as persons becomes aware of an injustice do they seek to correct it. Steere notes Woolman's emphasis on personal exposure.

In his later writings he is a strong advocate of personal exposure as a means of shaking us out of our lethargy and our acquiescence in wrongs which others suffer either at our hands or because we do not help protest them.[66]

Acquaintance with the condition of the oppressed sensitizes persons to the needs of the oppressed and confronts them with the question of complicity with the oppression. Steere quotes Woolman's counsel to the wealthy.

[I]t is good for all those who live in fullness to improve every opportunity of being acquainted with the hardships and fatigues of those who labor for their living, and think seriously with themselves, am I influenced with true charity in fixing my demands.[67]

Woolman followed his own counsel about personal exposure in his missions to southern Quakers. Steere describes one of the ways in which Woolman practiced personal exposure.

In the next decade, in addition to journeys in Pennsylvania, New Jersey, and New England, he made three journeys southward and made them on foot in order that he might be more completely exposed to the condition of those whose plight affected him so deeply and perhaps share in a small way in their suffering and witness to their masters by his actions as well as his words.[68]

It is clear from the above that personal exposure, along with the "awareness of creatureliness" that accompanies prayer, contributes to the "consciousness of solidarity."

Woolman's life and mission reveal the deepest expression of solidarity with the suffering. His solidarity even found expression in his unconscious life. Steere describes a dream Woolman experienced late in his life.

Some two and a half years before his death, John Woolman in a time of severe illness had a dream in which he saw a dull gray gloomy colored mass made up of suffering humanity and felt himself a part of it. His name was called out but he could not answer. Then a voice spoke the words, "John Woolman is dead." He took this to mean that God had extinguished something in himself and had mixed him indistinguishably with the gray mass of suffering mankind. The Quaker prayer "Lord lay on us the burden of the world's suffering" had been answered in Woolman's heart.[69]

This kind of solidarity leads to an expendability in the service of the suffering that links it to the willingness thesis. It brings to mind the theme of "dying to death," which was expressed in Steere's Ingersoll Lecture entitled "Death's Illumination of Life."

These are the main points in Steere's essay on Woolman that pertain directly to the organizing theses, the greatest contribution manifesting itself in the illumination of the first thesis. Woolman's life and mission also provide a sort of case study for the unfolding of a concern.

Before turning from this essay to the scattered references to Woolman in Steere's other writings, there are several recurring themes in Steere's spiritual theology which can be observed in his essay on Woolman. These themes, some of which have been mentioned in Chapter Two, are the costliness of spiritual faithfulness, the role of the cross in discernment, the detachment from results, and the affirmation that everything matters (even the "small things"). These will be examined briefly.

In the *The Hardest Journey*, Steere emphasized the costliness of the inward journey. In his treatment of Woolman's *Journal*, he stresses the costliness of following out a concern. He especially notes Woolman's knowledge that his outspoken opposition to slave-holding would cost him business as well as the good will of many in the community.

> Lest anyone think that this concern, once accepted, was followed out with ease, Woolman's own words are important to observe, "As writing is a profitable employ, and as offending people was disagreeable to my inclination I was straitened in my mind; but as I looked to the Lord, He inclined my heart to His testimony." Or again: "Tradesmen and retailers of goods who depend upon their business for living are naturally inclined to keep the goodwill of their customers; nor is it pleasant for young men to be under any necessity to question the judgment or honesty of elderly men, and more especially those such as have a fair reputation."[70]

These passages from Woolman's *Journal* also show how the costliness of following out of a concern tests the genuineness of the concern.

This costliness is directly related to one of the key themes in Quaker spiritual discernment: the role of the cross. Michael J. Sheeran in his book, *Beyond Majority Rule*, has noted that "The earliest major test of one's leading seems to have been whether one finds the Cross in what he is drawn to."[71] Steere observes the principle of the cross (a principle that will be more closely examined in Chapter Five) in Woolman's following out of a concern. He quotes from the *Journal*:

> I had a fresh confirmation that acting contrary to present outward interest from a motive of Divine love and in regard to truth and righteousness and thereby incurring the resentments of people, opens the way to a treasure better than silver, and to a friendship exceeding the friendship of men.[72]

Here the cross has not so much proved the validity of the concern as it has brought the one carrying out the concern into the fellowship of Christ's suffering.

Two other themes that resonate throughout Steere's writings are the importance of "small things" and detachment from results. Steere finds these principles confirmed in Woolman's *Journal* and takes note of them. The "small things" that Woolman pays attention to may strike some readers as being excessively scrupulous, but Steere sees them as the "logic of love." While traveling in England, Woolman refused to use the stagecoach post service (in spite of his longing for communication with his family) because the cruelty of the post service to the horses and the small boys employed by them was notorious. Woolman sent and received letters only when Friends would carry them. Steere writes that "John Woolman believed that for God there are no small things, that all that we do matters, and that, therefore, one's witness must be clear in those areas where light is given to us."[73]

The scrupulous logic of love in "small things" meshes smoothly with detachment from results, for "small things" seldom produce dramatic, visible results. During a time when fighting between Indians and whites was escalating dangerously, Woolman "felt a drawing to witness to a loving concern for the Indians whom he felt were being so badly mistreated."[74] Woolman followed out his concern at great personal inconvenience. Referring to this mission, Steere writes, "There is no record of the ultimate consequence of this journey, but Woolman [by this dangerous journey] had discharged his concern and left it in other hands to assess its worth."[75] Even the smallest motion of love is important and should be carried out regardless of the results.

There are many references to Woolman in Steere's other writings, but only one augments an understanding of the organizing theses. In the last essay of *Work and Contemplation*, Steere points to Woolman as a paradigm for the integration of prayer and social responsibility. In Woolman's *Journal* he perceives the life of one who had learned to "work collectedly."

If early in his life John Woolman is brought by contemplation to feel the incongruity of loving God and holding a fellow human being in slavery, and if his life is put in order, step by step, so that his witness to this insight can be shared with Quaker slaveowners in distant places, and if as he travels Woolman becomes more and more aware of his dependence upon the operativeness of what he has found in worship in the midst of the interviews he has with those whose hearts he would reach, it is once again apparent that it is not alternation but the simultaneous operation of work and worship, of work and contemplation, that has taken place and that in fact always takes place as a condition of sanctity emerges.[76]

Gradually, Woolman moves from alternation to a simultaneity that enriches both his worship and his action. Woolman's life serves as an illustration of the fifth thesis. Even beyond the fifth thesis lies a life that is caught up in such an integration. It appears that, for Steere, simultaneity or "working collectedly" may eventually lead to a "collected life," i.e., sainthood.

In *Quaker Spirituality* Steere writes that the *Journal* "is able to communicate a plain and honest account of a 'collected' life."[77] Steere's assertion that such a life has a special efficacy recalls his treatment of the saint in his essay entitled "The Saint and Society;" he writes:

Woolman's *Journal* is not only the story of a "collected" man but it is the recounting of the way in which a Quaker "concern" may unfold within a man's heart, and if attended to and followed out, may not only reshape his own life as its vehicle but spread to others, and become a transforming power in the history of his time.[78]

Steere not only affirms Woolman's success in ridding Quakers of slaveholding, but suggests that Woolman's method has special contemporary value.

In the course of his traveling in the ministry on this spiritually centered social mission, the *Journal* reveals the outlines of a highly creative, non-violent approach to the resolution of conflict, an approach that is striking in its contemporary relevance.[79]

It is this contemporary relevance that has made Woolman such an attractive model for Steere. Woolman's writings have guided Steere's spirituality in its intellectual expression and in its practical application.

Summary

This analysis of Steere's assimilation of von Hügel and Woolman has yielded persuasive insights into the origins of Steere's spiritual theology. These two authors, whom Steere encountered early in his career, have exerted a formative influence in Steere's vocation and writings. Although Steere draws from many sources, these two authors stand out as his key mentors in addressing the issue of the relation of prayer and social responsibility. In spite of the enormous cultural and religious differences separating Woolman and von Hügel, their approach to Christian experience is not so divergent that Steere cannot approximate a synthesis of their thought in his own spiritual theology.

In considering von Hügel's influence, it may be helpful to recall the first three (of seven) permanent values that Albert A. Cock discerned in von Hügel's spiritual theology.

First, the threefold analysis of the constituents of any world religion . . . Second, the delineation of the specific genius of Catholicism set in relation to a delicate appreciation of other religious systems, . . . Third, the steady maintenance of the note of Joy, or Bliss as ultimate in the Divine Nature with a full recognition of the Cross, of suffering [costliness] as the law of approach from the finite individual to the infinite Person of God . . .[80]

These first three values, when slightly altered, are evident in Steere's spiritual theology. First, Steere is constantly emphasizing a spirituality that includes a healthy balance of the institutional, intellectual, and mystical elements of religion. He is conscious of the Quaker tendency to undervalue the institutional aspect of religion. This is why Steere is so anxious to emphasize Woolman's rootedness in the corporate life of the Quaker community. Second, Steere seeks to delineate the specific genius of Quakerism while setting it in relation to a delicate appreciation of other religious systems. This can be seen in Steere's ecumenical writings as well as in his interfaith contacts. Third, Steere is able to maintain the note of joy as ultimate in the divine nature with a full recognition of the place of the cross and suffering (costliness) in the spiritual journey toward God. These similarities in the spiritual theology of Steere and von Hügel are remarkable.

With this summary of von Hügel's influence of Steere, it is reasonable to argue for the primacy of von Hügel as Steere's spiritual mentor. Nevertheless, it is important to remember that Steere writes as a committed Quaker and that Woolman is his Quaker guide. Woolman's great contribution is his account of the deeply spiritual way in which a concern unfolds and is followed out. It is Woolman's witness to the imperative of following the inward Guide that aided Steere in moving beyond von Hügel's largely academic interest in the relation of prayer and social responsibility to an actuation his spiritual theology in a life of spiritually-centered social mission.

NOTES FOR CHAPTER THREE

[1]Douglas V. Steere, *Doors into Life: Through Five Devotional Classics* (New York: Harper and Row, Inc., 1948; reprint ed. Nashville, Tenn.: The Upper Room, 1981), p. 158.

[2]Ibid., pp. 161-162.

[3]Joseph P. Whalen, *The Spirituality of Friedrich von Hügel*, foreword by Bishop B. C. Butler, (New York: Newman Press, 1971) pp. 17-18.

[4]Ibid., p. 20.

[5]Ibid., p. 22.

[6]Steere, *Doors into Life*, p. 167.

[7]John J. Heaney, *The Modernist Crisis: von Hügel* (Washington: Corpus Books, 1968), p. 201.

[8]Ibid., p. 202.

[9]Ibid., p. 202.

[10]Albert A. Cock, *A Critical Examination of von Hügel's Philosophy of Religion* (London: Hugh Rees, 1953), p. 17.

[11]Ibid., p. 154.

[12]Whalen, p. 30.

[13]Cock, p. 132.

[14]Ibid., p. 132.

[15]Ibid., p. 137.

[16]Michael de La Bedoyere, *The Life of Baron von Hügel* (London: Dent, 1951), p. xi.

[17]Ibid., p. xi.

[18]Ibid., p. 317.

[19]Ibid., p. xii.

[20]For Steere's agreement with this assessment of Bedoyere see the quotations with footnote numbers 46 and 47. Surprisingly, Whalen views the modernist controversy as peripheral

to von Hügel's key concern with spirituality.

[21]Bedoyere, p. 322.

[22]Heaney, p. 6.

[23]John J. Heaney, Review of *Spiritual Counsels and Letters of Baron Friedrich von Hügel* in *Heythrop Journal* 6 (Ja. 65):100.

[24]Cock, p. 18.

[25]Whalen, p. 221.

[26]Douglas V. Steere, *Critical Realism in the Religious Philosophy of Baron Friedrich von Hügel* (Unpublished dissertation at Harvard University, 1931), p. 305.

[27]Douglas V. Steere, *Spiritual Counsels and Letters of Baron Friedrich von Hügel* (New York: Harper and Row, 1964).

[28]Heaney, *Heythrop Journal*, p. 100.

[29]Steere, *Doors into Life*, p. 174.

[30]Steere, *Spiritual Counsels* . . ., p. 5.

[31]Ibid., p. 6.

[32]Whalen, p. 35.

[33]Ibid., p. 65.

[34]Steere, unpublished letter.

[35]Whalen, p. 183.

[36]Steere, *Doors into Life*, pp. 183-184.

[37]Steere, *Spiritual Counsels* . . ., p. 8.

[38]Whalen, p. 189.

[39]Ibid., p. 187.

[40]Ibid., p. 68.

[41]Ibid., p. 189.

[42]Ibid., p. 189.

[43]Ibid., p. 72.

[44]Ibid., p. 43.

[45]Ibid., p. 88.

[46]Steere, *Spiritual Counsels* . . ., p. 5.

[47]Ibid., p. 10.

[48]Steere, *Together in Solitude*, p. viii.

[49]Steere, *Doors into Life*, p. 11.

[50]Ibid., p. 85.

[51]*The Collected Letters of S. T. Coleridge*, ed. E. L. Griggs, (London, 1956), I, 302. Cited in the Introduction to *The Journal and Major Essays of John Woolman*, ed. Phillips P. Moulton, (New York: Oxford University Press, 1971), p. 3.

[52]Phillips P. Moulton, *The Journal and Major Essays of John Woolman*, ed. Phillips P. Moulton, (New York: Oxford University Press, 1971), p. 3.

[53]Ibid., p. 3.

[54]Ibid., p. 318.

[55]Steere, *Doors into Life*, p. 11.

[56]Ibid., p. 90.

[57]Ibid., p. 91.

[58]Ibid., p. 98.

[59]Ibid., p. 94.

[60]Ibid., p. 96.

[61]Ibid., p. 97.

[62]Ibid., p. 94.

[63]Ibid., p. 95.

[64]Ibid., p. 95.

[65]Ibid., p. 99.

[66]Ibid., p. 101.

[67]Ibid., p. 101.

[68]Ibid., p. 105.

[69]Ibid., p. 115.

[70]Ibid., p. 100.

[71]Michael J. Sheeran, *Beyond Majority Rule: Voteless Decisions in the Religious Society of Friends* (Philadelphia: Philadelphia Yearly Meeting, 1983), p. 24.

[72]Steere, *Doors into Life*, p. 100.

[73]Ibid., p. 110.

[74]Ibid., p. 108.

[75]Ibid., pp. 109-110.

[76]Steere, *Work and Contemplation*, p. 143.

[77]*Quaker Spirituality*, p. 161.

[78]Ibid., p. 162.

[79]Ibid., p. 162.

[80]Cock, p. 17

CHAPTER FOUR

OTHER LITERARY AND THEOLOGICAL SOURCES

This chapter will discuss the literary and theological sources, other than von Hügel and Woolman, that have exerted the most profound influence on Steere's philosophy and spiritual theology. Among these various sources, Soren Kierkegaard is of particular significance; his influence on Steere will be examined briefly. Finally, this chapter will indicate some other sources that Steere draws upon to develop his treatment of the relation of prayer and social responsibility.

In several places Steere has indicated those authors who have most enriched his life and thought. In the Introduction to *Together in Solitude*, Steere provides the most extended account of his key sources.

I have taught philosophy for a long generation at Haverford College. During that time I have been immeasurably enriched by feasting on the devotional treasures of the Roman Catholic tradition and particularly the writings of Nicholas of Cusa, the Spanish mystics, Pascal, Caussade, Grou, Baron Friedrich von Hügel and Gabriel Marcel. I have also been heartened by the Protestant writings of Lancelot Andrews, Thomas Traherne, William Law, Soren Kierkegaard, Evelyn Underhill, and Charles Williams, and in the company of my own contemporaries, a group that we charitably called the "Younger Theologians." This was a small gathering made up of men like Paul Tillich, Reinhold and Richard Niebuhr, Amos Wilder, Edwin Aubrey, Wilhelm Pauck, Henry Van Dusen, George Thomas, Roland Bainton, Robert Calhoun, John Mackay, and Joseph Hromadka, who for three decades met together for two long weekends each year and probed each others' minds and spirits.
If I were asked who, out of this long chain of witnesses who have blessed me, were my own most moving mentors, my debt and commitment to ecumenism in its deepest sense would be swiftly evident. For apart from my Quaker guides, Isaac Penington and John Woolman, I would be drawn to name Baron von Hügel, Soren Kierkegaard, and Romano Guardini. Each of these men in his own unique way has pointed me to the luminous center.[1]

This list suggests the ecumenicity and breadth of Steere's literary sources.

There are two notable omissions in this list. It is surprising that, in this list of those whom he says have blessed him, Steere fails to mention Gerhard Groote, to whom Steere attributes the *Imitation of Christ*, and Francis de Sales. They are both authors whose writings have been characterized by Steere as "doors into life for me."[2]

In an unpublished letter to a former student, Steere provides a brief intellectual profile that mentions other important philosophical and psychological sources. Two important philosophical sources are Maritain and Unamuno. Having taught abnormal psychology at Haverford for fifteen years, Steere is fully acquainted with the thought of Freud, Jung, Adler, and Kunkel; but, among these, Steere draws most on the work of Jung and Kunkel. These additions fill out Steere's intellectual profile but in no way encompass the scope of his learning.

The three "most moving mentors" for Steere, apart from his Quaker guides, are von Hügel, Kierkegaard, and Guardini. The inclusion of Guardini among his most moving mentors is rather surprising as Steere seldom mentions him or quotes him in his writings. On the other hand, the influence of Kierkegaard is abundantly apparent. Kierkegaard is the key author behind the existentialism of Steere's existential realism.

Kierkegaard: Steere's Existentialist Mentor

In Chapter Three, it was noted that Steere regarded von Hügel as a sort of pre-existentialist existentialist. Von Hügel's emphasis on the subject's response to the givenness of God marked the existential element in von Hügel's spiritual theology. Despite this inherent existentialist approach, Steere turns to Kierkegaard for a more searching analysis of the subject's response to God. Even here, though, the influence of von Hügel is felt because it was von Hügel who introduced Steere to Kierkegaard. Describing this introduction in *Doors into Life*, Steere writes:

> I first came across the name of Soren Kierkegaard in 1926-27 in reading Friedrich von Hügel's *Eternal Life*. The great balanced von Hügel called Soren Kierkegaard a fiercely passionate prophet of the transcendence of God, . . . And yet no modern writer has been more concerned than Kierkegaard with the transcending of the transcendence, with the overcoming of the cleft between man and God, with man's abandoning himself, yielding himself to God, with man's following Christ, with the nature of the Christian's dealing with this given cleft between man and God.[3]

In Kierkegaard, Steere found a bracing existential analysis of individual responsibility, an analysis that Steere found congenial to Quaker worship.

Steere outlines the development of his existentialism in a letter to a former student.

Philosophically I am, I suppose, an existential realist if that does not seem too ridiculous a description. The existentialist focus upon the subject and its freedom and power to choose has been what drew me to Pascal and Kierkegaard and Unamuno [later Steere mentions Maritain and Marcel] and that led me to learn Danish in order to translate *Purity of Heart* at a time (1934) when there was almost nothing on Soren Kierkegaard going in English translation. It has also led me to exalt in men and women their gift of contemplation and has led me to write on the deeper levels of prayer and the mystical dimension.[4]

This deeply revealing passage connects the existentialist focus on the subject's "power to choose" (or individual responsibility) with the subject's capacity for encounter with God. Here is the philosophical foundation for an interpretation of Quaker worship; in fact, *On Listening to Another* is grounded in just such an understanding.

The similarities between Steere's existential realism and Kierkegaard's existentialism are striking. In a passage dealing with Kierkegaard's dissatisfaction with Hegelian rationalism, the similarities are apparent.

The Hegelian rationalism that proved God's omnipresent operativeness, he found specious and if followed out he saw it dissolving away both God and the responsible individual subject in a misty immanentism, leaving no eternal encounter between man and God.[5]

The realism contained in this passage is supplied by Kierkegaard's religious faith. Without this religious grounding, Steere finds existentialism inadequate.

I have never regarded existentialism as an adequate philosophical position. It has no place for a philosophy of nature or of science, and finally no place for a religious ground that is *given* and that lures us on to respond to prior initiative. In the case of Pascal or Kierkegaard or Gabriel Marcel, this ground was already there having been supplied by a religious faith that they worked within, and in their case the existentialist account and analysis of the subject and its responsibility gave them fresh freedom to explore it and to probe it to its very core.[6]

So, Kierkegaard, as well as Pascal and Marcel, has a *given* (God) to which the subject responds. This accounts for the "realistic" nature of Kierkegaard's existentialism.

According to Steere, the purpose of *Purity of Heart* is to "undermine the reader's faith in the satisfying adequacy of this worldly life."[7] Kierkegaard accomplishes this purpose by relentlessly stripping away the reader's subtle subterfuges. Describing Kierkegaard's method, Steere writes:

It is a mood that determines his method. He will lay bare the will. He will expose that level in man from which the yielding, the committing, the abandoning comes. In every man there is an "infinite abyss that can only be filled by an infinite and immutable object, that is to say, only by God himself," declares Pascal. Kierkegaard will scrape way the coatings that have formed over this abyss in man; the lures of the world, the deceitful rationalizations of the divided self, the capacity to escape judgment by comparing oneself with others, by hiding in the crowd.[8]

This laying bare of the will supplies a clue to Kierkegaard's influence in the second thesis, which is "Prayer nurtures an awareness of God's infinite concern for every person and fosters a willingness to participate in God's redemptive order." Kierkegaard does not deal specifically with what *prayer* does to foster a willingness to participate in God's redemptive order, but since *Purity of Heart* is ostensibly a book written to help Christians prepare for the office of confession, the *prayerful* examination of conscience is understood. After stripping away all the barriers erected to shield the subject from an encounter with God, Kierkegaard confronts the reader with the imperative of responding to God.

Although there is little in Steere's analysis of Kierkegaard's work to indicate that Kierkegaard influenced the idea that "Prayer nurtures an awareness of Gods infinite concern for every person," there is evidence that Kierkegaard's insistence on the *equality* of God's concern for every person informs this part of the thesis. In Steere's Introduction to *Purity of Heart*, he writes:

> Kierkegaard saw only one solvent for these obvious inequalities, only one root of enduring equality between all men. That equality is in the equality of concern which a loving Eternal Father has for each individual that has ever existed. Hence only in the Christian sense of being children of a common Father are we all equal.[9]

For Steere, Kierkegaard's intuition of the equality of God's concern for every person implied God's *infinite* concern for all persons, the kind of concern that only a "loving Eternal Father" could possess.

In Steere's analysis of Kierkegaard, the emphasis is not so much on "*fostering* a willingness to participate in God's redemptive order" as on *exposing* the level of human freedom where the human person makes decisions; Steere writes:

> And it is the task of philosophy, of psychology and of all great religious writing and preaching to seek to bare this level in a man from which the deciding, the choosing, the committing come. It is equally their task to use reason against itself, that is dialectically, to expose the sham evasions by which a man draws away from facing his life situation and its deepest choices.[10]

Willingness can only exist when the human person becomes fully conscious of a choice, a decision that must be made. The great value of Kierkegaard's analysis for Steere's project is that it brings subjects to

> the infinite abyss in themselves and to the infinite and immutable pursuer who alone can fill that abyss, and it must leave them there. It must reveal what commitment is, what it involves, what it costs, in what ways men flee from it, and what follows on such abandonment.[11]

Kierkegaard's existentialist method confronts the subject with the necessity to choose, to will. Such a confrontation requires the subject to decide whether he or she will participate in God's redemptive order.

When the subject is brought to the edge of the abyss and confronted with a decision, it is the awareness of God's infinite concern that fosters a willingness to participate in God's redemptive order. Without this deep personal knowledge of God's infinite love, the subject is impotent to respond appropriately to God. Here Steere's approach (expressed in the second thesis) is shown to provide the subject with a spiritual motive for participating in God's redemptive order. It calls to mind the words of 1 John 4:19, "We love Him [and others?] because He first loved us."

Steere's appropriation of Kierkegaard's existentialism raises some issues concerning the value of existentialism as a philosophical partner for Christian theology. Christian theology has always developed in dialogue with philosophy (e.g., Augustine's use of neo-Platonism), but not all philosophical "schools" have exhibited equal value as a partner for it. John Macquarrie, one of the foremost authorities on existentialism, has examined the value of existentialism as a philosophical partner for Christian theology and his analysis will serve as an instrument for determining both the positive and negative aspects of an "existentialist theology," especially an existentialist theology profoundly influenced by Kierkegaard.

Macquarrie considers existentialism a particularly elusive philosophical category. It refuses to be neatly packaged; there is no set body of doctrine. It is not so much a philosophy as a style of philosophizing. The first and most important characteristic of this style of philosophizing is that it

> begins from man rather than from nature. It is a philosophy of the subject rather than of the object. But one might say that Idealism too took its starting point in the subject. Thus one must further qualify the existentialist position by saying that for the existentialist the subject is the existent in the whole range of his existing. He is not only a thinking subject but the initiator of action and a center of feeling.[12]

One of the summary phrases often used to characterize existentialist thought is Sartre's statement that "man's existence precedes his essence." By this statement Sartre means that

> man first of all exists, encounters himself, surges up in the world--and defines himself afterwards. If man, as the existentialist sees him, is not definable, it is because to begin with he is nothing. He will not be anything until later, and then he will be what he makes of himself.[13]

Some of the recurring themes in existentialism are freedom, decision, and responsibility--themes that sometimes have been regarded as inappropriate for philosophy. These themes became prominent for existentialism because they "constitute the core of personal being."[14]

Macquarrie's overall evaluation of existentialism as a philosophical partner for Christian theology is positive. In the closing pages of *Existentialism*,[15] he writes:

[T]he merits of this type of philosophy outweigh the objections. Existentialism has yielded many fresh and penetrating insights into the mystery of our own human existence, and it has thereby contributed to the protection and enhancement of our humanity in the face of all that threatens it today. . . . I still have to say that from existentialism we can learn truths that are indispensable to our condition and that will be essential to any sane, human philosophy of the future.[16]

Macquarrie arrives at this conclusion after examining five negative tendencies found in varying degree among existentialist philosophers; they are: irrationality, amoralism, excessive individualism, exclusive anthropocentrism, and pessimism. These tendencies in existentialism must be recognized and criticized, but they do not negate the value of existentialism for Christian theology as it seeks to probe the depths of personal being.

Soren Kierkegaard is commonly considered the father of modern existentialism. His emphasis on the subject and the themes of freedom, decision, and responsibility has already been noted. For Kierkegaard, the notion of the individual or the exceptional "man" became a major category. He also prized subjectivity and intensity as criteria for truth and genuineness.[17] Kierkegaard's thought is especially prone to the negative tendencies of irrationality and excessive individualism. H. J. Paton has written that "The rejection of reason finds it most elaborate modern expression in the voluminous writings of Kierkegaard."[18] When Macquarrie seeks evidence for an "undesirable degree of individualism" in existentialist philosophy, he turns first to Kierkegaard.[19]

[Kierkegaard's] individualism is explicit. He does not hesitate to say bluntly, in one of his most mature works, that '"fellowship" is a lower category than the "single individual," which everyone can and should be.[20]

These tendencies in Kierkegaard's thought indicate the need for caution in appropriating his philosophy.

While Steere cannot be faulted with succumbing to Kierkegaardian irrationality (Steere's criticism of existentialist inadequate philosophy of nature and science has already been noted), he is largely uncritical of the individualism that pervades Kierkegaard's thought. Steere prefers to interpret Kierkegaard's focus on the individual as a "universal note of the inward life of man."

The note that it [Kierkegaard's *Purity of Heart*] sounds is alien to modern ears which are tuned to collective thinking, collective action and collective salvation. It is, however, not an individualistic note that Kierkegaard sounds, but a universal note of the inward life of man, a note that even this age will be compelled to learn again when its present grim honeymoon with collective salvation has spent itself.[21]

Macquarrie also allows that existentialism may provide a helpful critique of collectivism; he writes that "Whenever individual judgment and responsibility are in danger of being submerged in some impersonal kind of collectivism, it is necessary to champion the rights of the individual . . ."[22]   Nevertheless, Macquarrie expresses deep concern about the excessive individualism of most existentialist philosophies. Rather than critique existentialism on this point, Steere gives evidence of being in substantial agreement. The issue of individualism in Steere's spiritual theology will receive closer attention in Chapter Five.

Macquarrie notes that "much of the most creative theological thinking in this century has sprung from the encounter with existentialism."[23]   He cites its significant influence on Barth, Bultmann, Tillich, Buri, Ott, Ebeling, and Rahner. In Macquarrie's analysis, the existential theologians (in regard to their language about God) can be divided into two fairly distinct groups. The first group, represented by Bultmann and Buri, suggests that God cannot become the object of thought but is known as the unconditioned demand that touches human life in certain specific moments. The second group, represented best by Tillich, seek an ontological as well as an existential basis for God-language. It is in this second group that Macquarrie situates himself.[24] Steere's existential realism would also fit most comfortably in this second group, as long as the ontology allowed for a realistic cleft between the subject and God, the I and Thou. (Steere and Tillich enjoyed a long friendship as participants in the group which styled itself the "Younger Theologians.")

In spite of the fact that Kierkegaard is a substantial source for the second thesis, Kierkegaard's importance for this study lies more in his role as a source for Steere's existential realism. Kierkegaard's existentialism provided Steere with a philosophical method for plumbing the depths of the subject's encounter with the Given. This focus on the subject along with von Hügel's critical realism supplied Steere with the material he needed to fashion his own approach to worship and the deeper levels of prayer.

Additional Sources for Steere's Development of the Organizing Theses

Having examined the three authors (von Hügel, Woolman, and Kierkegaard) whose writings have shaped the structure and content of Steere's spiritual theology, this study turns to the other scattered sources that Steere draws upon to illuminate or define the organizing theses. No single author is cited for more than one of the theses. In this section the study will proceed chronologically through the organizing theses.

There are two additional citations pertaining to the first thesis (the awareness thesis). In a section entitled "Creatureliness and Social Responsibility" in *Prayer and Worship*, Steere illustrates the relation of worship (and the awareness of creatureliness that accompanies it) and solidarity with a reference to a Quaker colleague's analogy.

Howard Brinton has expressed the effect of this approach to the center in the fellowship of worship by the figure of the spokes of a wheel. The nearer the spokes are to the center, the nearer they are to each other. If the worship is real this new sense of nearness to others will invade the rest of life.[25]

This analogy expresses the way worship may evoke a consciousness of solidarity with all persons and all creation--it is an especially apt analogy for Quaker worship. The other citation illuminating the first thesis pertains to the tiny promptings (the small things) that may be the "seeds of concern." In three of his books Steere quotes Adrienne von Speyr on the necessity of obedience in the small things.

It is hardly ever possible to see from the start all that God is to mean to one. . . . Once open to the light, man may ask God to claim him more essentially and more profoundly. But on one condition only, on condition he does not refuse the first small act God demands of him.[26]

This emphasis on the "small acts" is a key point in Steere's treatment of the unfolding of a concern.

Both Gabriel Marcel and St. Francis de Sales make important contributions to Steere's development of the second thesis (the willingness thesis). These authors reveal what devotion, meditation, and contemplation offer to "foster a willingness to participate in God's redemptive order." In his essay on St. Francis de Sales in *Door into Life*, Steere quotes Francis on devotion and meditation.

Devotion is simply the promptitude, fervour, affection and agility which we have in the service of God. And there is a difference between a good man and a devout man; for he is a good man who keeps the commandments of God, although without great promptitude or fervour; but he is devout who not only observes them but does so willingly, promptly and with a good heart.[27]

Meditation is no other thing than an attentive thought, voluntarily reiterated or entertained in the mind, to excite the will to holy and salutary affections and resolutions.[28]

Although Steere seldom quotes Francis when dealing specifically with the relation of prayer and social responsibility, these passages do help define Steere's understanding of devotional literature and prayer. Their purpose is to train the will in "swift and agile" obedience to God.

Steere's respect for Gabriel Marcel's philosophy was noted earlier in this chapter. Steere finds Marcel's treatment of contemplation especially helpful when it comes to moving contemplation beyond passive observance of the object of contemplation to availability to the object of contemplation; Steere writes:

The French Christian existentialist, Gabriel Marcel, has spoken in the words of the philosopher of this same participation, this *disponibilité* [availability] that has to be added to the simple, impartial, spectator-like recording of impressions, before contemplation at such a level [the level of mystical prayer] may arise. "There can be no contemplation without a kind of regrouping of one's resources, or a kind of ingatheredness; to contemplate is to ingather oneself in the presence of whatever is being contemplated, and this in such a fashion that the reality . . . itself becomes a factor in the ingathering."[29]

This quote supports Steere's conviction that in the highest level of prayer (mystical prayer) a transformation of the will, a "regrouping of one's resources," occurs and the prayer is made expendable in God's service. It should be noted, however, that this transformation is only an intensification of what happens in all genuine prayer.

The additional sources for the third thesis (the cleansing thesis) are Augustine, Whitehead, and Maritain. The third thesis, in an abbreviated form, reads: "Prayer cleanses action . . . and restores its frame of meaning." Steere quotes a passage from Augustine's writings that aptly expresses this idea.

Augustine, however, speaks for us all and goes to the heart of what happens in true prayer and worship when he says: "I was collected from the dispersion in which I turned from thee, the One, and was vainly divided." How better than in terms of dispersion could we describe the condition today of the overactive man? Yet how much easier it is to describe the uncollected, overactive man than to describe in detail the collected man or the means of his being collected.
Prayer is the principal agency for collection from dispersion.[30]

Prayer cleanses the "dispersion" of uncollected activity and restores to the pray-er a consciousness of the frame in which action is related to the end.

The first part of the third thesis states that "Prayer cleanses action, work, and service of its repetitive nature." Steere observes that much of human activity is automatic; there is little that is truly intentional. Prayer is able to break into this automatic existence. Here Steere finds an ally in Alfred N. Whitehead. "Professor A. N. Whitehead speaks of inward religion as 'an offensive against the repetitive mechanism of the universe.'"[31]   Inward religion, the life of prayer, reconnects action with the frame.

The saint is especially conscious of the force of habit, the tendency to run with the herd. Therefore, the saint turns to prayer as a means of being guided from within, rather than merely reacting to outward circumstances. Here Steere draws on an insight of Maritain.

As the saint finds his life laid open before the scrutiny of the All-Loving One, he is acutely aware that all of the projected sins of society are present within himself. And with God's help he is concerned to begin from within, in Maritain's words, "to purify the springs of history within his own heart."[32]

Again, inward religion purifies (cleanses) the outward life (history) so that the outward life may savor of the inward principle that has guided it.

There are no significant additional sources for the fourth thesis.

In his development of the ideas expressed in the fifth thesis, Steere weaves many sources. An additional source for the first part of the fifth thesis, viz., "both prayer and social responsibility are incomplete in themselves", is Immanuel Kant. Steere expresses the incompleteness by translating the categories of Kantian epistemology into spirituality.

> One might gather this up by paraphrasing the famous phrase of Immanuel Kant's to the effect that "percepts without concepts are blind" but that "concepts without percepts are empty" and say of work and contemplation that work without contemplation is bitter and blind, but that contemplation without work . . . is callow and empty.[33]

When it comes to the partial integration of work and contemplation achieved through alternation, Steere refers to the writings of William Ernest Hocking and, in one case, Charles Bennett.[34] Steere's most extended treatment of Hocking's alternation thesis is found in *Work and Contemplation*; Steere writes:

> In his *Meaning of God in Human Experience* William Ernest Hocking gives a much-quoted account of the alternation thesis in the matter of the relation of work and contemplation, of work and worship. In the course of working, the body becomes fatigued and has to stop to rebuild its strength. But this is not all. There is a deeper fatigue, a spiritual tiredness that accompanies the body's weariness, and this reveals itself by the bleeding away of our sense of purpose, of the goal of work, of the frame which contemplation has placed around the work to win the mind's approval and consent to it. Body and spirit are represented here by the analogy of a spring clock that has run down and has to be wound up. Contemplation or worship is the restoration of the frame, and it can begin only when the work stops.[35]

Although Steere acknowledges this conception as "helpful," it does not represent the full integration of work and contemplation that Steere advocates. Steere argues for a condition where work and contemplation interpenetrate each other, a simultaneity.

In his analysis of simultaneity, Steere turns to the philosophy of E. I. Watkin and the spiritual theology of Jacob Boehme, Dom Chapman, and Meister Eckhart. Perhaps the most succinct statement of simultaneity is that of Boehme who wrote, "Though my head and my hand be at labor, yet doth my heart dwell in God."[36] Dom Chapman describes simultaneity in terms of a simplification of life.

> Remember that the proper result of contemplative prayer is simplicity in the whole life; so that a contemplative is always doing the same thing all day and all night. He is praying, or having breakfast, or talking, or working, or amusing himself; but he is principally conscious that he is *doing God's will.* The different external activities seem to him a sort of varied outcome of one continuous internal intention as if in a long walk: one goes up hill and down, in rain or sun or wind, but the act of walking

remains the same all the time, the same movement of the legs, but sometimes easy, sometimes hard, sometimes pleasant, sometimes unpleasant.[37]

Steere's preferred term for the simultaneity of work and contemplation is "working collectedly," which he borrows from Meister Eckhart. The key passage from Eckhart is:

> One should learn to work with this contemplation in him, with him, and emerging from him, so that one allows his inner life to break into his activity and his activity into his inner life so that one becomes accustomed to *working collectedly*. If they can both happen in him, that is the best of all, for then he becomes a fellow workman with God.[38]

The witness of these spiritual authors to the reality of simultaneity is supplemented by the philosophy of E. I. Watkin, an English philosopher whose books *Philosophy of Form* and *Philosophy of Mysticism* influenced Steere's *Work and Contemplation*. In his *Philosophy of Mysticism*, Watkin describes the consciousness of the contemplative who has learned to "work collectedly."

> When the external activities supervene, the Divine possession is only felt at the root of consciousness and will always however be ready to fill both functions of the center thus consciously God-possessed.[39]

Here it must be remembered that, for Steere, the ultimate goal is not just moments of simultaneity, but a collected life. In such a life, periods of simultaneity give way to a life lived so near the root, the "luminous center," that work and contemplation interpenetrate each other thoroughly and continuously. This is the life Steere perceives in people like Francis Xavier, Catherine of Genoa, Vincent de Paul,[40] John Frederick Oberlin, and John Woolman.[41] It is the great goal of Christian living.

Conclusion

This concludes the analysis of the most significant sources, other than von Hügel and Woolman, in Steere's treatment of the relation of prayer and social responsibility. This chapter gives some indication of the breadth and depth of Steere's learning in the areas of philosophy and theology. On the other hand, this formidable host of sources raises the question of eclecticism. Has Steere simply gathered an impressive array of quotations and examples and strung them along an outline of the problem? What is original in his treatment? The answers to these questions will become clearer in the next chapter, but it is appropriate, in this chapter on sources, to examine briefly the question of eclecticism.

In reviews of two of Steere's books, the reviewers make critical comments on Steere's use of sources. At the end of a very positive review of Steere's *Dimensions of Prayer*, John B. Coburn writes:

> If a critical note is to be added it is to say that, however grateful we may

be for the many apt quotations on prayer from authors old and new, the book is best when the author speaks for himself out of his own experience and convictions. For penance, may his next book be without reference to any authority save that of the Holy Spirit working in his own life.[42]

More recently, in a review of *Together in Solitude* in *Quaker Religious Thought*, Arthur O. Roberts detects a "subtle name-dropping elitism" in Steere's writings.

Because strengths and weaknesses offer clues to where we stand in relation to each other, I have paired these qualities in reflecting upon this book. First, the book distills pertinent material on the spiritual life from a wide body of philosophical and religious literature, offering the reader a professionally competent religious travelogue through time. Steere also provides anecdotes of his own travels. Some shadow is cast on this strength by a subtle, name-dropping elitism--a sophisticated version of the VIP syndrome. One is conscious of it in such syntax as "Anker Larsen, a Danish mystic whom Rufus Jones always admired and with whom I once spent a day at his home in a suburb of Copenhagen." Although vital religious experience often serves vicariously at second hand it rarely does so at third hand.[43]

These critical remarks need to be viewed in the context of Steere's personalism and his attraction to "wisdom that is bound in human hide."[44] As a personalist and a realist, Steere places great emphasis on truth as it has been lived and incarnated. It was noted in Chapter Two that Steere draws on the lives of the saints (past and present) as a Biblical scholar draws on scriptures. E. Glenn Hinson writes that "He [Steere] is not a name-dropper, but his conversation, lectures, and writings are rich in personalia drawn from contacts with people everywhere."[45]

Another factor that has affected Steere's style is his appreciation for anecdote and illustration. While at Harvard, Steere developed a great admiration for Hocking's gift of using proverb-like statements and anecdotes to illustrate abstract ideas. Steere's desire to make ideas interesting and his attraction to "wisdom that is bound in human hide" account for his style and, perhaps, for his enormous popularity as a lecturer. Parker Palmer comments on this style in his biographical chapter on Douglas and Dorothy Steere.

I have always appreciated Douglas Steere's writing not only for its intellectual integrity and the spiritual guidance it offers but for its thoroughly human, anecdotal quality. In most of Douglas's books, one need not read too many paragraphs before one finds another story--a story about people, real or imaginary, which illustrates the tragedy, the comedy, the divine depths, or simply the dailyness of human life. This same quality is present in conversation with Dorothy and Douglas. Rather than speak about themselves and their ideas they will so often tell a story about people who have met and moved them.[46]

Coburn's critical note on *Dimensions of Prayer* should, in fairness to Steere, be seen in relation to the intended readership of the book. Steere wrote the book as a guide to prayer for lay women of the Methodist Church and hoped to introduce them to a broad spectrum of Christian devotional and spiritual writings. As a study guide and as a "professionally competent religious travelogue through time," the book succeeds quite well.

In examining the question of eclecticism as it pertains to the subject of this study, it must be remembered that, with the exception of Hocking's alternation thesis (which Steere finds inadequate), the theses are drawn from *Steere's* writings. The theses follow Steere's phrasing and Steere's arrangement of ideas. Steere marshalls his sources to develop an approach to the problem that is uniquely Steerean. This is no crude eclecticism; rather, it is a skillful weaving of themes to achieve a comprehensive treatment of the relation of prayer and social responsibility. The consistency of Steere's approach is rooted in his stance as an existential realist immersed in the ethical mysticism of Quakerism.

This chapter has discussed the significant sources, other than von Hügel and Woolman, for Steere's spiritual theology and for his approach to the relation of prayer and social responsibility. Although Steere cites hundreds of authors, the ones examined in this chapter have been singled out based on Steere's self-reflective observations and on their importance to Steere's treatment of the problem. Kierkegaard stands out among these as being of special significance. The analysis of these sources has broadened and deepened an understanding of the organizing theses. Chapters Five and Six will examine the value of Steere's teaching in the light of the needs of contemporary spiritual pilgrims.

NOTES FOR CHAPTER FOUR

ABBREVIATIONS:

DIL,	*Doors into Life*
DOP,	*Dimensions of Prayer*
BFW,	*On Beginning from Within*
LTA,	*On Listening to Another*
P&W,	*Prayer and Worship*
TIS,	*Together in Solitude*
W&C	*Work and Contemplation*

[1]Steere, *TIS*, pp. vii-viii.

[2]Steere, *DIL*, p. 11.

[3]Ibid., p. 121.

[4]Steere, Unpublished letter, p. 2. Jacques Maritain also advocates an "existential realism" (what he considers an authentic Thomism) in this book *Existence and the Existent*, trans. Lewis Galantiere and Gerald B. Phelan (Garden City, New York: Image Books, 1956), p. 12.

[5]Steere, *DIL*, p. 123.

[6]Steere, Unpublished letter, p. 2.

[7]Steere, *DIL*, p. 120.

[8]Ibid., p. 135.

[9]Douglas V. Steere, Introduction to *Purity of Heart* by Soren Kierkegaard, trans. with intro. by Douglas V. Steere, Harper Torchbooks ed. (New York: Harper and Row, 1956), p. 20.

[10]Steere, *DIL*, p. 130.

[11]Ibid., p. 135.

[12]John Macquarrie, *Existentialism* (Philadelphia, Pa.: The Westminster Press, 1972), p. 2.

[13]Jean-Paul Sartre, "Existentialism is a Humanism," *Existentialism from Dostoevsky to Sartre*, ed. Walter Kaufmann (Cleveland, 1956), p. 290. Cited in Macquarrie, p. 3.

[14]Macquarrie, p. 4.

[15]See footnote 12.

[16]Ibid., pp. 225-26.

[17]Ibid., p. 35.

[18]H. J. Paton, *The Modern Predicament* (New York, 1962), p. 120. Cited in Macquarrie, p. 220.

[19]Macquarrie, p. 223.

[20]Soren Kierkegaard, *Training in Christianity*, trans. W. Lowrie (Princeton, 1944), p. 218. Cited in Macquarrie, p. 223.

[21]Steere, Introduction to *Purity of Heart*, p. 26.

[22]Macquarrie, p. 222.

[23]Ibid., p. 215.

[24]Ibid., p. 217.

[25]Steere, *P&W*, p. 52.

[26]Adrienne von Speyr, *The Word*, Alexander Dru, trans. (London: Collins, 1953), p. 9. Steere cites Speyr in *DOP*, pp. 97-98. in *LTA*, p. 69. in *W&C*, p. 52.

[27]Francis de Sales, *Introduction to the Devout Life*, pp. 4-5. Cited in *DIL*, p. 68.

[28]Francis de Sales, *Treatise on the Love of God*, p. 236. Cited in *DIL*, p. 72.

[29]Gabriel Marcel, *The Mystery of Being* (London: Harvill, 1952) I, p. 126. Cited in *W&C*, pp. 52, 53.

[30]Steere, *TIS*, p. 24.

[31]Ibid., p. 26.

[32]Steere, *BFW*, p. 12.

[33]Steere, *W&C*, p. 22.

[34]Steere, *BFW*, p. 84.

[35]Steere, *W&C*, p. 141.

[36]Steere, *BFW*, p. 85.

[37]Dom Chapman, *Spiritual Letters*, p. 138. Cited in *BFW*, p. 86.

[38]Meister Eckhart, Pfeiffer, Sect. 50, p. 573. Cited in *BFW*, p. 86.

[39]E. I. Watkin, *Philosophy of Mysticism*, p. 308. Cited in *W&C*, p. 57.

[40]Steere, *W&C*, p. 57.

[41]Ibid., p. 143.

[42]John B. Coburn, Review of *DOP* in *Union Seminary Quarterly Review*, 19 (March '64): 279-280.

[43]Arthur O. Roberts, Review of *TIS* in *Quaker Religious Thought* 20 (Summer 1983): 31-32.

[44]E. Glenn Hinson, "Douglas V. Steere: Irradiator of the Beams of Love," p. 417.

[45]Ibid., p. 417.

[46]Palmer, p. 19.

CHAPTER FIVE

A CRITICAL EVALUATION
OF STEERE'S TREATMENT

The previous chapters have provided an analysis of Steere's treatment of the relation of prayer and social responsibility. This analysis has established that the organizing theses adequately summarize and represent Steere's approach to the problem. It has also traced the sources that Steere incorporates into his approach. With this understanding, this study will now seek to gain a critical perspective on Steere's treatment of the problem and to determine the adequacy of his approach for contemporary spirituality.

This critical evaluation will proceed by considering problems inherent in Steere's approach to the problem, examining Steere's treatment in the light of traditional concerns about Quaker enthusiasm and quietism, and appraising his approach in the light of recent studies on the role of ritual and liturgy in the formation of Christian community and Christian character. Each of these studies will provide a different critical angle by which to determine the value of Steere's spiritual theology.

Problems Inherent in Steere's Spiritual Theology

Of the various critical reviews of Steere's writings, there are none that offer substantive criticism of his treatment of the relation of prayer and social responsibility. Nevertheless, in studying his treatment several issues arise for the discerning reader. The first issue is related to the first thesis, viz. "Prayer (especially corporate prayer) deepens an awareness of creatureliness and evokes a consciousness of solidarity with all persons and all creation. Out of this solidarity 'seeds of concern' surface in the consciousness of the one who prays." The issue being considered here pertains to the development and following out of a concern.

In *Dimensions of Prayer*, Steere does not pay sufficient attention to the role of the active life in the formation of a concern. In it, Steere appears to teach that concerns only arise during prayer and worship. He writes that "In prayer, the seeds of concern have a way of appearing."[1] He neglects to mention that concerns might arise within the active life. In his earlier book, *Prayer and Worship*, he notes that concerns may arise in the midst of daily activities.

> During these active forms of work in the silence: in contrition, in purification, in simplification and refreshment, in petition, and in intercession, frequently if we are sensitive and listening, there come clear insights of things to be done [concerns]. Often they come in that receptive silent waiting after we have opened our needs and where we do nothing but wait for direction. Again they may come during the day and push their way in between events that seem to bear no connection to them.[2]

This quote indicates that the spiritual sensitivity developed in prayer may enable concerns to arise in the midst of the activity.

In his treatment of John Woolman, Steere is most attentive to the role of the active life in shaping a concern. Woolman was nurtured in the Quaker community and through his regular attendance at corporate worship became conscious of his solidarity with all persons and all creation; he writes, "my heart was tender and often contrite, and universal love to my fellow creatures increased in me."[3] Nevertheless, it appears that Woolman's particular concern with Quaker slaveholding arose as much from his business involvements as from his times of worship. It was in his business as a writer of legal documents that his concern became focused. When asked to prepare a bill of sale for a customer who had bought a slave, Woolman felt uneasy but wrote it through "weakness." His conscience had been pricked and the next time he was asked to prepare a bill of sale he refused. His convictions about slaveholding grew stronger as he continued to refuse to write legal documents for the sale of slaves. Woolman's example reveals that, although concerns are rooted in the consciousness of solidarity that is evoked in prayer, the active life plays a key role in focusing and shaping the concern.

The neglect of the role of the active life in the formation of concerns is peculiar to *Dimensions of Prayer*. Perhaps it is merely an oversight or a decision to focus exclusively on the dynamics of prayer. Nevertheless, abstracting the formation of concerns from the active life creates a sort of dualism that is inconsistent with Steere's usual approach.

Another issue pertaining to the first thesis arises in *Dimensions of Prayer*. Steere writes that "real prayer seldom concludes without some intimation of a work assignment."[4] If this is so, then many sincere Christians are not experiencing "real prayer." Some Christians come to prayer seeking to be made expendable in God's service without discerning any particular work assignment. Some Christians come to prayer seeking to be made sensitive and responsive to the needs of others as they present themselves within their daily activities. Isn't this also "real prayer?" Why is it necessary to receive the intimation of a work assignment during the time of prayer? Isn't it enough if the Christian's sense of vocation is deepened and his or her identification with Christ strengthened? Perhaps these are the kind "work assignments" that Steere is alluding to. Nonetheless, the concept of receiving regular work assignments in prayer is too mechanical. Steere says it better in *Prayer and Worship* when he writes, "frequently if we are sensitive and listening, there come clear insights of things to be done."[5] There is quite a leap from "frequently receiving insights of things to be done" to the assertion that "real prayer seldom concludes without a work assignment." The former perspective is more balanced.

One other issue concerning the first thesis remains. The first thesis can serve as an outline for Quaker worship and action. It has proved its value in the Quakers' exceptional record of service. Can this approach be adopted by other Protestant and Catholic Christians with the same efficacy that it is employed by Quakers? When translating this approach for other Christians, problems arise with evoking a "consciousness of solidarity with all persons and all creation" and with the discernment of concerns. This study will first examine the difficulty of evoking a "consciousness of solidarity with all persons and all creation."

As adoration plays a central role in all Christian worship, it would be difficult to maintain that Quaker worship is uniquely suited to "deepen an awareness of creatureliness." Certainly, corporate silent prayer often leads to an experience of awe (creatureliness) but so can inspirational congregational singing. But, the "awareness of creatureliness" that is common to all forms of Christian worship does not automatically evoke a "consciousness of solidarity with all persons and all creation." In some Christian circles, particularly among fundamentalists, it appears that the awe experienced in worship heightens a sense of separation from unbelievers and "sinners." The central Quaker affirmation of the universal inward Light provides strong conceptual encouragement for the experience of solidarity. Nonetheless, the consciousness of solidarity with all persons and all creation is not an uncommon experience among worshipers, especially contemplatives, of various communions.

Thus far, the first thesis presents no major problems. But, the expectation of divine guidance in the formation of concerns creates some problems pertaining to spiritual discernment. The Quaker community has made wise provision for communal discernment by creating the committee for clearness and the business meeting. These two bodies assist the person exercised by a "major" concern in discerning God's will. Should Christians without such assistance in spiritual discernment be encouraged to look for and follow out the "leadings" that come in prayer?

Dimensions of Prayer provides insights into the way in which Steere adapts his Quaker process of discernment for non-Quaker--in this case Methodist--readers. In many ways the process of discernment described in it follows the outline of Steere's other writings on the subject. He begins his treatment with the disclaimer that the leadings that come in prayer are not infallible. "Certainly these leadings come to us by the route of our own psychological mechanism and are capable of being distorted."[6] The leading must be submitted to "rational scrutiny" in which "we have unleashed our own private detective agency upon it and examined it from all of the searching angles that this bureau is capable of unearthing."[7] The leading should also be discussed with "wise and trusted people."[8]

The only difference between the process of discernment outlined in *Dimensions of Prayer* and the discernment process in Steere's Quaker writings is the provision for communal discernment. As communal discernment is suggested only in the case of major concerns, Steere's basic method of discernment is possible for all Christians. Along with the awareness of the fallibility of leadings, rational scrutiny and wise counsel provide sufficient basic guidance in responding to the concerns that arise in prayer. If Steere were writing today for Methodists, he could recommend discussing concerns with a spiritual director or with participants in a covenant discipleship group[9]; however, neither of these were options in 1962.

It is surprising that in his treatment of discernment Steere fails to mention "the presence of inner peace" as a principle of discernment. Howard Brinton characterizes "the presence of inner peace" as "the main Quaker test of right guidance."[10] Perhaps the presence of inner peace is too subjective for Steere. Certainly, rational scrutiny and the counsel of wise and trusted friends are steps toward seeing a concern from a more objective perspective. Nevertheless, since the presence of inward peace is such an important factor in traditional Quaker discernment, it is peculiar that Steere fails to mention it.

Another traditional element in Quaker discernment--whether one finds the *cross* in what he or she is drawn to--does not appear in Steere's treatment. Of course, Steere emphasizes the costliness of carrying out a concern, but this is different from the principle of the cross. The principle of the cross is based on the conviction that Spirit guidance normally contradicts natural inclination, and natural preference. "Actions from the true Spirit were . . . seen by Friends as always contrary to self-will."[11] This principle of discernment implies a certain Nestorian anthropology that is inconsistent with Steere's spiritual theology and, happily, finds no place in his approach to discernment.

For most Catholics and Protestants scripture serves as a normative guide for faith and practice, but "For Fox, his comrades, and successors, only the Spirit of God--the Inner Light--was normative."[12] Steere follows in this tradition and does not mention scripture when writing about discernment. Nevertheless, when dealing with scripture, Steere emphasizes the help it affords in interpreting Christian experience. In his treatment of devotional reading in *Prayer and Worship*, Steere first discusses Bible reading:

> You come to find something that will speak to your condition. You are searching for something that will interpret for you the meaning of the experience you have just had or the choice that lies immediately before you.[13]

Also, in his Introduction to *Quaker Spirituality*, Steere writes that the Bible plays "a considerable role in helping them [Quakers] to keep within the Christian stream and to cross their inward experience with its searching power and witness."[14] This important addition to the instruments of discernment described earlier (i.e., rational scrutiny and wise counsel) is most welcome. It is unfortunate that Steere fails to mention the role of scripture in his treatment of the discernment of concerns.

Before leaving the subject of spiritual discernment, it will be valuable to examine Steere's approach to spiritual discernment in light of the limitations of early Quaker discernment. Michael J. Sheeran has distinguished three key limitations in the early Quakers' tests of leadings.

> First, belief in corruption of nature led Friends to replace reason solely with direct inspiration. . . . Secondly, Friends lacked--at least at the beginning--

a theological tradition. . . . Finally, strictly in the area of assessing a person's inner motivations, Friends clearly seem to have been deprived of a working knowledge of the literature of discernment that preceded them.[15]

These limitations do not apply to Steere's spiritual theology for Steere has more than a working knowledge of the literature on spiritual discernment; he is rooted in what is now a fairly well-defined theological tradition, and he exhibits a great appreciation for what the intellect and learning can bring to the life of the spirit.

This analysis of the first thesis has shown that Steere's approach to prayer and the formation of social concerns can be adopted with some alterations by Christians (especially contemplatives) of other communions. But, it has also shown that the Quaker affirmation of the universal inward Light proves especially congenial to the experience of solidarity with all persons and all creation. As Dermot Lane and Richard Woods have shown, all religious experience is interpreted through some conceptual framework.[16] The point here is that the consciousness of solidarity, which is so central in the formation of a concern, is most likely to occur among those with theological or philosophical convictions about the interconnectedness of all creation. Nevertheless, having recognized the importance of theology for religious experience, the consciousness of solidarity is not limited to those with a theological or philosophical predisposition for it. Theological convictions may also be affected by religious experience. If Steere is accurate in suggesting that one of the powers of contemplation is the apprehension of unity,[17] then the consciousness of solidarity may arise directly out of contemplative prayer. So, the consciousness of solidarity is most likely experienced in prayer by contemplatives or those with a theological or philosophical conviction of the interconnectedness of all creation.

Although the consciousness of solidarity with all persons and all creation may be less accessible to some Christians, a Christian reading Steere's work will be conceptually disposed for the experience. In his writing on prayer, especially intercessory prayer, Steere emphasizes the interconnectedness of souls in God. He also emphasizes God's infinite concern for all creation and envisions a cosmic redemption. The sympathetic reader will incorporate this into his or her theology and be conceptually prepared for the experience of solidarity.

The final problem inherent in Steere's treatment of the relation of prayer and social responsibility concerns Steere's failure to articulate the way in which acts of social responsibility are reappropriated before God in prayer. Steere has given careful attention to how prayer informs and shapes social concerns, but less attention to how acts of social responsibility affect prayer. The fully dialectical dimension of the reciprocity between prayer and social responsibility cannot be understood without a clearer explication of how acts of social responsibility are incorporated into prayer.

The fourth thesis, which is "Acts of social responsibility clarify and test the genuineness of prayer," summarizes Steere's interpretation of what action offers prayer. Contemplation, which intuits the frame of meaning, needs work in order for the intuition to find form. Without work, the vision revealed through contemplation remains disincarnate. For Steere, contemplation that does not issue in action is defective. True prayer bears fruit; it expresses the active caring of the One contemplated in prayer. The genuineness of prayer is tested by action.

Although this emphasis on the necessity of action and the embodiment of contemplation is helpful, Steere offers little guidance on *how* action can be reappropriated before God in prayer. Primarily, it appears that work and acts of social responsibility serve as a call to deeper prayer, more penetrating contemplation. Here it will prove helpful to review an illustration in Steere's writings that exemplifies this understanding. In a passage from the gospels, Steere shows how acts of social responsibility clarify prayer. In this gospel passage (Mark 9:14-29) the disciples have been unable to exorcise a young man possessed by a demon. Jesus comes and exorcises the man and the disciples ask him why they were not able to accomplish the exorcism. Jesus answers, "This kind cannot be driven out by anything but prayer."(Mark 9:29) For Steere this failure in the disciples work helped clarify what was still lacking in their prayer.

> Here in the work of healing we have the insertion of contemplation into the resistances of creation, and we have the simultaneous revealing of the contemplation itself as still too callow, still too empty. It believed it had grasped the root of the way to heal, but clearly it had not. Greater abandonment to God, greater caring for the one to be healed, greater identification with the creation, greater faith in the redemptive healing power that is available, all are needed by the workman. What a clarification of the original contemplation, what an illumination of what is still wanting, the work brings to bear on contemplation in this instance![18]

Here the disciples' work has revealed to them the shallowness of their prayer and the insufficiency of their faith. They felt called to join Jesus in his healing ministry, but such an experience reveals to them their unreadiness to fulfill this calling. Action has served as a call to deeper prayer; prayer that will lead to greater caring, greater abandonment to God, greater identification with the creation, and greater faith in the healing power of God. But, how is their action to be reappropriated before God in prayer? This remains unclear.

The closest Steere comes to offering guidance in this area is in *On Listening to Another*. In his treatment of the unfolding of concerns, he mentions some queries that serve as a reflective tool in the life of the person exercised by a concern.

> The Society's experience, however, has been that those who from the first entry into a concern have learned to listen, have learned to keep open, have asked the question about each turn of events, "What may I learn from this? What has this to teach me about where I am to go?" have been the ones whom nothing could deter, and have had operating in them a process of correction which did not fail them in any situation that arose. The faith in the accessibility of the Divine Listener that has marked the carrying out of Quaker concerns and the subsequent listening temper with its flexibility and openness to admit errors and correct it, have had a cleansing effect upon the diseases of private fanaticism that may readily infect such action.[19]

Although prayer is not mentioned in this passage, it is safe to assume that "learning to listen" and "learning to keep open" represent attitudes of prayer. At each turning point in the following out of a concern, the concerned person prayerfully reflects on the queries, "What may I learn from this? What has this to teach me about where I am to go?" Out of such reflection on action may come both correction and further guidance. This process certainly provides guidance for the outward journey, but what does it offer the inward journey? This is where Steere's guidance stops.

In *Mutual Irradiation* there is a hint of what acts of social responsibility may offer the journey inward. In discussing Quaker conversations with Zen Buddhists, he writes, "But we [Quakers] have experienced often that 'the mountain' [a reference to Zen meditation] where we meet another's need, may open the way to the 'inward mountains,'. . . ."[20] Here is an acknowledgement that acts of social responsibility may open new depths within the life of prayer, but Steere has little to say about how action may be reappropriated in prayer in such a way that it will open the inward mountains.

Within Steere's writings on the relation of prayer and social responsibility, there are enough hints about how action might be reappropriated before God in prayer to warrant an attempt here at such a construction. In *Prayer and Worship* Steere examines the issue of autosuggestion in prayer.

> There is no fear here of the charge of autosuggestion in prayer that so haunted the last generation. It is freely admitted from the outset that large elements of prayer are and should be of that character. One wise writer has suggested that the very purpose of the active cultivation of the interior life is to transform the gifts of grace into an effective autosuggestion.[21]

In this case, the term is used to describe a "conscious" psychological mechanism as opposed to the typical use of the term to denote an "unconscious" mechanism. Here "autosuggestion" effectively means working to effect a productive stewardship over imagination and memory. Such autosuggestion could play a key role in reappropriating action before God in prayer. Through autosuggestion previous action could be recapitulated in prayer. There might be reflection on resistances encountered, both within the pray-er and the situation which the pray-er hopes to affect. Resistances within the pray-er might be the focus of sustained attention. Very likely such resistances in the outward journey of faithfulness are revelatory of reservations and obstacles along the path of the inward journey as well. In this way, the life of action would prove to be a valuable aid for the journey of prayer.

The obstacles to spiritual growth that seem so elusive in prayer and contemplation may become painfully clear in action. Resistances in the situation itself might evoke prayers of intercession or lead to openness to new strategies in responding to the situation. There might also be reflection on providential aid that helped speed social action towards its goal. The renewed awareness that "one is not working alone" would quite naturally lead to prayers of gratitude. This heightened awareness of providence would lead to greater abandonment to God and to greater participation in God's redemptive order.

Also through autosuggestion a situation that created a "stop in the mind" or a crisis of conscience might be reimaged in prayer. The main actors might be envisioned within the context of "God's infinite concern for every person." The sinful actions of various parties, including the person praying, may be viewed in the light of God's judgment and mercy. Then, by conscious attention, the person praying may focus on the "active nature of Divine Love" [22] until the will is engaged. Finally, the pray-er could practice the listening and openness that would lead afresh into the world of action.

This construction, although nowhere set out in Steere's writings, is consistent with his approach. It assists this study by supplying a brief but vital element required for a full appreciation of the reciprocity of prayer and social responsibility. If prayer must penetrate action, then action must also penetrate prayer.

A broader issue concerning Steere's spiritual theology is the relative lack of specificity in his social vision. Compared with the social vision and ethics of liberation theology (which prizes analysis of sinful structures and vivid portrayal of corporate injustice) Steere's writings, though eloquent, are comparatively vague. Steere's Quaker instincts and his existentialism mesh in a powerful emphasis on individual responsibility for the social order rather than on social or political solidarity with the oppressed.

Some of the problems inherent in an existentialist theology were noted in Chapter Four, the tendency to individualism being the key concern. This focus on the individual limits existentialism's value as an instrument for social and political analysis. Macquarrie's critique reveals the limitations of existential political thought.

> I have pointed out that the political role of existentialism may be simply that of criticizing all dehumanizing forms of collectivism . . . But we need some positive guidance in these areas, and it is doubtful if insistence that all existence is inescapably a being-with-others, most existential philosophies take the existence of the individual as the starting-point, and when this first step is taken, perhaps the bias toward the existence of the single individual makes itself felt in all the subsequent analysis.[23]

Steere's determination to "begin from within" indicates his preference for taking individual existence as his starting-point. The primacy of the individual makes itself felt in all his writings and discloses both the strength and the limitations of his spiritual theology. E. Glenn Hinson can write that "in periods of great skepticism about whether individuals matter, it is good to have a Douglas Steere in our midst."[24] On the other hand, in an otherwise favorable review of *On Beginning from Within*, Charles Brodhead suggests that "against social and theological collectivists, who begin from without, this book's emphasis is upon the half truth of individualism." [25] Brodhead's critique is a bit of an overstatement; an emphasis on individual responsibility is not synonymous with individual*ism*. Nevertheless, Steere's spiritual theology does not lend itself to an analysis of systemic evil or corporate injustice.

In liberation theology, the project of "conscientization" has been to help the oppressed person reject the oppressive consciousness and commit him or herself to social transformation and the building up of society.[26] Social analysis is the second major tool for the project of liberation theology. Along with conscientization, social analysis assists the oppressed in recognizing that apparently legitimate social realities (such as the concentration of farm lands in the hands of a few wealthy land-owners) are inherently unjust and oppressive.

Spiritual and social solidarity with the oppressed also represents a major element of liberation theology. The "solidarity with all persons" expressed in the first thesis represents Steere's conviction that all souls are interconnected in God. The awareness of this interconnectedness is deepened in prayer. It is a universal spiritual solidarity that expresses itself in concrete acts of social responsibility. Gutierrez's definition of spirituality expresses a similar attitude concerning solidarity; he writes that "spirituality is a concrete manner, inspired by the spirit, of living 'before the Lord,' in solidarity with all men . . . It arises from an intense spiritual experience, which is later explicated and witnessed to."[27]   But, the solidarity takes on a specificity that is absent in much of Steere' spiritual theology. Gutierrez writes that "A spirituality of liberation will center on conversion to the neighbor, the oppressed person, the exploited social class, the despised race, the dominated country."[28]   This preferential option for the poor does not negate the universality of human solidarity, but it does express an evangelical concern for the poor. Segundo Galilea writes that

> the demand of a universal brotherhood avoids the possibility that the option for the poor, which is proper to the Gospel, become sectarian or classist. A sense of brotherhood and a sense of the poor are dialectically complementary demands.[29]

The option for the poor expresses itself in what Sobrino calls a "praxis of socio-political love." This means that love must be applied within the configuration of the whole of society; it is a love that becomes justice.[30]

To the degree that Steere's writings can be viewed as a practical approach to Christian social ethics, the lack of specificity in his social vision must be noted. On the other hand, his life and social leadership show his predilection for the oppressed person, the exploited social class, the despised race, the dominated country. This concern for all who suffer is characteristic of a Quaker social vision and finds full expression in his life. Steere's broad appeal to solidarity with all persons and all creation, though lacking specificity, fosters a global consciousness and an identification with all who suffer. It should be noted that most of Steere's writings come well before liberation theology became an important theological force.

This concludes the analysis of problems inherent within Steere's spiritual theology. It has raised several issues pertaining to the unfolding and following out of a concern. But two limitations in Steere's spiritual theology have been noted-- the absence of guidance for reappropriating action before God in prayer and the lack of specificity in Steere's social vision. A method for reappropriating action before God in prayer (a method implicit in Steere's spiritual theology) has been suggested in order to achieve a full reciprocity of prayer and action. The lack of specificity in Steere's social vision does not vitiate Steere's contribution to an understanding of the relation of prayer and social responsibility, but it does situate his contribution and its limits.

Traditional Concerns about Quaker Enthusiasm and Quietism

Although no one has accused Steere of enthusiasm or quietism, he represents a tradition that often is associated with these two tendencies in the spiritual life. (Of course, Anabaptists, Moravians, Methodists, and Pentecostals, have all been accused of enthusiasm.) Despite the fact that enthusiasm is usually limited to the early years of a new spiritual movement (the years before a theological tradition has developed), this study would not be complete without examining Steere's writings to see if traces of these tendencies are found in his spiritual theology.

Before examining Steere's work, it will prove helpful to establish working definitions of enthusiasm and quietism. The key sources for arriving at such a definition are Ronald Knox's classic entitled *Enthusiasm*[31] and the *Westminster Dictionary of Christian Spirituality*.[32] As enthusiasm is the broader term, it will be studied first.

The definition of enthusiasm offered by Roland Walls in the *Westminster Dictionary of Christian Spirituality* is very broad.

> The derivation of the word (nowhere found in NT Greek) is from relatively late classical Greek *entheos* and the corresponding verb *entheazein*--to be God-possessed--to be caught up in a psychic excitement transcending the rational. . . .
> Enthusiasm is also the term used specifically in spirituality for a perennial tendency (usually though not always ending in a sect) to claim additional revelation of an ecstatic nature.[33]

This study will deal only with the former type of enthusiasm--the type that claims divine authority for extra-biblical literature goes beyond the scope of this paper. The key element in the former type is the transcendence of the rational.

Ronald Knox acknowledges that enthusiasm is more of a tendency than a discrete category. He refers to this tendency as 'ultrasupernaturalism'.[34] It emphasizes "direct personal access to the Author of our salvation with little of intellectual background or of liturgical expression."[35] The enthusiast

> decries the use of human reason as a guide to any sort of religious truth. A direct indication of the Divine will is communicated to him at every turn, if only he will consent to abandon the 'arm of flesh'--Man's miserable intellect, fatally obscured by the Fall.[36]

In his analysis of enthusiasm, Knox makes a helpful distinction between "evangelical" and "mystical" enthusiasm.

> One [the mystical], taking its point of departure from the incarnation, rather than the Atonement, by-passes the theology of grace and concentrates on the God within; not repelling, necessarily, the Unitarian. The other [the evangelical], more acutely conscious of man's fallen state, thinks always in terms of redemption; to know, somehow, that your sins are forgiven, that you are a new creature in God's sight, is all that matters.[37]

Of course, the early Quakers tended toward the mystical type of enthusiasm.

Eventually, the enthusiast sect develops a theological tradition and within a hundred years becomes, to some degree, institutional.[38] Therefore, it would be a mistake to label a denomination--whether Anabaptist, Quaker, Moravian, or Methodist--with some theological tradition and history as enthusiast. For the enthusiast will always react against any form of institutional religion.[39]

The relation of quietism to enthusiasm is not defined by Knox, but it appears that quietism is an excessively passive form of mystical enthusiasm. Owen Chadwick has indicated that the term 'quietism' is often abused; he writes, "It [the accusation of quietism] sometimes seems to be used of any author when teaching about contemplation what another author disapproves."[40] Gordon Wakefield also considers the term to be abused and suggests that the term be confined "to a small seventeenth-century group, the most notable of whom are Molinos; Petrucci (1636-1701); Madam Guyon; Fenelon."[41] Nonetheless, the term is still broadly used for certain unhealthy tendencies in spirituality and deserves closer attention.

Knox presents quietism as an exaggeration of a healthy, orthodox mysticism. In it, "there is a tendency to exalt contemplative prayer as if it were the only exercise of the human spirit really pleasing to God, really efficacious in promoting man's salvation."[42] Some of the other key elements that Knox discerns in quietism are: 1.) an insistence on the passivity of the soul--almost excluding human effort,[43] 2.) a depreciation of the value discursive meditation in prayer,[44] 3.) a scruple against the use of mental images in prayer (even images of Christ),[45] 4.) a conviction that prayers of petition are inconsistent with perfect love of God,[46] 5.) a renunciation of the consolations of prayer and all preferences in time or eternity,[47] and 6.) a scorn for virtues because they represent conscious action of the part of the soul.[48]

With this understanding of enthusiasm and quietism, this study can examine Steere's writings in order to determine what role, if any, these tendencies play in his spiritual theology. Fortunately for this study, Steere has responded to Knox in his Introduction to *Quaker Spirituality*.

> The questions that he [Knox] puts are searching and the early Society of Friends provides some fertile ground for witnessing both to the confirmation of his darkest predictions and to the refutation of them in almost the same breath.[49]

Then, after summarizing some of the enthusiastic excesses that threatened the very survival of the Quaker movement, Steere points to the limitations in Knox's analysis.

> Knox's book leads to but neither raises nor answers a further question as to what else the Society of Friends had that enabled it to survive these threats that Ronald Knox so brilliantly depicts. . . . As far as the Quakers were concerned, something has already eluded Ronald Knox's analysis and has eluded his predictions. Only as we look more carefully at the different dimensions of Quaker practice can the secret of their survival, if there is one, be fully discovered.[50]

Steere suggests several key factors played a central role in keeping Quakers within the Christian stream. First of all, Steere emphasizes the role of the scriptures.

> It is important to note that the Quaker movement as a third force never sought to replace the infallible authority of the Church by the infallible authority of the Bible as classical Protestantism had done. Nevertheless the Bible played, and must always play, a considerable role in helping them to keep within the Christian stream and to cross their inward experience with its searching power and witness. . . . The regular reading of the Bible, both in private and in family devotions, was standard practice for the early Friends, and many are seeking to restore this in our time.[51]

Some other key factors in the Quaker survival are: the Quaker "Queries" that were meant to guide Quaker thought and practice,[52] the mutual enrichment that came from the practice of Quaker "visitation under concern,"[53] the regular use of family worship,[54] the influence of Quaker grammar schools,[55] the central importance of the corporate meeting for worship,[56] and, of course, the provision for communal discernment in the committee for clearness and the meeting for business.[57]

The treatment above serves as a summary of Steere's apologetic for Quakerism, but it does not address the issue of whether Steere's spiritual theology contains tendencies of enthusiasm. Certainly, enthusiasm as defined by Roland Walls can be eliminated immediately. Steere's spiritual theology does not lend itself to being "caught up in psychic excitement transcending the rational."[58] The type of enthusiasm represented in Walls's definition is more of the evangelical type. Knox's characterization of enthusiasm as "direct personal access to the Author of salvation with little of intellectual background or of liturgical expression"[59] is more to the point. Nonetheless, Steere's teaching does not fit this description either. "Direct" personal access to God implies an infallibility that Steere rejects.[60] Early Quakers claimed infallibility for their leadings,[61] but Steere rejects this claim. Steere also acknowledges that these leadings come by way of "psychological mechanisms and are capable . . . of being distorted."[62] This acknowledgement of the possibility of distortion calls for the "rational scrutiny" that Steere recommends and for the guidance of wise and trusted friends.

So, Steere cannot be accused of the grosser forms of enthusiasm, but what about the more subtle error of quietism. This excessively passive form of mystical enthusiasm troubled the Quakers in the eighteenth century and some people still associate it with Quakerism. Steere notes in his Introduction to *Quaker*

Spirituality that Quakers read widely in the spiritual literature of other Christian traditions and that the writings of Fenelon and Madame Guyon (both condemned for quietism) were among their favorite readings. Steere's treatment of the Quietist period in Quaker history reveals his approach to this issue.

Steere combines a sympathetic appreciation for some of the Quaker leaders during the "so-called Quietist period"[63] with a recognition of the error of their dualistic psychology. In *On Speaking Out of Silence*, Steere writes:

> The psychology that marked the Quietist period in 18th century American Quakerism, which saw the ideal Quaker minister as a hollow tube or an open trumpet for the Lord to blow through, is one that we have laid aside.[64]

Nevertheless, in fairness to these quietists, Steere recognizes what they were protesting.

> It was a ministry of words, a ministry that had not been freshly tempered, hammered out, and reshaped in the powerful forge of the listening meeting. They were pleading instead for longer and more attentive listening to keep the forward, wordy part of themselves back and to be permeated by the all-searching, all-transforming presence of the eternal Christ who could be met only in that way. They were asking those who lead others to stay seated in that presence until their own frosted hearts were melted down and they were fused with the needs of those immediately present and of those everywhere who suffer.[65]

In this sympathetic treatment of the quietist protest, it is not clear whether Steere is writing only of the quietists or of his own convictions as well, but the phrase "the eternal Christ who could be met only in that way." is problematic. Can the eternal Christ only be met in the silent listening meeting? Certainly not. It must be assumed that Steere is writing of the quietists because earlier in the same book he speaks of the presence of the "living Listener" in all dimensions of prayer and worship.

Steere contends that the 18th century Quaker quietists can teach contemporary Quakers about the deeper levels of prayer, but

> Such a reading . . . will not close our eyes to the need for prizing more highly than they do the gifts which the Quaker worshipper brings to the ministry, nor will it tempt us to belittle, as they did, what these gift's in God's keeping can contribute to ministry.[66]

The quietist distrust of the intellect and, indeed, of every form of preparation for ministry arose out of the dualistic psychology mentioned earlier. Here is Steere's analysis of that psychology of prayer.

> It would seem that the principal ground for this Quietist error lay in their curious psychology that failed to distinguish between an inward clarification in which the ministering worshipper was indeed given an insight to be shared, and the different levels on which this insight might be

searched and communicated. Failure to distinguish between these, resulted in the first place in a radical depreciation of all natural and cultivated gifts which the ministering worshipper might lay in God's hands for use in searching and communicating this disclosure.[67]

This dualistic psychology believes that the "natural man" must be repressed in order that the inward Light not be contaminated by any human element.[68]

Steere counters this conception with a balanced appreciation for what all human faculties can bring to God's service. He emphasizes that George Fox and John Woolman, though having little formal education, cultivated their minds through the study of the Bible and other edifying literature. He also mentions how the great learning of Rufus Jones and Henry T. Hodgkin enriched their ministry.

This in no sense suggests that formal education necessarily cultivates or prepares the spirit for ministry or that the humble spirit-tipped word of an utterly unlearned man or woman or child in a meeting may not minister to its deepest need, but it does propose that nothing is too good for God and that over the years there is no preparation of the mind and heart and will that God cannot use and use with power to further his ministry.[69]

Here a cultivated mind, purified emotions, and a disciplined will all have a part to play in the service of God.

This teaching cuts right across one of the key elements in quietism. The quietist will have nothing to do with the training of the will--the human will is to be erased so that God's will is all. The passivity of the soul, so valued by the quietist, is disturbed by human effort.

Of the six characteristics of quietism listed earlier in this section, the first (dealing with the passivity of the soul) and the sixth (dealing with the disdain for virtues) are eliminated by Steere's emphasis on the will. All but one of the remaining four characteristics of quietism can be dismissed quickly. The depreciation of discursive meditation, mental images, and prayers of petition (the second, third, and fourth characteristics of quietism listed earlier) is totally absent from Steere's writings. Although Steere obviously has a high regard for contemplative prayer, he presents adoration, confession, meditation (including mental images), petition, and intercession with deep appreciation. As far as the renunciation of the consolations of prayer and all preferences in time and eternity (the fifth characteristic), Steere is largely silent. Steere seems more concerned with desolations than consolations. Steere recognizes that sometime during the life of prayer every Christian will experience dry times, night shifts, dark nights. These desolations will come, but the Christian must persist in the life of prayer. Steere has no objection to consolations, but he will not allow desolations to hinder the life of devotion.

In view of this examination of Steere's spiritual theology for traces of enthusiasm and quietism, Steere is seen to possess a wholesome spiritual theology. In fact, his deep spiritual sensitivity and balanced approach to the life of prayer would make his writings especially helpful for those contemporary Christians with tendencies toward enthusiasm or quietism. In the final section Steere's treatment of the relation of the relation of prayer and social responsibility will be considered in dialogue with some of the contemporary theologians who are making the greatest contributions to understanding this issue.

The Role of Ritual and Liturgy in the Formation of Christian Character and Christian Community

Just as human beings are inherently social beings and come to know themselves only in relation to others, their intellectual constructions achieve clarity only through dialogue with other intellectual constructions. The purpose of this section is to present an alternate approach to the relation of prayer and social responsibility and to bring Steere's approach into dialogue with it. This dialogue will enable this study to achieve greater clarity in determining the value of Steere's approach.

Choosing a dialogue partner for Steere's religious thought presents something of a problem. Should the dialogue partner be another spiritual writer such as Thomas Merton (Glenn Hinson has already noted that Steere's approach resembles Merton's in some significant ways) or another Quaker writer or, perhaps, a more divergent tradition? Certainly, each of the authors cited in the notes for the Introduction (see note #12, p.10) would make a valuable dialogue partner, but the concern here has been to choose a dialogue partner that offers a significant *contrast* model for Steere's religious thought, one that can provide a critique at a fundamental level. It has also been a concern to choose an alternative approach that is on the "cutting edge" of contemporary Christian thought. The alternative approach chosen for this dialogue is that of Stanley Hauerwas, William Willimon, and Donald Saliers. Although Hauerwas specializes in ethics and Willimon and Saliers specialize in worship, they represent a fairly coherent approach to the relation of worship and ethics. Hauerwas is widely recognized as a leading thinker in contemporary Christian ethics and Willimon and Saliers have earned respect as sacramental-liturgical scholars.

These three authors are particularly valuable as dialogue partners for Steere's spiritual theology. Each approaches the problem of relating worship and ethics in a slightly different fashion, but all three share a high view of the role of ritual, liturgy, and narrative in the formation of Christian community and character. Individual Christian character is shaped through corporate worship that represents the Christian story through ritual and liturgy. From this perspective, the conscience and the values of the individual Christian are formed as the Christian interacts with these elements in the worship experience. These elements are not completely exterior, as they must be internalized by the worshiper to achieve potency in his or her life. Nevertheless, this approach differs significantly from that presented in Steere's writings. For Steere, the conscience and the values of the individual Christian, though also shaped through corporate worship, are formed through interior attentiveness to the workings of divine grace. Whatever vocal ministry is expressed during corporate worship should come out of this interior encounter with God. As representatives of a worship tradition that values highly the role ritual and liturgy in the formation of Christian character, Hauerwas, Willimon, and Saliers present an approach to the relation of worship and ethics that provides a fresh critical angle by which to determine the value of Steere's spiritual theology. As Hauerwas's work addresses the underlying theological issues involved in this study, it will be examined first.

Hauerwas has become well known for his studies in character and virtue, for his emphasis on narrative in theology, and for his exploration of the role of community in ethics. Consequently, his theology may be expected to put a heavier stress on communal structure than does Steere's.

Hauerwas suggests that "Every theological ethic involves a central metaphor that shapes its conception of moral existence . . ."[70] His work arises out of a concern to situate theological ethics in the metaphors of character and virtue. This approach is opposed to the traditional Protestant ethics that sets the Christian moral life within a "command-obedience metaphor." He summarizes the "command-obedience metaphor" in this way:

> Protestant theological ethics has tended to shape its conception of the moral life around the metaphor of command. The Christian's obligation, in the light of this metaphor, is obedience to the law and performance of the will of God. The object of the moral life is not to grow but to be repeatedly ready to obey each new command. Of course the status of the law and the content of God's will and how it is known has been a matter of controversy within the Protestant tradition. Nonetheless, it has generally assumed that God's relation to man is fundamentally to be understood in terms of command and obedience.[71]

Hauerwas does not deny the value of the command-obedience metaphor but suggests that language of command should be placed "in the larger framework of moral experience"[72] represented by the language of character.

Part of the problem with the command-obedience metaphor is its inability to articulate the nature of the Christian moral life.

> This inadequacy has become more apparent with the gradual loss of the vitality of central Christian symbols. The decay of our language has revealed the systematic inadequacies that have been endemic to the Protestant understanding of the Christian life. . . . [T]he dominance of the metaphor and the language of command in Protestant thought encouraged an occasionalistic ethic concerned with decisions and judgment about specific acts. Situation ethics is a natural development of a theological tradition that provided no means to develop an ethic of character.[73]

Hauerwas's ethics of character is an attempt to shift the focus from specific acts and decisions to the relation of belief and behavior. "The ethical issue is not just what we do but what we are and how what we are is formed by our fundamental convictions about the nature and significance of Christ."[74] From this perspective, Christian ethics is intimately related to systematic theology and the way Christian symbols are interpreted.

Hauerwas has defined character as "the qualification of man's self-agency through his beliefs, intentions, and actions, by which a man acquires a moral history befitting his nature as a self-determining being."[75] This definition assumes a certain understanding of the self. The self is not some ahistorical essence but the person formed by a particular history and language. "The self that gives rise to agency is fundamentally a social self, not separable from its social and cultural environment."[76] Nevertheless, the person formed by a particular culture and language exists as a free, self-determining person.[77]

This understanding of character and character formation indicates the crucial role of the community that serves as the bearer of particular beliefs and symbols.

The relation of the community and the ethics of character . . . is the proper context to suggest the significance of the community's central symbols for the formation of character. The ethics of character places its emphasis on how our fundamental symbols provide the self with duration and unity amid our many beliefs and practices.[78]

Of course, the central Christian symbol is Jesus Christ, but this symbol alone is not sufficient. The Christian community must creatively represent this symbol in such a way that it has a formative influence on the persons making up the Christian community.

Hauerwas defines community as "a group of persons who share a history and whose common set of interpretations about that history provide the basis for common actions."[79] Where there is no shared history there is no community.[80] The shared Christian "history" is expressed through the narrative or story of the Bible. It is this shared tradition that creates Christian community.

The nature of Christian ethics is determined by the fact that Christian convictions take the form of a story, or perhaps better, a set of stories that constitutes a tradition, which in turn creates and forms a community.[81]

The shared story creates the community that, in turn, remembers and retells the story. Worship serves as the instrument for remembering and retelling the story. "Because the Christian story is an enacted story, liturgy is probably a much more important resource than are doctrines and creeds for helping us to hear, tell, and live the story of God."[82]

The creation of a community that hears, tells, and lives the story of God constitutes the ethics of character that Hauerwas champions. At first glance this appears to be ecclesiology rather than ethics. Isn't this a prescription for ecclesial faithfulness? Yes, it is, and this is Hauerwas's point.

I am in fact challenging the very idea that Christian social ethics is primarily to make the world more peaceable or just. Put starkly, the first social ethical task of the church is to be the church--the servant community. Such a claim may well sound self-serving until we remember that what makes the church the church is its faithful manifestation of the peaceable kingdom in the world. As such the church does not have a social ethic; the church is a social ethic.[83]

As the church and the world are relational concepts, it is only possible for the world to recognize itself as the world if the church fulfills its true nature as the church.[84] "The church must learn time and time again that its task is not to make the world the kingdom, but to be faithful to the kingdom by showing the world what it means to be a community of peace."[85]

But, for the church to be a community of peace, a people who can hear, tell, and live the story of God, a certain kind of people is required--a people of virtue.

> For the church to *be* rather than to *have* a social ethic moreover means that a certain kind of people are required to sustain it as an institution across time. They must, above all, be a people of virtue--not simply any virtue, but the virtues necessary for remembering and telling the story of a crucified savior. They must be capable of being peaceable among themselves and with the world, so that the world sees what it means to hope for God's kingdom.[86]

Hauerwas makes a distinction between virtue and the virtues. Virtue "denotes the power of anything to fulfill its function. Thus the virtue of the eye is seeing; the virtue of the knife is cutting; the virtue of a horse is running, and so on."[87] "To be a person of [moral] virtue, therefore, involves acquiring the linguistic, emotional, and rational skills that give us the strength to make our decisions and our life our own."[88] On the other hand, "The individual virtues are specific skills required to live faithful to a tradition's understanding of the moral project in which its adherents participate."[89] Nowhere does Hauerwas attempt to list and describe all the virtues necessary for faithfulness to the Christian tradition, but he does emphasize the virtues of patience, courage, hope, and charity.

> The virtues of patience, courage, hope, and charity must reign if the community is to sustain its existence. For without patience the church may be tempted to apocalyptic fantasy; without courage the church would fail to hold fast to the traditions from which it draws its life; without hope the church risks losing sight of its tasks; and without charity the church would not manifest the kind of life made possible by God.[90]

These are the key virtues required for hearing, telling, and living the story of God.

It is within this context that Hauerwas seeks to ground Christian decision making. Decisions are made within the process of sanctification represented by growth in character, virtue, and virtues. Here the command-obedience metaphor may be renewed but it is no longer the center for moral reflection.[91] The focus then of Christian ethics is the creation of a people of sufficient character and virtue to hear, tell, and live the story of God.

This brief summary of Hauerwas's ethics of character provides only the barest sketch of his intricate and nuanced ethical thought. Nevertheless, it offers a foundation for understanding the role of ritual and liturgy in the formation of

Christian community and Christian character. As community requires the existence of a shared history, ritual and liturgy represent the Christian story in such a way that people can claim and own that story. At the same time, ritual and liturgy are the production of the Christian community as it seeks to express its self-understanding. Ritual and liturgy create Christian community by helping a people remember their history; at the same time, the Christian community creates ritual and liturgy to sustain this remembering. Ritual and liturgy are also intended to produce people of character instilled with the virtues necessary for hearing, telling, and living the story of God.

An initial question for Steere, therefore, in the light of Hauerwas's vision of a community of character is this: Does Steere's Quaker praxis possess the potential for the formation of a community by shared story, ritual, and commitment?

Hauerwas's theology of character is complemented by the studies of Saliers and Willimon in the area of worship. Willimon acknowledges Hauerwas's influence on his thought in the preface of *The Service of God: How Worship and Ethics Are Related*.[92] Hauerwas indicates the congeniality of Saliers's thought in a footnote in *A Community of Character*; he writes: "For an account of the passions very similar to my own analysis, see Don Saliers' marvelous book, *The Soul in Paraphrase: Prayer and Religious Affections* (New York: Seabury, 1980)."[93] These studies by Willimon and Saliers will further an understanding of the role of ritual and liturgy in the formation of Christian community and Christian character.

Willimon's definition of worship encompasses the whole spectrum of Christian worship.

By "worship" I mean all those formal and informal, written and unwritten, spontaneous and rigidly prescribed, high-church and low-church words and acts by which Christians meet and are met by God in intentional, corporate gatherings of the church. By defining worship in this manner I make it clear that I am not advocating one style or form of public worship as more ethically formative than another. I want to draw from the richness of Christian worship practices--from the gorgeous processions of Eastern Orthodoxy, to the inner directed quiet of a Quaker meeting, to the toe-tapping jubilation of a Free Will Baptist hymn-sing--a multifarious, multidimensional, liturgical setting that is the context of all Christian life and work.[94]

All worship, according to Willimon, assumes a particular shape through liturgy. Liturgy is the pattern or form that worship takes. "All churches have a liturgical life that can be observed, defined, predicted, and that influences the moral life in important ways."[95]

For the purpose of studying the relation of worship and ethics, Willimon defines ethics as "a study of the conscious and unconscious, subjective and objective, personal and institutional ways that form and re-form a responsible and responding Christian."[96] This definition of ethics is remarkably close to what this study has termed "social responsibility." The remarkable affinity of Willimon's project with the theme of this study makes it an especially appropriate contrast model.

Willimon contends that the ethical thought of James Gustafson and Stanley Hauerwas "provides the best opportunity for viewing worship and ethics as mutually enriching."[97] The similarity of Willimon's approach with that of Hauerwas is observed in his treatment of community and character. A summary of Willimon's approach is outlined in three key points. First, "Character is formed in a social matrix, a community. . . . We come to our ethical dilemmas with a history that is more social than psychological, out of an ethical community . . . "[98] Second, "Character is formed by a lifelong cultivation of virtues."[99]   Third, "Christian character is formed . . . by sharing the Christian vision. . . . My moral self not only comes out of my past history or my present decisions but also out of my vision of the future."[100] This approach follows closely that presented earlier in the thought of Hauerwas.

Willimon links his own conception of worship with Hauerwas's ethics. Willimon conceives of ritual as having a powerful effect upon ethics. Ritual, which Willimon defines as "patterned, predictable, public, purposeful worship behavior,"[101] takes the form of crisis rites and cyclic rites. Crisis rites enable a person to deal creatively with painful transformations in life.

> The crisis of transition threatens to overwhelm us. Crisis rites help us cope by giving us the knowledge, skills, and vision needed to negotiate the journey from one state of being to another.[102]

Cyclic rites are rites repeated for the sake of group maintenance. They enable a community to revision and rehearse participation in its myth. Cyclic rites provide imaginative rehearsal for religious/ethical behavior.

> It [ritual] helps us encounter a new world without fully owning that world, a new selfhood without fully relinquishing our old self. Out of such experimental, playful, ritualized encounters comes the opportunity for creative adaptation and growth.[103]

Ritual, in this understanding, affects both the formation of Christian community and Christian character.

After a general treatment of the effects of ritual upon ethics, Willimon turns to the specific ways Christian liturgy may influence Christian character. This outline of Willimon's treatment of the relation of liturgy and character will follow in his own words. First, "Liturgy helps form Christian identity."[104] "The only way the church will remain distinctive and lively in this world is through close attention to her identity-forming liturgies and rites."[105] Second,

> Liturgy creates a world for the Christian, world in the sense that it is often used in the New Testament. When Paul refers to "the world" (*cosmos*) he is not referring to the physical world, the planet, but to the social reality; the world of values and institutions into which we have been socialized.[106]

Third, "Liturgy is a primary source of the symbols and metaphors through which we talk about and make sense out of our world."[107] "Social change is primarily symbolic change. In order for us to change, our symbols must change because they determine our horizons, our limits, our viewpoints and visions."[108] Fourth, "Liturgy aids in Christian imagination."[109] "Liturgy is mind-expanding work on a Christian's imagination. It helps us to transcend our immediate situation, to see 'a new heaven and a new earth,' to release the tight grip of the status quo."[110] Fifth, "Liturgy is a primary source of Christian vision."[111] "We must periodically withdraw from the world in order to worship because our vision needs the focus and concentration that occurs in worship. Such withdrawal is confrontation rather than escapism."[112] Sixth, "Liturgy is a major source of our Christian tradition which enables us to rise above the present and envision the future."[113]

> In affirming the wealth of the church's tradition, the liturgy is not only holding onto what is important in our past, but is also prodding us forward to everwidening realms of importance. Memory is a major source of foresight. We push into the future mainly on the basis of images inherited from the past.[114]

These six points, presented in Willimon's own words, offer a compelling argument for the power of liturgy in forming Christian character.

This summary of the relation of liturgy and the formation of Christian character provides the context in which Willimon's work unfolds. Within this conception, Willimon develops certain ideas that closely resemble several of the organizing theses. Although these ideas are nowhere expressed in the same order or form as in Steere's writings, their resemblance is worth examining.

Although Willimon grounds the awareness of creatureliness (first thesis) in *belief* rather than in *prayer*, creatureliness still plays a significant role in his ethics. "Christian ethics must commend a different path [different from Aristotle's aristocrat of the moral life], one that advocates a humility due to our honest awareness of creatureliness . . . derived from our belief in a Creator."[115] Willimon makes no connection between the awareness of creatureliness and the consciousness of solidarity.

As was noted earlier in the treatment of Hauerwas's ethics, there remains a place for the command-obedience metaphor in the ethics of character. The command-obedience metaphor must be situated in a broad understanding of the formation of Christian character. Willimon's treatment of ethics expresses this same understanding in a way that resembles Steere's conception of the development of a concern.

> The lone individual . . . lacks the moral equipment, the skills of discernment, and the coherent convictions to be moral. Our moral lives are cumulative. The "command of God," in which Barth posits so much value, is not always a crisis intrusion into human life. The divine command is more often a divine leading that arises out of qualitative human experience.[116]

As was demonstrated in Steere's analysis of the development of Woolman's concern, corporate worship and the Christian community provide the necessary environment for the formation of a concern. In such an environment, a "divine leading" may arise and be nurtured.

In the cleansing thesis, prayer is seen as cleansing action of its repetitive nature and as restoring to action a frame of meaning. Ritual serves the same purpose in Willimon's approach. "When we become lost in the familiar words, patterns, gestures, and beat of liturgy, ritual relaxes the tight grip of the status quo and frees us from the frantic treadmill of reason and reflection."[117] Here the "tight grip of the status quo" is analogous to the "repetitive nature of action." In each case prayer or ritual provides an opportunity for revisioning the frame of meaning.

The first part of the fifth thesis, which is "both prayer and social responsibility are incomplete in themselves," is mirrored in the first chapter of *The Service of God.*

> In recent decades, those allegedly religionless Christians who claimed they need not pray or worship because "work is our prayer" might testify that without prayer one's work quickly falls short of the glory of God. On the other hand, church history is full of evidence that pious folk who think prayer is Christian work enough end with something less than full Christian discipleship. . . . worship and work are distinct and inseparable Christian activities.[118]

Willimon's emphasis on the distinction of worship and work is opposed to those who would collapse worship and work and thereby neglect one or the other.

Willimon does not mention the word alternation but the alternation theme is implied in his treatment. "Both action in the world and worship in the sanctuary may be done by the same person for the same purpose, for the 'glory of God,' but we rarely do both at the same time."[119] Later he writes that, "We must periodically withdraw from the world in order to worship because our vision needs the focus and concentration that occur in worship."[120] Both these quotes indicate the need for a rhythm of work and worship. Nevertheless, Willimon also presents a more complete integration of work and worship.

The integration that Willimon envisions is rooted in the Biblical understanding of service. "The Hebrew '*Abad* (to serve) is used for both work and worship. . . . The term *leitourgia* means literally 'service' or 'work' of 'the people.'"[121] The service of God and service in the world are both understood as a Christian's liturgy.

> The line between liturgy and life is significantly blurred in the New Testament. The whole of a Christian's life is liturgical life.
> While warning against any reductionism that simply equates worship with service in the world, or work in the world with cultic work in the sanctuary, we must note at the outset the New Testament's constant linking of these two modes of a Christian's service.[122]

These two modes of service "ought to be complementary, reciprocal, [and] mutually enriching."[123]

At the end of his chapter entitled "The Work of Worship," Willimon offers an account of work and worship that resembles Steere's account of how alternation gives way to the experience of simultaneity.

> The memory and hope they [Christians] receive in their *leitourgia* thrusts them into, and sustains them within, their *diakonia*. Their *diakonia* provides the context and the need for their *leitourgia* until, in *leitourgia* and *diakonia*, worship or service, it becomes difficult for the Christian to distinguish between the two. This may, after all, be the point of it all.[124]

There is no mention here of "working collectedly" or simultaneity but the integration of worship and service that Willimon articulates here is analogous to Steere's integration of prayer and social responsibility.

Having presented this summary of Willimon's approach to the relation of worship and ethics and having noted some similarities to the organizing theses, a more critical dialogue between Steere's and Willimon's approaches may be attempted. One of the difficulties in attempting this dialogue is that the authors represent such divergent worship traditions. The authors appear to speak in different languages about worship.

How then may these two approaches be brought into dialogue? Here, an effort to characterize each approach may provide insights. It would be possible to speak of Willimon's approach as the "sacramental-liturgical" approach to worship and of Steere's as the "contemplative" but this would be creating a false dichotomy. Willimon has demonstrated that all corporate worship exhibits some form of ritual or liturgy and Steere writes of the contemplative dimension of all genuine prayer. Certainly there is a contemplative dimension to sacramental-liturgical worship and there is patterned, predictable, public, purposeful worship behavior in a classical Quaker meeting. This understanding indicates that these two traditions are not so divergent as they appear at first glance. Both are forms of Christian worship that can question the adequacy of the other and, thus, enrich an understanding of Christian worship. As some classification is necessary for analysis, Willimon's approach will be referred to as the "liturgical" approach and Steere's will be referred to as the "classical Quaker" approach. The purpose here is to bring these two approaches into mutually enriching dialogue and, finally, to determine the adequacy of Steere's approach.

Willimon claims that his treatment incorporates the catholic (liturgical) and free church traditions. "Because I am a United Methodist, I intend to do justice to both the catholic and free church traditions when I speak of worship, for we United Methodists have roots in both."[125] He also says that "I am not advocating one style or form of worship as more ethically formative than another."[126] Nevertheless, it is clear that Willimon's preference lies with the catholic form of worship and, despite his claims of neutrality, he considers the catholic form to be more "ethically formative."

Those churches which do not observe the liturgical year often find that they suffer from a truncated story. Their worship fails to hit the full range of notes within the Christian narrative. The result can only be a truncated ethical life. It is important to tell the Story, the whole Story, again and again until it is our own.[127]

A truncated ethical life is certainly a sign of malformation. The problem with free church worship exists not only in its failure to tell the whole story but also in its dearth of images for ethical reflection.

A rich multifarious tradition can be a great help to a church. Churches whose liturgies are less "rich," tend to have a paucity of images, themes, metaphors, and patterns to draw from when confronting ethical dilemmas.[128]

These quotes reveal Willimon's preference for the catholic form of worship.

On the other hand, Steere's worship tradition represents the most extreme form of the free church tradition. In spite of Steere's appreciation for other forms of worship, he is an advocate of the classical form of Quaker worship. In *On Listening to Another*, Steere points out some of the problems inherent in free church and liturgical worship that do not trouble the classical Quaker form of worship.

The most ardent free churchman or devoted adherent of a liturgical church would be the first to admit that the Quaker type of lay religious fellowship with its worship of silent waiting and its waiting ministry is spared certain problems which afflict their forms of worship. When the late Dean Willard Sperry of the Harvard Divinity School in what is generally acknowledged to be his finest book, *Reality of Worship*, begins to detail some of the defects and troubles of free church worship with elements that are "assembled and not grown"; with its "pilfered prayers secured through predatory raids on the liturgy"; its responsive reading of blood-curdling psalms that cannot but outrage the discerning, or if expurgated of these elements, excite the criticism of "whole Biblelists"; its pre-fabricated sermons; its prayers over the collection; the garbled architecture and the treacly hymns, a Quaker may heave a grateful sigh. The liturgist, also, with his problems of rote and purely mechanical habits that groove both clergy and congregation, often enough inoculating them with a kind of assured immunity to the meaning and to the costly surrender which the words demand, presents another set of obstacles that are not found to disturb a Quaker service of corporate waiting worship.[129]

Later in the same book, Steere suggests that "One of the tragedies of formal Protestant services is their wordiness, their forensic character."[130]

The liturgical approach emphasizes the central importance of language, ritual, and memory in the formation of Christian community and character. Hauerwas and Willimon make this approach to the formation of Christian character intelligible and compelling. It is much harder to grasp how Christian community and character is formed through classical Quaker worship. All the outsider notices in classical Quaker worship is what is missing.

> But it is not what is missing, but what is present that makes this plain Quaker form of corporate renewal so natural and so adequate. For the worshippers are present, and the living Listener is present, and the worshipper's needs are there in abundance, together with the needs of the community and the world, and the living Listener's magnetic transforming caring is present and able to meet those needs and to draw the worshippers into his service.[131]

In Quaker worship, Christian character is formed by a corporate intuition of the presence of the living Listener (the universal inward Christ) and by corporate attentiveness to the leadings of the Holy Spirit. Steere's analysis of John Woolman's development provides an example of how such worship can form a Christian of extraordinary character.

If, as Willimon suggests, churches that do not observe the liturgical year often fail to tell the whole Story and, subsequently, form ethically truncated Christians; then the Quakers, who tell no Story (at least in liturgy and preaching), could hardly form Christians at all. Something in classical Quaker worship has obviously eluded Willimon's analysis. It would be hard to argue that the Quakers, as a community of Christians, are ethically malformed. Their record of service and compassion is exemplary. With Willimon, Steere affirms the need for the full Christian Story but does not find adherence to the liturgical year the only means of achieving this completeness.

> There is no Quaker liturgical cycle of the Christian year. Yet it can be said that a meeting whose members read and inwardly digest the Bible, who pray, and who are exposed to the needs of one another and of those who suffer in the world around them, will not fail to be drawn down into the great Christian themes of the love, the joy, and the greatness of God; of suffering, sin, redemption, atonement and resurrection.[132]

Although this quote shows how the full Christian Story can be appropriated in classical Quaker worship, it assumes great commitment on the part of the worshiper. It assumes that the worshiper reads and inwardly digests the Bible, prays, and is exposed to the needs of the congregation and those who suffer around the world. Most Christians seek the assistance of a well-planned worship program that exposes them afresh to the Christian Story and the needs of the community and the world.

Willimon's contention that "churches whose liturgies are less 'rich,' tend to have a paucity of images . . . to draw from when confronting present ethical dilemmas"[133] is not really addressed by Steere. Because most Quaker meetings exist in close proximity with other Christian churches, it may be that Quakers draw on the images and themes represented in the liturgical churches. Such a parasitical explanation is not likely to please Quakers. It is more accurate to suggest that the Quakers are the bearers of an apophatic tradition that finds the kataphatic tradition unnecessary, and in some cases unhelpful, for Christian worship. It may be remembered that Steere sees some marked similarities between the Zen-Buddhists and their relation to the Buddhist world and Quakers to the Christian community. Both are "anti-liturgical, iconoclastic, unconventional witnesses to the spirit."[134]

One other point of tension in this dialogue is the question of whether worship alone is self-vindicating. In his book, *Work and Contemplation*, Steere asks whether *contemplation* alone is self-vindicating. His answer is that true contemplation is inseparably linked with work. "In this earthly life it is this indispensable engagement of contemplation with action, with deeds, with work, that clarifies and confirms what the very contemplation contains."[135] It should be remembered that Steere also wrote that "real prayer seldom concludes without some intimation of a work assignment."[136] This perspective arises out of Steere's conviction that those who truly worship God become participants in God's redemptive order. Although Willimon also emphasizes that worship and work are inseparable, he views worship itself as moral activity.[137] "Like ethics, worship is response to what is good and right."[138]

> While worship is not an escape from ethics, neither is worship the mere servant of ethics. . . . *Leitourgia* must be celebrated for its own sake, not simply as a means of rallying the faithful for *diakonia*.[139]

Willimon considers worship to be like good art--it is sufficient that it presents a compelling vision of reality. Worship does not need to provide a work assignment. "We rarely finish a service of worship with a recipe for action. If we do, we have probably participated in a moralistic pep rally, which is less than true worship of God."[140]

These contrasting conceptions of the self-sufficiency of worship are more differences of style than substance. Both authors contend that worship and work are inseparable. Neither would suggest that worship is the mere handmaid of ethics. Their differing approaches are more related to the positions they are opposing. Steere's opposes a spirituality that would separate piety and ethics. Willimon, who was in seminary in the 1960s when many were suggesting that worship was irrelevant, opposes those who say that worship is valuable only in as much as it leads to social responsibility. Moreover, classical Quaker worship can hardly be conceived of as a "moralistic pep rally." Rather, Steere's "work assignments" are the result of sensitivity to the intimations and leadings of the Holy Spirit.

This dialogue has pointed out some significant points of tension in the approaches of Steere and Willimon. The most significant difference is situated in their varying accounts of how worship forms Christian community and Christian character. For Willimon, Christian community and Christian character are formed by retelling and remembering the Story (through ritual, liturgy, and preaching). For Steere, they are formed through corporate attentiveness and responsiveness to the living Listener. Of course, corporate worship is not the only way Christians are formed and classical Quakers, more than other Christians, must supplement corporate worship with Bible and devotional reading. Having recognized these varying accounts of how worship forms Christian community and character, this study will examine some similarities that go beyond the organizing theses.

In *Character and the Christian Life: A Study in Theological Ethics*, Hauerwas suggests that one of the problems with contemporary Christian ethics has been its neglect of sanctification and overemphasis on justification. He writes that "the concentration on justification tended to impede the development of an ethic concerned the nature and formation of the moral self."[141] He also writes that "A theme often associated with the idea of sanctification is the concept of growth or development."[142] Although Steere does not write as an ethicist, his emphasis on social responsibility develops in the context of sanctification or Christian growth. From the outset of his career as a writer, Steere addressed the theme of growth in the Christian life. In Chapter Two it was noted that Steere "is deeply concerned about the 'mediocrity of soul that fills the Christian ranks.' Steere's life work may be understood as an effort to evoke and nurture great souls within the Christian community."[143] Steere's emphasis on Christian growth and his attention to sainthood show that his conception of the ethical life relies on the formation of Christian character. Moral decisions and even the concerns that arise in prayer are rooted in the cumulative life of Christian devotion.

It should also be noted that Hauerwas's ethics of virtue has some affinity with Steere's treatment of the saint. The very qualities that make the saint such an effective agent of social change are the virtues that Hauerwas commends as expressive of Christian character. Hauerwas emphasizes the virtues of patience, courage, hope, and charity. In Steere's essay on "The Saint and Society," the characteristics of the saint--staying power, joyous heroism, faith that group life is redeemable, and caring--are analogous to the virtues of patience, courage, hope, and charity.

It is important to remember that Steere's interest in spiritual (character) formation came during a time when American theologians had little interest in this area as it related to ethics. Willimon writes that "American theological ethics (between 1930 and 1965) has been dominated largely by practical, pragmatic, moral concerns of deciding and doing."[144] The idea of the cultivation of virtues (of emphasis on spiritual growth) has also been suspect. "Virtue implies long-term habitual, and intentional effort on the part of the moral agent--discipline, ritual, continuity--all of which are suspect in today's church."[145] Willimon and Hauerwas locate this attitude in the ethics of Barth and Bultmann with their emphasis on the command-obedience metaphor.

> The principle weakness of the metaphor of command-obedience, in the ethics of theologians like Barth and Bultmann, is that it forecloses an adequate appreciation of the larger framework of ethical experience--the long- term communal formation of the moral self.[146]

> Protestant ethics neglected the Christian's growth and sanctification. In this view, the purpose of the moral life was not divinization, maturity, and depth of the moral self but rather an intentional ignorance, a repeated readiness to hear and obey freely each new command in each new situation.[147]

Steere objects to this same attitude in his article entitled "Common Frontiers in Catholic and Non-Catholic Spirituality." In this article Steere tells about a visit (during the time Steere was staying at Maria Laach) he had with Barth at Bonn.

I spoke of the role of private prayer as means of putting us in the stream of grace and even spoke of how impressed I had been by the rhythm of the daily Benedictine liturgical cycle as a means of exposing a community to this baptism of grace. Barth repudiated both roles and denied that either had the slightest significance as far as my own, or the monks', redemption was concerned. He insisted that for himself he knew that he hung suspended between heaven and hell, that the weight of his sins would most certainly sink him to hell, and that only the intervention of the supreme act of grace wrought in Christ would be sufficient to lift and to overcome this terrible gravitational force of his sin. He implied that this act of Jesus Christ was enough, that anything else was utterly irrelevant, and that anyone who wasted his time or trust on these practices was to be pitied.[148]

This text reveals Steere's appreciation of discipline, ritual, and continuity in the formation of Christian character.

Don Saliers's approach, although similar to that of Hauerwas and Willimon, enriches this dialogue in several ways. His book, *The Soul in Paraphrase*,[149] provides an analysis of the relation of prayer and religious affections. His account offers a new perspective on some of the organizing theses and especially broadens the dialogue on the role of language and silence in worship. This study will examine first his perspective on concepts related to the organizing theses.

The first part of the first thesis states that "Prayer (especially corporate prayer) deepens an awareness of creatureliness." Saliers begins his treatment of intercessory prayer by calling for a recovery of the corporate dimension of intercessory prayer. He writes that "for the early church, praying was always praying in community, even when it was prayer alone. The distinction between individualistic devotional prayer and the church's common prayer is foreign to the earliest periods of the church."[150] For Saliers, all intercessory prayer should bear this communal dimension. This insight makes a valuable contribution to this analysis of intercessory prayer but it should not depreciate the value of a flesh and blood community for intensifying intercessory prayer. For Steere, one of the values of the corporate worship is that it confronts worshipers with the needs and burdens of their fellow worshipers.

Although Saliers does not mention the power of prayer for deepening an awareness of creatureliness, he does indicate the power of prayer to evoke a sense of solidarity with all people.

In interceding for the world and for others, we identify with others and enter into the capacity to bear their burdens. . . . Genuine intercessory prayer arouses and sustains the affective kinship with all who suffer. In it we are profoundly affected by the sense of solidarity with the whole race.[151]

Saliers's account of the power of intercessory prayer to "arouse and sustain the affective kinship with all who suffer" shares much in common with Steere's treatment of intercessory prayer.

Saliers's work also illuminates an understanding of the integration thesis (fifth thesis). Along with Willimon and Steere, Saliers views worship and religious faith as inseparable from service and action. "Affections which do not become the wellspring and motive for action turn in upon themselves. Faith contemplating only itself leads to sickness."[152] This seems to bear out Steere's contention that contemplation alone is not self-vindicating.

Saliers's thought on the integration of prayer and action draws on the model offered in the life of Christ.

Tensions are built into the Christian life itself because they are built into the very concept of praying and the call to holiness at the heart of the gospel. This is the focal point of Christian existence: Christ's own life is one of active prayer and prayerful action. It is fitting to speak of his whole life as a prayer, a continual self offering to the Father.[153]

This "prayerful action" that marks the life of Christ has marked similarities with Steere's concept of "working collectedly." This integration is also the goal of Saliers's spiritual formation.

Thus we must consider the notion of the pervasiveness of prayer as a mark of Christian maturity. We must extend the concept of prayer from its application to specific acts of worship . . . to its application over the whole of one's life. As Origen and others have said, the whole of the life of the saint is one continuous prayer.[154]

The reference here to Origen refers to a quotation earlier in Saliers's book. Origen links prayer to action in unceasing prayer.

The man who links together his prayer with deeds of duty, and fits seemly actions with his prayer is the man who prays without ceasing, for his virtuous deeds or the commandments he has fulfilled are taken up as a part of his prayer. For only in this way can we take the saying "Pray without ceasing" as being possible, if we can say that the whole life of the saint is one mighty integrated prayer.[155]

These quotations show how close Saliers's integration comes to that previously presented in the analysis of Steere's spiritual theology.

Saliers manages to maintain a healthy tension between the apophatic and kataphatic traditions when examining the role of language and thinking in the life of prayer. Along with Hauerwas and Willimon, his analysis emphasizes the powerful formative influence of language on character. "In corporate worship, Christians engage in language and actions which articulate and shape how they are to be disposed to the world."[156] In the chapter entitled "Praying and Thinking," Saliers indicates how crucial the use of liturgical language is in the formation of Christian identity. He writes that a "Theological understanding of the Christian faith depends partly on a person's being habituated in the 'liturgical' use of religious language."[157] Liturgical language evokes, shapes, and informs the very capacities required for religious understanding. This high view of the role of language in the formation of Christian identity is tempered by an appreciation of the role of silence, of wordless awe. Saliers begins this same chapter with a quote from Bishop Ignatii Brianchaninov, a representative of the apophatic tradition.

> Do not theologize, do not be carried away by following up brilliant, original, and powerful ideas which suddenly occur to you. Sacred silence, which is induced in the mind at the time of prayer by a sense of God's greatness, speaks more eloquently than any human words. "If you pray truly," said the Fathers, "you are a theologian."[158]

Saliers himself writes that "Theology which begins and ends in prayer honors the silence which surrounds our language about God."[159]

Steere recognizes the necessity of language, for without it "existence would be hidden and mute."[160]   Quaker history also reveals that a Christian community cannot flourish without a measure of vocal ministry.

> This relation of words to the Word has been a central problem for Quakerism from the beginning. For it soon enough became clear that a meeting for worship that was habitually "starved for words", habitually silent, tended to wither and dwindle.[161]

Nevertheless, as an advocate of the apophatic tradition, Steere commends an approach that emphasizes the priority of silence.

> A contemporary German philosopher, Martin Heidegger, in a happy phrase refers to language as "the dwelling place of being". Language is indeed the foreground of reality, its articulate shore. But back of language and clinging to it, when it is real, is the receptive sea of silence. Language is always tempted to make reality more articulate than it is. And the words of language are always being rebuked and overrun and swallowed up again by the silent ocean of existence from which they once emerged. It is obvious that without some form of language, existence would be hidden and mute, but only when words come up fresh and breathless, come up still moist and glistening from the sea of existence, do they carry power and authority.[162]

"Language torn away from the background of silence, of existence becomes stale, emaciated, and powerless."[163]   These quotes establish Steere's priority on silence. This emphasis on the priority of silence is consistent with Steere's accent "on beginning from within."

Steere and Saliers both express a deep appreciation for the role of silence in worship and prayer. Nevertheless, Steere's priority on silence indicates a certain tension in their approaches that enriches this dialogue. Steere is concerned that the wordiness of worship may rob language of its vitality. For Saliers, the language of worship evokes the very feelings that Steere believes should precede vocal ministry. These differing perspectives are basic to the two traditions of worship.

As both liturgical and classical Quaker approaches to the relation of prayer and social responsibility are rooted in their worship traditions, it is important that this study examine the practical way in which these worship traditions may enrich one another. So far, the enrichment has been limited to the theoretical explication of this relationship. A practical enrichment most likely will result from a mutual experience of the other's worship tradition. To this end, this study will suggest ways in which each tradition can incorporate aspects of the other.

First of all, it should be understood that contemporary Quakers do not reject the worship of traditional Christian churches. Harold Loukes writes at the end of his book *The Quaker Contribution*, that "As we have considered the Quaker story through its three hundred years it has become clear that it is not, as the first Friends thought, about a complete substitute for the traditional Christian church."[164] Rather, Loukes sees the Quakers as the bearers of a tradition that sounds a particular theme in the Christian symphony.

Quakerism is the antithesis of the thesis of the Christian tradition, an element in the total Christian conversation, a theme in the Christian symphony. Other Christians, from time to time, state the Quaker theme, but no other Christians have disposed their worship and church order around this theme alone. There is here, therefore, a unique Quaker role, a special message from the Quakers to the Church, which is laid on them to sustain until the time comes when the Christian symphony sounds in its fullness from the whole orchestra.[165]

Although the Quakers have a particular theme to play, Loukes recognizes that the Quakers carry a fragile theme; it needs the support of the larger, more articulate tradition. "The theology in all this remains, as it did in Fox's thought, implicit, inarticulate, naïve; and to the degree that it is naïve, Quakerism cannot stand alone, a church in its own right carrying by itself the Christian meaning."[166] Nevertheless, this very naïveté--"the concentration on the moment, the raw experience, the felt simplicity"[167]--has its place in the Church. He writes that "Friends make poor Dominicans, but they still sound the Franciscan note."[168]

This modest and thoughtful appraisal of the Quaker theme in the Christian symphony indicates the vulnerability of the Quaker tradition. Perhaps more than most Christian communities, the Quakers need the larger tradition. Their approach poses little threat of overwhelming the liturgical tradition; rather, the greater danger is that the Quaker theme be lost from the Christian symphony.

Nevertheless, the Quakers have their own methods for sustaining their own community. No less than the liturgical churches, the Quakers are people who share a history and a set of interpretations about that history. They also have ways of remembering and retelling the Story. Much of this remembering and retelling must come outside the meeting for worship. Steere has noted the Quaker practices that assist in the formation of Quaker community: regular Bible reading (both in private and family devotions), the Quaker queries, Quaker visitation, family worship, devotional reading, and education in the Quaker schools. These practices, along with classical Quaker worship, have provided for the spiritual and ethical formation of the community.

While recognizing the value of this Quaker approach to Christian formation, this study suggests that it can be enriched through experience with a liturgical Christian community. Steere's appreciation for his experience at Maria Laach has already been noted, especially his appreciation for the "rhythm of the daily Benedictine liturgical cycle."[169] Periodic visits to a monastic community rooted in the daily offices would certainly complement the Quaker worship experience. But, being a small minority within predominantly liturgical Christianity, the Quakers have many opportunities to experience liturgical worship. Perhaps more difficult to determine is how classical Quaker worship can be incorporated into the life of the liturgical churches.

Steere has made some suggestions in his writings about how the liturgical and free churches might incorporate Quaker worship into their services.

My own experience is that the gathered meeting provides a nurturing ground for effective ministry. It is such a precious instrument that I have often suggested to ministers in other denominations that if they could get their communities to gather for a half hour before the service and persuade these groups to hold their minister in the atomic-pile of this kind of corporate gathered silence in which whatever message they had brought might be remade and requickened for the group's use, it might revolutionize their whole service of worship.[170]

This way of incorporating Quaker worship into the liturgical and free churches seems highly improbable. Most pastors carefully prepare their sermons (seeking to be open to the Holy Spirit and sensitive to the needs of the congregation) during the week prior to worship and are not interested in having their sermons "remade" one half hour before the service of worship. Steere's suggestion also fails to account for the "average" churchgoers unwillingness to sit for more than an hour during any type of worship. What would be the classical Quaker community's response to a suggestion that they remain for a half hour of liturgy and preaching following their usual meeting for worship?

In *On Listening to Another*, Steere offers a more plausible way of incorporating Quaker worship into other churches. In his treatment of vocal ministry, Steere writes:

How blessed any Protestant minister might feel if he could have the privilege of sitting for an hour in silent waiting with a little inner company of his congregation that week. How that message might be clipped, how it might be refocused, and upon occasions how it might be completely recast as he was swept by a deeper sense of both the need of his group and of the abundance of God's power to meet the need. In such an experience, how it might be charged with power!

How helpful, too, it might be if this occasion might become a regular spring and source of his ministry, if the ministry were required of him that week, or a place where one of the lay group sitting with him might from time to time be inwardly drawn to discharge the vocal ministry of the meeting and on that occasion relieve him of the exercise. If to this little group could in time be added the whole congregation who would gather with him to wait in this way, with the freedom to minister shared still more widely, and the message straight from a freshly touched mind and heart, is it impossible to see some, at least, of the steps by which this Quaker treasure of a silent waiting ministry could be shared with the whole free church family?[171]

This type of service could become a part of the congregational life of some churches, but it is doubtful that any regular weekday service would ever involve the whole congregation.

In spite of Steere's hope that classical Quaker worship might be incorporated into the worship life of other Christian churches, it seems unlikely. Most Christians would need training in the dynamics of classical Quaker worship. More importantly, for many Christians, raised in a tradition that values ritual, liturgy, and celebration, such a worship experience might feel empty and foreign. Nonetheless, such a practice would certainly enrich the worship experience of those willing to participate in it.

The difficulty of incorporating classical Quaker worship into the worship life of the liturgical churches becomes less problematic if one considers the Quaker worship tradition as an expression of the Christian contemplative tradition. Steere seldom suggests that other churches adopt supplementary Quaker worship services--his main concern is with the deepening of the spiritual life of all Christians. He especially values silent, corporate, contemplative prayer as a means of deepening the spiritual life. This raises the question of whether classical Quaker worship is synonymous with silent, corporate, contemplative prayer. The answer must be that Quaker worship is more than contemplative prayer, although it may certainly contain moments of contemplative prayer. Therefore, Steere's teaching about deepening the life of prayer and contemplation does not require the adoption of classical Quaker worship services. There are other ways the the apophatic tradition of silent, contemplative prayer can be incorporated into the liturgical , kataphatic tradition. Steere has influenced two of the most promising efforts to introduce a more contemplative dimension into the Protestant churches.

In a recent issue of the *Shalem News*,[172] Dr. Gerald May, Shalem's Director of Spiritual Guidance, developed a computer sketch illustrating some of the historical influences on the Shalem Institute for Spiritual Formation. The sketch was entitled "A Stream of Spiritual History: Some Important Historical Influences for Shalem." The "stream" begins in Judaism and flows through the New Testament, the early church, etc.; the most contemporary historical influence entering the stream is Douglas Steere.

In the metropolitan Washington, D.C. area, the Shalem Institute offers long term contemplative prayer groups for deepening the spiritual life. The Shalem ministry includes a two-year graduate program in Christian spiritual guidance. Many of the clergy and laity who have participated in this program offer opportunities for group contemplative prayer in their local churches.

Steere also assisted in the planning for the Upper Room's Academy for Spiritual Formation and continued to play an active role as an Adjunct Professor in it until he stopped lecturing in 1990. This academy offers a program in spiritual formation that shares a family resemblance with the Shalem program. Here too clergy and laity from liturgical (and non-liturgical) churches are exposed to the contemplative tradition.

Both these institutions are providing leadership in the spiritual renewal of the American church. Each presents the value of corporate, silent, contemplative prayer as one of the disciplines for deepening spiritual life. Although the classical Quaker meeting is not likely to become a supplementary worship service in most Protestant churches, it does seem that the value of corporate silent prayer is becoming more deeply appreciated in the liturgical churches.[173]

This dialogue between the liturgical approach of Hauerwas, Willimon, and Saliers and the classical Quaker approach of Steere has indicated some surprising similarities in these two approaches. They hold in common some key elements of the organizing theses. The dialogue also has pointed out some significant areas of tension. These two approaches represent two poles of Christian worship that should enrich and complement each other.

It is not the purpose of this study to determine which approach is more ethically formative; rather, the purpose here is to determine the value of Steere's approach. It has been established that Steere's work anticipates some of the insights of an ethics of character. His emphasis on sanctification and growth (based primarily in prayer and worship) as the foundation for ethical action came during a period when Protestant ethics emphasized justification (based on command and obedience) as the primary ethical foundation. Steere's thought, represented in the organizing theses, finds broad support in the work of these other authors. In sum, Steere's approach to the relation of prayer and social responsibility provides a valuable and compelling approach to this enigmatic relation. Nonetheless, Steere's approach can be enriched by bringing it into dialogue with the liturgical approach to the formation of Christian community and Christian character.

Summary

This chapter has examined Steere's approach to the relation of prayer and social responsibility from several different angles in order to determine its value for contemporary Christian spirituality. The problems inherent in Steere's approach were examined and two limitations in his spiritual theology were noted, viz., the absence of a method for reappropriating action in prayer and the lack of specificity in his social vision. These two limitations do not vitiate the value of the integration of prayer and social responsibility achieved in Steere's writings. This examination has also established that Steere's spiritual theology cannot be accused of enthusiasm or quietism. Finally, this chapter has presented the liturgical approach to the formation of Christian character and Christian community and has brought it into dialogue with Steere's classical Quaker approach to the relation of worship and ethics. These two approaches have been shown to be complementary and mutually enriching. Each of these angles on Steere's spiritual theology has contributed to the judgment that his approach presents a valuable and balanced explication of the relation of prayer and social responsibility which contributes harmoniously to the emerging tradition of contemporary Christian spirituality.

NOTES FOR CHAPTER FIVE

ABBREVIATIONS

CCL:STE,	*Character and Christian Life: A Study in Theological Ethics*
CC:TCCSE,	*A Community of Character: Toward a Constructive Christian Social Ethic*
DIL,	*Doors into Life*
DOP,	*Dimensions of Prayer*
LTA,	*On Listening to Another*
PK:PCE,	*The Peaceable Kingdom: A Primer in Christian Ethics*
P&W,	*Prayer and Worship*
QS,	*Quaker Spirituality*
TIS,	*Together in Solitude*
W&C,	*Work and Contemplation*
WDCS,	*Westminster Dictionary of Christian Spirituality*

[1]Steere, *DOP*, p. 97.

[2]Steere, *P&W*, pp. 41-42.

[3]John Woolman, Quoted by Steere in *DIL* p. 94. No citation from Woolman's *Journal*.

[4]Steere, *DOP*, p. 95.

[5]Steere, *P&W*, p. 41.

[6]Steere, *DOP*, pp. 99-100.

[7]Ibid., p. 100.

[8]Ibid., p. 100.

[9]In the early 1980s United Methodists began to use the term "spiritual formation" for the process of forming Christian disciples. This acceptance of the term is represented in the formation in 1984 of a Division of Spiritual Formation within the General Board of Discipleship. Along with this new development, there has been a growing acceptance of the ministry of "spiritual direction," a ministry once considered exclusively Roman Catholic. Group spiritual direction played a key role in the discipleship of early Methodists and has been recovered in David Lowes Watson's book entitled *Accountable Discipleship: Handbook for Covenant Discipleship Groups in the Congregation*, (Nashville: Discipleship Resources, 1984).

[10]Michael J. Sheeran, *Beyond Majority Rule* (Philadelphia, Pa.: Philadelphia Yearly Meeting, 1983), p. 27.

[11]Ibid., p. 25.

[12]Ibid., p. 26.

[13]Steere, *P&W*, p. 68.

[14]Steere, *QS*, p. 21.

[15]Sheeran, pp. 28-29.

[16]Richard Woods, Introduction to *Understanding Mysticism* ed. Richard Woods (Garden City, New York: Image Books, 1980), p. 4. and
Dermot A. Lane, *The Experience of God* (New York: Paulist Press, 1981), p. 20.

[17]Steere, *W&C*, p. 37.

[18]Ibid., p. 132.

[19]Steere, *LTA*, p. 71.

[20]Steere, *Mutual Irradiation* (Wallingford, Pa: Pendle Hill, 1971), pp. 19-20.

[21]Steere, *PW*, pp. 16-17.

[22]Ibid., p. 16.

[23]John Macquarrie, *Existentialism* (Philadelphia: The Westminster Press, 1972), p. 224.

[24]Charles Daniel Brodhead, "The Way to Sainthood" in *The Christian Century*, April 5, 1944, p. 435.

[25]E. Glenn Hinson, "Douglas V. Steere: Irradiator of the Beams of Love" in *The Christian Century*, April 24, 1985, p. 419.

[26]Gustavo Gutierrez, *A Theology of Liberation*, trans. and ed. Sister Caridad Inda and John Eagleson, (New York: Orbis Books, 1973), pp. 90-91.

[27]Ibid., p. 204.

[28]Ibid., p. 204.

[29]Segundo Galilea, *Following Jesus*, trans. Sister Helen Phillips, M.M., (New York: Orbis Books, 1981), p. 31.

[30]Jon Sobrino, "Following Jesus as Discernment" in *Discernment of the Spirit and of Spirits*, ed. Casiano Floristan and Christian Duquoc, (New York: The Seabury Press, 1979), p. 19.

[31]Ronald A. Knox, *Enthusiasm: A Chapter in the History of Religion*, (First series), (London: J.M. Dent and Sons Ltd., 1921).

[32]*The Westminster Dictionary of Christian Spirituality*, ed. Gordon S. Wakefield, (Philadelphia: The Westminster Press, 1983).

[33]Roland Walls, "Enthusiasm" in the *WDCS*, p. 133.

[34]Knox, p. 2.

[35]Ibid., p. 2.

[36]Ibid., p. 3.

[37]Ibid., p. 581.

[38]Ibid., p. 590.

[39]Ibid., p. 590.

[40]Gordon Wakefield, "Quietism" in the *WDCS*, p. 328.

[41]Ibid., p. 328.

[42]Knox, p. 261.

[43]Ibid., p. 263.

[44]Ibid., p. 263.

[45]Ibid., p. 263.

[46]Ibid., p. 270.

[47]Ibid., p. 274.

[48]Ibid., p. 279.

[49]Steere, *QS*, p. 20.

[50]Ibid., pp. 20-21.

[51]Ibid., p. 21.

[52]Ibid., p. 22.

[53]Ibid., p. 23.

[54]Ibid., p. 24.

[55]Ibid., p. 25.

[56]Ibid., p. 26.

[57]Ibid., p. 43.

[58]Walls, *WDCS*, p. 133.

[59]Knox, p. 2.

[60]Steere, *DOP*, p. 99.

[61]Sheeran, p. 23.

[62]Steere, *DOP*, pp. 99-100.

[63]Steere, *QS*, p. 33.

[64]Steere, *On Speaking Out of Silence* (Wallingford, Pa.: Pendle Hill, 1972), p. 19.

[65]Steere, *LTA*, p. 52.

[66]Ibid., pp. 52-53.

[67]Ibid., p. 53.

[68]Howard Brinton, *The Religious Philosophy of Quakerism* (Wallingford, Pa.: Pendle Hill, 1973), p. 56.

[69]Steere, *LTA*, pp. 54-55.

[70]Stanley Hauerwas, *Character and Christian Life: A Study in Theological Ethics* (San Antonio: Trinity University Press, 1975), p. 1.

[71]Ibid., p. 2.

[72]Ibid., p. 3.

[73]Ibid., pp. 229-230.

[74]Ibid., p. 230.

[75]Ibid., p. 11.

[76]Ibid., p. 33.

[77]Ibid., p. 26.

[78]Ibid., p. 232.

[79]Stanley Hauerwas, *A Community of Character: Toward a Constructive Christian Social Ethic* (Notre Dame, Ind.: University Press, 1981), p. 60.

[80]Ibid., p. 53.

[81] Stanley Hauerwas, *The Peaceable Kingdom: A Primer in Christian Ethics* (Notre Dame, Ind.: University of Notre Dame Press, 1983), p. 25.

[82] Ibid., p. 26.

[83] Ibid., p. 99.

[84] Ibid., p. 101.

[85] Ibid., p. 103.

[86] Ibid., p. 103.

[87] Hauerwas, *CC:TCCSE*, p. 111.

[88] Ibid., p. 115.

[89] Ibid., p. 115.

[90] Ibid., p. 68.

[91] Ibid., p. 115.

[92] William H. Willimon, *The Service of God: Christian Work and Worship* (Nashville: Abingdon Press, 1983), p. 13.

[93] Hauerwas, *CC:TCCSE*, p. 267.

[94] Willimon, p. 16.

[95] Ibid., p. 17.

[96] Ibid., p. 18.

[97] Ibid., p. 28.

[98] Ibid., p. 29.

[99] Ibid., p. 32.

[100] Ibid., p. 34.

[101] Ibid., p. 17.

[102] Ibid., p. 43.

[103] Ibid., p. 46.

[104] Ibid., p. 48.

[105]Ibid., p. 50.

[106]Ibid., p. 51.

[107]Ibid., p. 56.

[108]Ibid., p. 57.

[109]Ibid., p. 58.

[110]Ibid., p. 59.

[111]Ibid., p. 63.

[112]Ibid., p. 65.

[113]Ibid., p. 69.

[114]Ibid., pp. 70-71.

[115]Ibid., pp. 81-82.

[116]Ibid., p. 30.

[117]Ibid., p. 47.

[118]Ibid., p. 15.

[119]Ibid., p. 15.

[120]Ibid., p. 65.

[121]Ibid., p. 18.

[122]Ibid., pp. 18-19.

[123]Ibid., p. 19.

[124]Ibid., p. 72.

[125]Ibid., p. 17.

[126]Ibid., p. 17.

[127]Ibid., p. 70.

[128]Ibid., p. 71.

[129]Steere, *LTA*, p. 32.

[130]Ibid., p. 46.

[131]Ibid., p. 32.

[132]Ibid., pp. 64-65.

[133]Ibid., p. 71.

[134]Steere, *Mutual Irradiation* (Wallingford, Pa: Pendle Hill, 1971), p. 18.

[135]Steere, *W&C*, p. 128.

[136]Steere, *DOP*, p. 95.

[137]Willimon, p. 20.

[138]Ibid., p. 20.

[139]Ibid., p. 42.

[140]Ibid., p. 60.

[141]Hauerwas, *CCL:STE*, p. 229.

[142]Ibid., p. 215.

[143]From Chapter Two of this book, p. 26.

[144]Willimon, p. 22.

[145]Ibid., p. 34.

[146]Ibid., p. 27.

[147]Ibid., p. 28.

[148]Steere, *TIS*, p. 4.

[149]Don E. Saliers, *The Soul in Paraphrase: Prayer and the Religious Affections* (New York: Seabury Press, 1980).

[150]Ibid., p. 99.

[151]Ibid., p. 39.

[152]Ibid., p. 102.

[153]Ibid., p. 101.

[154]Ibid., p. 102.

[155]Ibid., p. 42.

[156]Ibid., p. 37.

[157]Ibid., p. 82.

[158]Ibid., p. 74.

[159]Ibid., p. 74.

[160]Steere, *LTA*, p. 48.

[161]Ibid., p. 49.

[162]Ibid., p. 48.

[163]Ibid., p. 48.

[164]Harold Loukes, *The Quaker Contribution* (London: SCM Press, Ltd, 1965), p. 117.

[165]Ibid., pp. 117-118.

[166]Ibid., p. 124.

[167]Ibid., p. 124.

[168]Ibid., p. 124.

[169]Steere, *TIS* p. 4.

[170]Douglas V. Steere, *On Speaking Out of Silence* (Wallingford, Pa.: Pendle Hill, 1972), pp. 19-20.

[171]Steere, *OLTA*, p. 67.

[172]Gerald May, *Shalem News*, X (February 1986): 5.

[173]One model that I have found especially valuable for experiencing the mutually enriching aspects of the liturgical and contemplative traditions is based on the common lectionary and contemplative prayer. While in campus ministry at James Madison University in Harrisonburg, Virginia, I met weekly on Wednesday mornings with a group of clergy and laity from area churches. We would read the lections for the coming Sunday and discuss them briefly. This would be followed by a period of extended silence (roughly a half hour). During the silence, some of those present chose to meditate on the scriptures and others sought simply to focus their attention on the presence of God. The silence ended with the recitation of the Lord's Prayer. The lections were read and discussed again. I found this particular approach deeply satisfying. It incorporated the contemplative tradition into the liturgical life of the Church.

CHAPTER SIX

STEERE'S CONTRIBUTION TO CONTEMPORARY SPIRITUALITY

The critical perspective achieved in Chapter Five will yield, in this chapter, to a broader appraisal of what Steere's approach to the relation of prayer and social responsibility contributes to contemporary spirituality. Steere's approach will be viewed in the larger context of his ecumenism, his role as a bearer of the Christian "spiritual" tradition, and his role as a Quaker leader. This appraisal will begin by examining Steere's work under the rubric of "ecumenical spirituality" and conclude with an evaluation of Steere's contribution to contemporary spirituality.

Steere as a Pioneer in Ecumenical Spirituality

Emmanuel Sullivan contends, in an article entitled "Ecumenical Spirituality" in the *Westminster Dictionary of Christian Spirituality*, that spiritual ecumenism is at the heart of the ecumenical movement.

> Ecumenical spirituality expresses the common life shared by Christians in spite of the separation of their churches. . . . The rediscovery by many Christians of their obligation to live together in the spirit of the gospel has inspired the modern ecumenical movement. The very soul of that movement has been spiritual ecumenism.[1]

The particular contribution that ecumenical spirituality makes to the ecumenical movement is its focus on the "life of prayer and worship, especially prayer for Christian unity."[2] This understanding of ecumenical spirituality is descriptive of much of Steere's work. (It should be remembered that Steere's first book was entitled *Prayer and Worship*.)

The most significant characteristics of ecumenical spirituality are abundantly present in Steere's life and writings. Without documenting the evidence of these characteristics in Steere's writings (there being sufficient evidence in the previous chapters), the characteristics noted by Sullivan will be examined briefly. One of the central characteristics of ecumenical spirituality is a "mutual evaluation and appreciation of particular spiritual gifts and practices found in various churches and Christian communities."[3] Throughout his career Steere has sought to present the unique genius of Quakerism along with a deep appreciation for the spiritual treasures of other churches, especially the Roman Catholic Church.

Another central element in ecumenical spirituality is that it

entails some sort of conversion or change of heart towards Christians of other churches. This takes the form of a commitment to pray and work for the renewal of one's own church or community in order to let the essential elements of church life surface and prepare the way for Christian unity.[4]

Steere's approach to ecumenism, expressed in the phrase "mutual irradiation," represents just such a conversion or change of heart toward other Christians. And, of course, it has always been the Quaker attitude to emphasize the essential elements of church life.

Finally, one of the most basic elements of ecumenical spirituality has been friendship that crosses denominational boundaries.

His [Jesus's] precept of charity is the true sign of discipleship (John 15:12-17). In the short history of the ecumenical movement a particular form of this charity is Christian friendship; friendship has proved itself an indispensable element in the process of Christian unity.[5]

This aspect of ecumenical spirituality has been especially evident in Steere's work. E. Glenn Hinson writes that

Long before the Second Vatican Council, Steere was opening doors between Catholics and Protestants, drinking and leading others to drink at the broad stream of spirituality that flows through Christian history, and cultivating friendships with communities of Catholic religious around the world.[6]

Steere is certainly one of the pioneers of ecumenical spirituality, building bridges of friendship across denominational lines early in the 1930s.

Steere's approach to interfaith encounter (also expressed in terms of "mutual irradiation") has proved its value in the continuing Zen-Christian Colloquiums and has also proved to be amazingly farsighted. John Cobb, one of the leading contemporary figures in interfaith dialogue, has called for an approach toward other religious faiths that goes beyond dialogue to mutual transformation. Cobb's call to move beyond dialogue, represented in his book *Beyond Dialogue: Toward a Mutual Transformation of Christianity and Buddhism*,[7] came in 1982 while Steere's call for mutual irradiation came in 1968. The similarity of these two approaches is evident in the following quotations. Steere writes that mutual irradiation is a relationship in which each religion

is willing to expose itself with great openness to the inward message of the other, as well as to share its own experience, and to trust that whatever is the truth in each experience will irradiate and deepen the experience of the other.[8]

This kind of interfaith encounter "is not likely to leave any of the participants as they were when they started."[9] Cobb contends that

> authentic dialogue must lead beyond dialogue to the radical transformation of the dialogue partners. Christians must cross over, genuinely and deeply exposing themselves to the wisdom of the other. Then we must come back, facing the task of restructuring our heritage in the light of what we have learned.[10]

Steere has practiced and presented an approach to interfaith encounter that continues to be relevant today.

Despite Steere's important contribution to ecumenism and interfaith encounter, he has sometimes undervalued the theological and institutional elements of the ecumenical movement. In 1963 Steere wrote an article for the *Quaker Quarterly Review* entitled "Beyond Diversity to a Common Experience of God." In that article, Steere showed little appreciation for any approach other than an experiential one. He writes:

> For it has not been in the area of faith and order (in the hammering out of some lowest common denominator of theological doctrine), or of liturgy and sacraments, or of the discipline of church government, that the Protestant and Orthodox churches have made the real strides in overcoming their diversities. It has rather been in their common experiences of God and in finding that they understood each other because they love the same Lord. If Quakers have any witness to make to the ecumenical work of other Christian denominations, it may well be in accenting this discovery that it is not in doctrine or liturgy or church discipline but alone in the common devotional experience of loving the same Lord and serving him in situations of acute human need that diversities can melt away.[11]

In his emphasis *solely* on the "common devotional experience," Steere depreciates the important contribution made through efforts to arrive at doctrinal and liturgical understanding. This devaluation of the theological element appears especially shortsighted in the light of the recent progress in sacramental theology represented in the Lima text of the document *Baptism, Eucharist, and Ministry*.[12]

Paul Lacey was invited to respond to Steere's article and made valuable critical remarks about Steere's approach.

> Though I strongly endorse Douglas' position, I cannot help feeling that to say our diversities melt away in our loving the same Lord neglects the fundamental problem . . . [13]

Certainly, the shared experience of loving the same Lord provides a foundation for ecumenical worship and service but the experience cannot be separated from interpretation without abstracting two elements that are essentially united. Lacey writes:

> We cannot chose between doctrine and devotion, and this is so because

doctrine, even at its worst, has grown out of devotion. And at its best, doctrine is continually growing out of devotion; it has put down living roots into the soil of the devotional life. The formula and the experiment must always be checking each other, so that the truth they both represent can have the power to convince us.[14]

It is also true that exclusive emphasis on the experiential aspect of religion limits dialogue as much as excessive intellectual posturing (or what the early Quakers called "notions").

If we absolutize the experiential, we have sealed ourselves off from full dialogue with others every bit as much as if we had proposed a verbal shibboleth as a test of orthodoxy.[15]

Once again it is necessary to contrast Steere's approach with one that gives full attention to the role of language and interpretation.

Though I value the emphasis Douglas Steere has made in this paper, I feel something by way of counterbalance is needed. Douglas has taught us the value of learning where words come from; in what I have written I have tried to remind us that one way to do this is to listen to what the words actually say, to give the letter its proper valuation in relation to the spirit.[16]

Steere must have assimilated Lacey's critique because in his later writings (most of Steere's "ecumenical" writing appears after this article) he acknowledges the legitimate role for dialogue seeking greater theological and institutional agreement. Although he continues to maintain that the Quakers have the most to offer at the level of experience, he also suggests that in the Quaker witness to the universal inward Christ the Quakers may have something to offer the Christian community as it seeks to articulate an image of Jesus Christ that is truly universal. At the institutional level, the Quaker's minimal and flexible structural requirements may provide some insights for churches struggling with heavy bureaucratic machinery.[17]

With the exception of his early depreciation of the theological and institutional elements of the ecumenical movement, Steere has provided sound leadership in spiritual ecumenism. He has helped numerous Protestants evaluate and appreciate the treasures of the Roman Catholic spiritual tradition. In a recent telephone conversation with John Oliver Nelson, founder of Kirkridge (a retreat center dedicated to spiritual renewal and social transformation), Nelson told me that Steere was responsible for introducing disciplined silent retreats at Kirkridge, including silence at meal times. He also volunteered that when Roman Catholic monks visited Kirkridge they would sometimes complain that these were just the sort of practices they were seeking to get away from! According to Nelson, Steere's great contribution was helping Protestants appreciate the Roman Catholic mystical tradition. Conrad Hoover, former retreat leader for the Church of the Savior in Washington, D.C., spoke to me of Steere as being a guiding influence on those who founded Dayspring Retreat Center, one of the first (mid-1950s) Protestant spiritual retreat centers offering silent retreats. Dorothy Devers, one of the founders of Dayspring, confirmed Hoover's remarks and added that the founders first came under Steere's influence while on a retreat at Pendle Hill. This group met with Steere to make plans for Dayspring. She said, with a laugh, that Steere had insisted on "acoustical integrity," meaning that they should attend to the need for quiet. Here also Steere aided Protestants in understanding and appreciating the Roman Catholic spiritual tradition.

Having emphasized Steere's role in helping Protestants appreciate the Roman Catholic spiritual tradition, one caveat must be added. Steere seldom acknowledges the importance of the sacramental piety that is so fundamental to Roman Catholic spirituality. Godfrey Diekmann, while speaking to me warmly about Steere's leadership in the Ecumenical Institute for Spirituality, said that Steere was "nervous" about sacramental piety and "suspicious" (as might be expected of a Protestant) of the Roman Catholic teaching represented in the phrase *ex opere operatum*. In Diekmann's view, Steere placed so much emphasis on individual responsibility that he had little appreciation for the eucharist as being wholly the "act of Christ."

In fairness to Steere, however, it should be noted that he never belittles sacramental piety in his writings; in fact, at times Steere gives evidence of warm appreciation for it. Steere writes of von Hügel's devotion to the eucharist with apparent warmth. Steere's appreciation for sacramental piety is most strongly expressed in his biography of Arthur Shearly Cripps, an Anglican missionary to the nations then know as Rhodesia. Commenting on Cripps's deep devotion to the eucharist, Steere writes:

> The One who gave all that he had and all that he was, and asks of us no less than all that we are and all that we have, seemed to Cripps to be peculiarly present upon those occasions, and like the priest and shepherd that he was, he carried around his neck on all his journeyings a small phial of the consecrated elements for sharing with the sick.[18]

This passage indicates Steere's appreciation for sacramental piety, even though it has little influence in his own spirituality.

As the Quakers have no outward sacraments, it not surprising that Steere neglects this element of Roman Catholic spirituality. Steere prefers to emphasize those elements of the Roman Catholic tradition that are most congenial to his spiritual theology, the elements of devotional or spiritual reading (*lectio divina*), prayer, manual labor, silence, contemplation, and service. This selective emphasis indicates the limits of Steere's role as an interpreter of the Roman Catholic spiritual tradition. Nevertheless, this same selectivity has contributed to his ability to introduce many Protestants to these elements of Roman Catholic spirituality.

Through his writings and ecumenical efforts, Steere has helped soften the hearts of many Christians toward their sisters and brothers in other communions. More importantly, Steere has created bonds of friendship where none existed. Parker Palmer describes this ministry well.

> Douglas Steere is surely one of the best-known figures in the world of ecumenical relations--not through such visible structures as the World

Council of Churches [although Steere did participate in WCC and NCC committees], but through the invisible bonds of the Spirit which connect the most diverse sorts of seekers.[19]

These invisible bonds of friendship, along with the visible bonds expressed through the Ecumenical Institute of Spirituality, indicate Steere's significance for American ecumenical spirituality. Of course, Steere's most important intellectual contribution to the larger Christian community has been his Quaker approach to relating prayer and social responsibility. This approach will be evaluated in the context of Steere's leadership in the Religious Society of Friends.

An Appraisal of Steere's Contribution to Contemporary Christian Spirituality

Although it is not the purpose of this study to determine Steere's place in the history of the Religious Society of Friends, his leadership in the Quaker community deserves brief consideration. One of Steere's concerns within the Religious Society of Friends has been to preserve its "religious" and Christian character. According to Elton Trueblood, many people join the Quakers as spiritual refugees from "churches in which creeds are overarticulate and binding. The danger . . . is that they, in their new sense of emancipation, will leave out Christ."[20] In his address to the Philadelphia Yearly Meeting in 1965, Steere addressed this problem.

We have now and I predict that we shall have increasingly in the future, men and women in our ranks who treasure our tenderness with those who, out of inner honesty, dare not formulate the cosmic redemptive scene in even as rigid a way as I may seem to have done in this swift statement. I would be the last one who would want to crowd or compel these precious seekers whom God may have called into our company to go beyond what their integrity or their experience up to now has disclosed to them as valid. But I would not want these persons to be deprived of facing the fact that the Quaker experience of the centuries, joined with that of other Christians over the years, has found this windowing of God's own nature in Jesus Christ of compelling significance.[21]

Along with this emphasis on the revelatory nature of Jesus Christ, Steere's stress on the importance of corporate worship serves to preserve the religious nature of the Society of Friends. Without this deep appreciation for corporate worship, Steere is concerned that the Quakers might evolve into an "ethical culture society."

I do not see how Friends can escape turning into an ethical culture society met together for thinking about their highest ideals unless they enter a meeting for worship with the expectation that something tremendous is going on and that in silence they are baptized inwardly into this very redemptive process and enlisted in the ranks ready to face their families, their communities, and their world as emissaries of this overwhelming love that was revealed in Jesus Christ and that is actively present among us today.[22]

This emphasis on the absolute centrality of corporate worship characterizes all of Steere's work, from his first published book to his recent Introduction to *Quaker Spirituality*. This emphasis has helped preserve the religious character of the Religious Society of Friends.

But, Steere's greatest contribution to the Quaker community is the same contribution he has made to the ecumenical movement, namely, the integration of prayer and social responsibility achieved in his life and writings. For Steere, this integration represents the genius of the Quaker spirituality and it is the gift of the Quaker community to the Christian community and the world. In a lecture delivered at the Friends World Committee for Consultation at Sitguna, Sweden in 1970, Steere points to this integration as the Quaker contribution to social transformation.

> If we [Quakers] are to play some minute part in this process of liberation and sharing, however, it will not be by reason of our succumbing to all the diseases of overactivism to which Quakers are so prone in our day, but it will be because we have kept our involvement in the world in intimate touch with our inward involvement, and there dare be no humbug of merely outward conformity to piety about it. Only the Friend who knows what it is to feel inwardly drawn by a concern and to have his work steadily under the scrutiny of the inward Guide, to have it sorted out and layers in him broken down and resistances in him overcome and who knows what it means to be tendered again and again, and knows also what it means to be told that "now is not the time to rest" when he periodically proposes a withdrawal, only this species of Friend is likely to have much to share that our hard driven colleagues in other churches and other world religions can profit from.[23]

Steere presents this linkage of the inward journey toward God and the outward journey of social responsibility as the great heritage of the Quaker community.

Steere has sought to share this heritage of Quaker spirituality with the larger Christian community through scholarship, lectures, retreat work, ecumenical involvement, and writing. Steere's contribution to spirituality is evidenced in the third volume of the Doubleday Devotional Classics. The third volume treats 19th and 20th century Protestant devotional literature. The three classics represented in this volume (i.e., Soren Kierkegaard's *Purity of Heart*, Thomas Kelly's *A Testament of Devotion*, and Steere's *On Listening to Another*) are all works with which Steere has had significant involvement. Steere translated and introduced Kierkegaard's classic to English speaking world; he wrote the biographical memoir to Kelly's work; and, of course, wrote *On Listening to Another*. E. Glenn Hinson, editor of this series of devotional classics, writes in his preface to *On Listening to Another* that:

> I think it not inappropriate to say here, however, that the Church owes a great debt to Douglas Steere for his contribution to spirituality. A man of obvious brilliance--Rhodes Scholar at Oxford (1925-27), Phi Beta Kappa-- and honored in many ways in the academic world, he has channeled his best thought and experience into a search for the divine in the midst of our

lives.[24]

Steere has made the treasures of Christian spirituality accessible to many twentieth century Christians.

Steere has kept the Christian devotional tradition alive among Protestants during a period when this dimension of the Christian tradition was largely ignored or scorned. It often was scorned because the advocates of piety appeared oblivious to social imperatives of the gospel. The respect accorded to Steere's work is evidence of his ability to articulate a spirituality which refuses to bifurcate the life of prayer and social ministry. Charles Daniels Brodhead's review of Steere's *On Beginning from Within*, published in *The Christian Century* in 1944, indicates the freshness and power of Steere's integration.

> . . . it is indeed a choice book, not for beginners in religion but for travelers further along the Christian highway. Only such a spirit as "St. Douglas of Haverford" could have written it. For its illumination and inspiration we are deeply grateful.
>
> Here then is the Quaker contribution of practical mysticism, a response to the inner light that amid the darkness of these times glows all the more brightly.[25]

"St. Douglas of Haverford" has been able to articulate the Christian spiritual tradition in a way that commends itself to the contemporary demand for a holistic spirituality.

Steere understood the contemporary need for a holistic spirituality long before it became a popular concern in Christian circles. In an article entitled "Protestant Piety Today" written for *Religion in Life* in 1950, Steere discerned a need that would find full expression only in the 1970s. After analyzing the piety of various groups in Protestant Christianity, he writes:

> [As] Noble a Protestant piety as these groups represent, however, they draw attention to a further factor in perhaps the highest flower of Protestant devotion that has yet to be attained, namely, the very limited conception of social or political responsibility that is connected with it. . . . This crossing of the Christian devotional life with this corporate sense of responsibility for one's fellows would seem to be the mark of the Protestant devotion of the future.[26]

Steere's work has anticipated, to a degree, this "highest flower" of Protestant devotion. He has been able to cross the devotional life with a corporate sense of responsibility for others.

Although the need for such a spirituality is urgently felt today among both Protestant and Roman Catholic Christians, there are few models for such an integration. In his writings, Steere presents an adequate and compelling explication of the relation of prayer and social responsibility. It is an approach that has much to offer the contemporary search for a holistic spirituality.

Of course, the Church needs more than intellectual and theological explications of a holistic spirituality; the Church needs lives that embody such models. The majority of Christians are moved more by living examples than by intellectual formulations. Steere's life provides just such a example, as does the life of John Woolman. Perhaps the story of his life will prove more important than his notable efforts to provide a viable intellectual understanding of the intimate relation of prayer and social responsibility. But, that story is still unfolding.

The urgent need for what Steere's spiritual theology offers becomes apparent in a recent Gallup poll on religious beliefs and practices of Americans. The poll documents a renewed interest in religion and an exceptionally high percentage of Americans who believe in God. But, at the same time, the poll revealed a "self-centered kind of faith."[27]   It showed that more Christians "pray, read the Bible, and engage in other religious practices because 'it makes me feel good' than because it makes them 'realize the need for repentance or the need to do God's will regardless of the cost.'"[28]   Steere's spiritual theology is valuable because it not only exposes the shallowness of the current narcissism but it also presents the costly imperatives of the gospel in the context of God's infinite concern for every person.   Steere makes the life of Christian discipleship compelling and attractive without watering down its costly demands.

Steere's spiritual teaching is valuable for contemporary spirituality precisely because the world can seem so scattered and Christians often feel impotent before massive problems and difficulties.   Steere's Quaker instincts cut through the surface commotion and reach to a level of solidarity with God and fellows, a listening to the still quiet Voice that empowers rather than distracts.   At this level, the Christian appropriates a new freedom to participate in God's redemptive order. Steere's integration suggests a way in which both the life of prayer and the life of action can be mutually enriching.

Here, then, is an approach to prayer and social responsibility that speaks eloquently to the needs and aspirations of contemporary Christian spirituality. This approach can certainly benefit from dialogue with the liturgical approach, but it makes a significant contribution in its own right. Moreover, Steere has achieved an integration, both in his life and writings, that will make a lasting contribution to the history and literature of Christian spirituality.

NOTES FOR CHAPTER SIX

[1]Emmanuel Sullivan, "Ecumenical Spirituality" in *The Westminster Dictionary of Christian Spirituality* ed. Gordon S. Wakefield (Philadelphia: The Westminster Press, 1983), p. 125-126.

[2]Ibid., p. 126.

[3]Ibid., p. 126.

[4]Ibid., p. 126.

[5]Ibid., p. 126.

[6]E. Glenn Hinson, "Douglas V. Steere: Irradiator of the Beams of Love," in *The Christian Century*, April 24, 1985, p. 418.

[7]John B. Cobb, Jr., *Beyond Dialogue: Toward a Mutual Transformation of Christianity and Buddhism* (Philadelphia: Fortress Press, 1982).

[8]Steere, *Mutual Irradiation*, p. 8.

[9]Ibid., p. 8.

[10]Cobb, p. 140.

[11]Douglas V. Steere, "Beyond Diversities to a Common Experience of God," in *Quaker Religious Thought*, V (Autumn 1963): 5.

[12]*Baptism, Eucharist, and Ministry* (Geneva, Switzerland: World Council of Churches, 1982).

[13]Paul Lacey, "Comments," in *Quaker Religious Thought*, V (Autumn 1963): 18.

[14]Ibid., p. 19.

[15]Ibid., p. 20.

[16]Ibid., p. 22.

[17]Steere, *Mutual Irradiation*, p. 30.

[18]Douglas V. Steere, *God's Irregular: Arthur Shearly Cripps* (London: SPCK, 1973), p. 37.

[19]Parker Palmer, "Douglas and Dorothy Steere: More Than the Sum of the Parts," in

Living in the Light: Some Quaker Pioneers of the 20th Century ed. Leonard S. Kenworthy, (Kennett Square, Pa.: Friends General Conference, 1984), p. 229.

[20]Elton D. Trueblood, *The People Called Quakers* (New York: Harpers, 1966), p. 277.

[21]Steere, Cited by Trueblood, p. 277.

[22]Steere, "Three Areas of Concern," undated manuscript at the Quaker Collection at Haverford College.

[23]Douglas V. Steere, "Emerging Horizons," *Friends Quarterly*, (April 1971): 61.

[24]*Doubleday Devotional Classics, Vol. III* ed. E. Glenn Hinson, (Garden City, New York: Doubleday and Company, Inc., 1978), p. 203.

[25]Charles Daniel Brodhead, "The Way to Sainthood," in *The Christian Century*, April 5, 1944, p. 435.

[26]Douglas V. Steere, "Protestant Piety Today," in *Religion in Life*, 19 (1950): 8.

[27]George Gallup, Jr., "Religion in America: 50 Years (1935-1985)," in *The Gallup Report*, Report No. 236, May 1985, p. 12.

[28]Ibid., p. 12.

CONCLUSION

The purpose of this conclusion is to summarize the results of this study and to present the contributions it makes to contemporary spiritual theology.

The Introduction established that the relation of prayer and social responsibility represents a perennial problem for Christian spirituality. I argued that the problem has been addressed with varying degrees of adequacy throughout church history, but that the Religious Society of Friends, with its history of uniting experiential religion with prophetic social engagement, represents one of the more satisfying answers to the problem. Among contemporary Friends, Douglas V. Steere was singled out as the one who has addressed the issue with the greatest cogency.

Chapter One demonstrated that Steere's spiritual theology expresses a type of Quaker praxis arising out of his efforts to incarnate God's infinite concern for all persons and all creation Those efforts found clarity and expression in his work with the American Friends Service Committee and the Friends World Committee for Consultation.

In Chapter Two, I examined Steere's writings over a period of almost fifty years in order to distill his teaching on the relation of prayer and social responsibility. The nature of that relation, as it is expressed in the full scope of Steere's spiritual theology, represented something of a mystery. The examination ascertained that the most appropriate term to characterize the relation disclosed in Steere's writings is "integration." This integration is never a simple oneness, for prayer and social responsibility are never collapsed, but it is an integration in which prayer and social responsibility are interdependent, inseparable, mutually clarifying, and mutually enriching. The analysis also established that the five theses drawn from Steere's writings accurately convey his approach to the problem. Finally, the study demonstrated that the spiritual theology expressed in the first thesis grounds Steere's approach to ecumenical and interfaith encounter.

Chapters Three and Four analyzed the influence of von Hügel, Woolman, Kierkegaard, and other writers on Steere's spiritual theology. Although these authors exert a profound influence on Steere's spiritual theology, the analysis demonstrated that Steere's spiritual theology represents his own interaction with and critical appropriation of the thought of these authors.

Chapter Five examined Steere's spiritual theology from several different critical perspectives in order to determine its value for contemporary Christian spirituality. The analysis revealed two limitations in Steere's spiritual theology: the absence of a method for reappropriating action in prayer and the lack of specificity in Steere's social vision. I addressed the absence of a method for reappropriating action in prayer by outlining a method, consistent with Steere's spiritual theology, in which the full dialectical reciprocity of these elements could be realized. The examination demonstrated that Steere's spiritual theology cannot be accused of the errors of enthusiasm or quietism. Finally, the evaluation brought Steere's classical Quaker approach to the relation of prayer and social responsibility into an extensive dialogue with a liturgical approach. The evaluation showed that these approaches can complement each other and described ways in which a more productive symbiosis may be established. The chapter concluded with the judgment that Steere's spiritual theology presents a balanced and cogent approach to the relation of prayer and social responsibility that commends itself to the needs of contemporary Christian spirituality.

Chapter Six offered a broader appraisal of Steere's contribution to contemporary Christian spirituality by evaluating his role as a leader in ecumenical spirituality, as a bearer of the Christian spiritual tradition, and as a leader in the Quaker community. This appraisal noted Steere's early depreciation of theological and institutional elements of the ecumenical movement, but showed that this does not vitiate his extraordinary contribution to spiritual ecumenism. The capstone of Steere's contribution, both to the Quaker community and larger Christian community, is the integration of prayer and social responsibility conveyed in his life and writings.

This study has demonstrated the merit of Steere's integration of prayer and social responsibility, but what in his approach makes it noteworthy? First, it has been his ability to retain the integrity of what is essentially his own Quaker approach to the relation of prayer and social responsibility while weaving into it some of the most penetrating insights of Roman Catholic spirituality and existential thought. These elements give his writings a depth and intensity that are extremely rare in a Protestant devotional writer. Second, Steere's engagement with the issue has never been purely academic. His writings bear the stamp of one who has struggled with the issue in his own life and in the social order. Third, Steere writes and speaks with an eloquence that is rare in this age of pedestrian language. Steere's style is probably at least partially the result of Steere's encounter with von Hügel, whose style is at once both brilliant and ponderous.

One of the more promising byproducts of this study is its analysis of the way in which a concern unfolds in prayer and in Quaker worship. The examination of Steere's description of the formation of a concern and the way in which a concern reshapes the life of pray-er might well serve as a preliminary study to Michael J. Sheeran's analysis of the corporate disposition of concerns in the Quaker meeting for business. Together they would provide a comprehensive guide to spiritual discernment in the Quaker tradition.

Writing this book, a personal "concern," has proved both more costly and more rewarding than I could have anticipated. The greatest rewards have come from swimming in the stream of Christian devotion that Douglas Steere expresses in his life and writings. My greatest hope is that others as well may be swept along by that stream and made ever more willing to participate in God's redemptive order. I also hope that this study, having clarified Steere's solution to the problem of relating prayer and action, may serve as a foundation for further study in the academy and in the churches.

SELECT BIBLIOGRAPHY OF QUAKER SPIRITUALITY

Barbour, Hugh. *The Quakers in Puritan England*. New Haven: Yale University Press, 1964.

_____. and Roberts, Arthur O. *Early Quaker Writings*. Grand Rapids: Eerdman, 1973.

Braithwaite, William C. *Spiritual Guidance in Quaker Experience*. (Swarthmore Lecture). London: Headley Bros., 1909.

Brayshaw, A. Neave. *The Quakers*. New York: Macmillan, 1938.

Brinton, Howard H. *Friends for 300 Years*. New York: Harper, 1952.

_____. *Ethical Mysticism*. Pendle Hill Pamphlet no. 156, 1967.

_____. *The Religion of George Fox*. Pendle Hill Pamphlet no. 161, 1968.

_____. *The Religious Philosophy of Quakerism*. Wallingford, Pa.: Pendle Hill Publications, 1973.

Grubb, Edward. *The Historic and Inward Christ*. (Swarthmore Lecture). London: Headley Bros., 1914.

_____. *Quaker Thought and History* New York: Macmillan, 1925.

Hinson, Glenn. "Douglas V. Steere: Irradiator of the Beams of Love." *The Christian Century*, April 24, 1985.

Jones, Rufus M. *Studies in Mystical Religion*. London: Macmillan, 1909.

_____. *The Faith and Practice of Quakers*. London: Methuen, 1928.

The Journal and Other Essays of John Woolman. ed. Phillips P. Moulton. New York: Oxford University Press, 1971.

The Journal and Other Writings of John Woolman. ed. Amelia Mott Gummere. New York: The Macmillan Company, 1922.

Kelly, Thomas R. *A Testament of Devotion*. Edited with biography by Douglas V. Steere. New York: Harpers, 1941.

_____. *The Eternal Promise*. New York: Harpers, 1941.

Living in the Light: Some Quaker Pioneers of the Twentieth Century. ed. Leonard S. Kenworthy. Kennett Square, Pa.: Friends General Conference and Quaker Publications, 1984.

Loukes, Harrold. *The Quaker Contribution.* London: SCM, 1965.

Newman, Daisy. *A Procession of Friends* New York: Doubleday, 1972.

Nuhn, Ferner. *Friends and the Ecumenical Movement.* Philadelphia, Pa.: Friends General Conference, 1970.

Nuttall, Geoffrey, *The Holy Spirit in Puritan Faith and Practice.* Oxford: Blackwell, 1946.

Palmer, Parker. "Douglas and Dorothy Steere: More Than the Sum of the Parts." *Living in the Light: Some Quaker Pioneers of the Twentieth Century.* ed. Leonard S. Kenworthy. Kennett Square, Pa.: Friends General Conference, 1984.

Quaker Spirituality. Edited with introductory essay by Douglas V. Steere and preface by Elizabeth Gray Vining. New York: Paulist Press, 1984.

Sheeran, Michael J. *Beyond Majority Rule: Voteless Decisions in the Religious Society of Friends.* Philadelphia, Pa.: Philadelphia Yearly Meeting, 1983.

Trueblood, D. Elton. *The People Called Quakers.* New York: Harpers, 1966.

_____. *Robert Barclay.* New York: Harpers, 1967.

Vining, Elizabeth G. *Friend for Life: Rufus M. Jones.* Philadelphia: Lippincott, 1958.

_____. *William Penn: Mystic.* Wallingford, Penn.: Pendle Hill Pamphlet no. 167, 1969.

SELECT BIBLIOGRAPHY FOR A STUDY OF THE SPIRITUAL
THEOLOGY OF BARON FRIEDRICH VON HÜGEL

Barman, Lawrence F. *Baron Friedrich von Hügel and the Modernist Crisis in England.* Cambridge: University Press, 1972.

Cock, Albert Arthur. *A Critical Examination of von Hügel's Philosophy of Religion.* London: H. Rees, 1953.

De La Bedoyere, Michael. *The Life of Baron von Hügel.* London: Dent, 1951.

Heaney, John J. *The Modernist Crisis: von Hügel.* Washington: Corpus Books, 1968.

Hügel, Friedrich von. *Essays and Addresses on the Philosophy of Religion.* (First series) New York: E. P. Dutton and Company Inc., 1921.

_____.*Essays and Addresses on the Philosophy of Religion.* (Second series) New York: E. P. Dutton and Company Inc., 1921.

_____. *Letters from Baron von Hügel to a Niece.* Edited with introduction by Gwendolyn Green. London: J. M. Dent and Son Ltd., 1928.

_____. *The Mystical Element in Religion as Studied in St. Catherine of Genoa and Her Friends.* New York: E.P. Dutton and Company Inc., 1909. (Second edition in 1923).

_____. *The Reality of God, and Religion and Agnosticism: Being the Literary Remains of Baron Friedrich von Hügel.* Edited by Edmund G. Gadner. New York: E. P. Dutton and Company Inc., 1931.

Steere, Douglas V. *Critical Realism in the Religious Philosophy of Baron Friedrich von Hügel.* Unpublished dissertation at Harvard University, 1930.

_____. *Spiritual Counsels and Letters of Baron Friedrich von Hügel.* New York: Harper and Brothers, 1963. and London: Darton, Longman, and Todd, 1964.

Whalen, Joseph P. *The Spirituality of Friedrich von Hügel.* Foreword by B. C. Butler. New York: Newman Press, 1971.

WORKS CONSULTED TO GAIN A CRITICAL PERSPECTIVE ON THE SPIRITUAL THEOLOGY OF DOUGLAS V. STEERE

Allport, Gordon Willard. *The Individual and His Religion: A Psychological Interpretation.* New York: Macmillan, 1950.

Arasteh, Reza. *Final Integration in the Adult Personality.* Leiden: E. J. Brill, 1965.

Brown, Robert McAfee. *Spirituality and Liberation: Overcoming the Great Fallacy.* Philadelphia: The Westminster Press, 1988.

Cobb, John. "The Identity of Christian Spirituality and Global Consciousness." Unpublished paper written for the faculty of the School of Theology at Claremont, Ca., Fall 1975.

Dorr, Donal. *Spirituality and Justice.* Maryknoll, New York: Orbis Books, 1984.

Dulles, Avery. *Models of the Church.* Garden City, New York: Image Books, A Division of Doubleday Inc., 1978.

Galilea, Segundo. *Following Jesus.* trans. Sister Helen Phillips, M.M., New York: Orbis Books, 1981.

Gutierrez, Gutavo. *A Theology of Liberation.* trans. and ed. by Sister Caridad Inda and John Eagleson, (New York: Orbis Books, 1973.

Homes, Urban T. *A History of Christian Spirituality: An Analytical Introduction.* New York: Seabury Press, 1981.

Hood, R. W., Jr. "Psychology Strength and the Report of Intense Religious Experience," *Journal for the Scientific Study of Religion.* 13 (1974):65-71.

_____. "Religious Orientation and the Report of Religious Experience," *Journal of the Scientific Study of Religion.* 9 (1970):285-291.

Hauerwas, Stanley. *Character and Christian Life: A Study in Theological Ethics.* San Antonio: Trinity University Press, 1975.

_____. *A Community of Character: Toward a Constructive Christian Social Ethic.* Notre Dame, IN.:Notre Dame University Press, 1981.

_____. *Vision and Virtue: Essays in Christian Ethical Reflection.* Notre Dame, IN.: Notre Dame University Press, 1981.

_____. *The Peaceable Kingdom: A Primer in Christian Ethics*. Notre Dame, IN.: Notre Dame University Press, 1983.

_____. and William Willimon. *Resident Aliens*. Nashville: Abingdon Press, 1989.

Knox, R. A. *Enthusiasm: A Chapter in the History Religion*. (First series). London: J. M. Dent and Sons Ltd., 1921.

Macquarrie, John. *Existentialism*. Philadelphia: The Westminster Press, 1972.

Merton, Thomas. *Contemplation in a World of Action*. Introduced by Jean Leclerq, O.S.B. Garden City, New York: Doubleday and Company Inc., 1971.

Niebuhr, H. Richard. *Christ and Culture*. New York: Harper and Row, Publishers, 1951.

Saliers, Don E. *The Soul in Paraphrase: Prayer and the Religious Affections*. New York: Seabury Press, 1980.

_____. *Worship and Spirituality*. Philadelphia: Westminster Press, 1984.

Willimon, William H. *The Service of God: Christian Worship and Work*. Nashville: Abingdon Press, 1983.

_____. *Sighing for Eden: Sin, Evil, and the Christian Faith*. Nashville: Abingdon Press, 1985.

BIBLIOGRAPHICAL NOTE

This bibliography lists Steere's key books, pamphlets, articles, and contributions to books. It is not intended to provide a complete listing of his writings but to present those writings that are most important and most accessible. A complete bibliography would include three pages for lectures and six pages for travel letters. Most of these, however, are only available at The Quaker Collection at Haverford College.

Ms. Eva Walker Myer compiled a complete bibliography while serving as a bibliographer at The Quaker Collection at Haverford College. Since completing that bibliography, she has moved to Mississippi, but her new address is provided below for those interested in a complete bibliography.

I have also included the addresses for The Quaker Collection and Pendle Hill, two key sources for publications on Quaker spirituality and Douglas Steere.

Ms. Eva Walker Myer
4427 Deer Creek Drive
Jackson, MS 39211

The Quaker Collection
Magill Library
Haverford College
Haverford, PA 19041-1392
(215) 896-1175

Pendle Hill Publications
338 Plush Mill Rd.
Wallingford, PA 19086
(215) 566-4514

BOOKS BY DOUGLAS STEERE

Steere, Douglas V. *Dimensions of Prayer.* Woman's Division of Christian Service. Board of Missions, The United Methodist Church, 1962. and New York: Harper and Row, 1963.

_____. *Doors into Life Through Five Devotional Classics.* New York: Harper, 1948. (Includes essays on *The Imitation of Christ*, Francis de Sales' *Introduction to the Devout Life, Journal of John Woolman, Purity of Heart*, and *Selected Letters* of Friedrich von Hügel).

_____. (with Dorothy Steere) *Friends Work in Africa.* London: Friends World Committee for Consultation, 1954.

_____. *Gebet und Andacht.* Bad Pyrmont: L. Friedrich, 1948.

_____. *Gegenseitetige Erleuchtung.* Berlin Germany: Religiöse Gesellschaft der Freunde (Quäker) in Deutschland, 1968.

_____. *Gleanings: A Random Harvest.* Nashville: The Upper Room, 1987.

_____. *God's Irregular: Arthur Shearly Cripps.* London: SPCK, 1973. and Wallingford, PA: Pendle Hill Publications, 1973.

_____. *On Beginning from Within* New York: Harpers and Brothers, 1943.

_____. *On Listening to Another.* New York: Harper and Brothers, 1955. First published as *Where Words Come From.* The book is drawn from the 48th annual Swarthmore Lecture that Steere delivered in May of 1955 at the opening session of the London Yearly Meeting.

_____. *Prayer and Worship.* Richmond, Indiana: Friends United Press, 1978. (First published in 1938 by the Association Press).

_____. *Quaker Spirituality.* Edited with introduction by Douglas Steere and preface by Elizabeth Gray Vining. New York: Paulist, 1984.

_____. *Time to Spare.* New York: Harper and Brothers, 1949.

_____. *Spiritual Counsels and Letters of Baron Friedrich von Hügel.* London: Darton, Longman, and Todd, 1964.

_____. *Together in Solitude.* New York: Crossroads, 1982.

_____. *Work and Contemplation.* New York: Harper and Brothers, 1957.

KEY PAMPHLETS BY DOUGLAS STEERE

Steere, Douglas V. *Bethlehem Revisited*. Wallingford, Pa: Pendle Hill Publications, 1965. 18 pp.

_____. *Community and Worship*. Wallingford, Pa: Pendle Hill Publications, 1940. 34 pp.

_____. *Contemplation and Leisure*. Wallingford, Pa: Pendle Hill Publications, 1975. 34 pp.

_____. *The Hardest Journey*. Wallingford, Pa: Pendle Hill Publications, 1968. 30 pp.

_____. *Inward Preparation for the Life of Peace*. New York: The Episcopal Pacifist Fellowship, 1956. 8 pp.

_____. *A Manual on the Need, the Organization, and the Discipline of Cells for Peace*. New York: Fellowship of Reconciliation, 1947. 15 pp.

_____. *Mutual Irradiation: A Quaker View of Ecumenism*. Wallingford, Pa: Pendle Hill Publications, 1971. 32 pp.

_____. *On Being Present Where You Are*. Wallingford, Pa: Pendle Hill Publications, 1967. 36 pp.

_____. *On Speaking Out of Silence*. Wallingford, Pa: Pendle Hill Publications, 1972. 20 pp.

_____. *The Open Life*. Philadelphia: Book Committee of the Religious Society of Friends, 1937. (William Penn Lecture Delivered at Arch Street Meeting House).

_____. *The Peace Team*. New York: The Fellowship of Reconciliation. n.d. 16 pp.

_____. *Prayer in the Contemporary World*. Published by the National Council of Churches of Christ for the United Church Women, 1966. 32 pp.

_____. *The Soil of Peace: The Human Factor in Reconstruction*. Washington: Human Events, Inc., 1946. 20 pp.

_____. *Toward the Practice of Prayer*. Philadelphia: Friends Book Store. Undated, probably 1931. 12 pp.

KEY ARTICLES BY DOUGLAS STEERE

Steere, Douglas V. "Beyond Diversity to a Common Experience of God." *Quaker Religious Thought* V (Autumn 1963).

_____. "Caring is All That Matters." *Monastic Studies* 8 (Spring 1972): 14-17.

_____. "A Chapter in Protestant-Catholic Encounter: 1918-62." (Autumn 1963).

_____. "Common Frontiers in Catholic and Non-Catholic Spirituality." *Worship* 39 (December 1968): 605-18.

_____. "Contemplation and Leisure." *Humanitas* (Nov. 1972).

_____. "On Dove's Feet." (report on creative religious movement in Europe). *Christianity and Crisis* 9 (1951): 66-8.

_____. "Emerging Horizons." *Friends Quarterly* (April 1971).

_____. "The Evangelical Academics in Germany." *The Friends Quarterly* V (April 1951): 79-86.

_____. "Evangelism and Christian Fellowship." *Religion in Life*. VIII (Winter 1939): 3-13.

_____. "Foreword to an Anatomy of Worship." *Pastoral Psychology*. 11 (March 1960): 10-15.

_____. "A Fresh Look at Retreats." *Religion in Life* 36 (1967): 100-107.

_____. "Hope of Glory and This Present Life." *Theology Today*. 10 (October 1953): 367-74.

_____. "Is the Social Gospel Adequate to Become the Religion of the Next Generation?" *The Crozer Quarterly* XII (April 1935): 128-141.

_____. "The Life of Prayer as the Ground for Unity." *Worship* 45 (May 1971): 250-61.

_____. "The Meaning of Mysticism within Christianity." *Religion in Life* XXII (Autumn 1953): 515-526.

_____. "In the Morning Sow Your Seed." *Friends World News* (Winter

1972).

_____. "Mutual Irradiation." *Religion in Life* XXVII (Summer 1959): 395-405.

_____. "Mystical Experience." *Review and Expositor* 71 (Summer 1974): 323-44.

_____. "On Apprehending God." Phonotape. Wesley Theological Seminary Convocation Series, Spring 1962.

_____. "Opening Address." The Ecumenical Institute on the Spiritual Life. *Worship* (December 1965).

_____. "Peace, War and Conscientious Objection: Vatican Council Deliberations." *Friends World News* 78 (April 1966): 10-12.

_____. "Protestant Piety Today." *Religion in Life* 19 (1950): 3-15.

_____. "A Quaker at the Central Committee Meeting of the World Council." *Religion in Life* VXL (Summer 1971): 267-272.

_____. "A Quaker Looks at the Vatican Council." *Religion in Life* 33 (1964): 5690-576.

_____. "The Quaker Message." *The Christian Century* August 1955).

_____. "Reconstruction Training at Haverford." *The Haverford Review* 3 (1944).

_____. "Solitude and Prayer." *Worship* 55 (March 1981): 120-36.

_____. "Spiritual Renewal in Our Time." *Union Seminary Quarterly Review* 17 (November 1961): 33-56.

_____. "The Spiritual Task of Teachers Today." *Sisters* 45 (1975): 5-13.

_____. "The Spirituality of Friedrich von Hügel." *Worship* 47 (November 1973): 540-6.

_____. "That Which We Apprehend." Phonotape. Wesley Theological Seminary Convocation Series, Spring 1962.

_____. "Thy Will Be Done: The Spiritual Basis of Our Christian Service." *Friends Journal* (August 1, 1961).

CONTRIBUTIONS TO BOOKS

Beyond Dilemmas: Quakers Look at Life. Edited by Scera Bright Laughlin with introduction by Douglas Steere. Port Washington, NY: Kennekat Press, 1969.

Break the New Ground. Edited by Charles W. Cooper with introduction by Douglas Steere. Birmingham, England: Friends World Committee for Consultation, 1969.

Brooks, Edgar Harry. *Three Letters from Africa.* Foreword by Alan Paton with introduction by Douglas Steere. Wallingford, PA: Pendle Hill, 1965.

Chambers, William Nesbitt. *Responsibility and Illness.* Foreword by Caroline Newton with introduction by Douglas Steere. Berwyn, PA,: n. pub., 1961.

Coburn, John. *Feeding Fire* (poems) Foreword by Douglas Steere. Wilton, CT: Morehouse-Barlow Co., 1980.

Herman, Nicholas. *The Practice of the Presence of God.* Arranged and edited by Douglas Steere. Nashville: The Upper Room, 1950.

The Imitation of Christ. Arranged and edited by Douglas Steere. Nashville: The Upper Room, 1952.

Introduction to the Devout Life. Translated and edited by John Ryan with introduction by Douglas Steere. New York: Harper, 1952.

Kelly, Thomas R. *Heiliger Gehorsam.* mit Biographischen von Douglas Steere. Bad Pyrmont: L. Friedrich, 1960.

_____. *A Testament of Devotion.* Edited with biography by Douglas Steere. New York: Harper and Brothers, 1941.

Kierkegaard, Soren. *Purity of Heart is to Will One Thing.* Translated with introductory essay by Douglas Steere/ Harper and Brothers, 1938.

_____. *Works of Love.* trans. David F. Swenson and Lillian Marvin Swenson. Introduction by Douglas Steere. Princeton, NJ: Princeton University Press, 1946.

Mather, Eleanor Price. *Pendle Hill: A Quaker Experiment in Education and Community.* Foreword by Douglas Steere. Wallingford, PA: Pendle Hill, 1980/

Merton, Thomas. *The Climate of Monastic Prayer.* Foreword by Douglas Steere. Shannon, Ireland: Irish University Press, 1969.

_____. *Contemplative Prayer.* Introduction by Douglas Steere. Garden City, NY: Image Books. a division of Doubleday and Company Inc., 1971.

O'Connor, Elizabeth. *Letters to Scattered Pilgrims.* Foreword by Douglas Steere. San Francisco: Harper and Row, 1979.

Prayer and Liberation: The Ecumenical Institute of Spirituality. Foreword by Douglas Steere. New York: Alba House, 1976.

Quaker Spirituality. Edited with introduction by Douglas Steere. New York: The Paulist Press, 1984.

Sheeran, Michael John. *Beyond Majority Rule: Voteless Decisions in the Religious Society of Friends.* Foreword by Douglas Steere. Philadelphia, PA: Philadelphia Yearly Meeting, 1983.

Swearer, Don K. *Dialogue: The Key to Understanding Other Religions.* Foreword by Douglas Steere. Philadelphia: Westminster Press, 1977.

Steere, Douglas V. "Common Frontiers in Catholic and Non-Catholic Spirituality." and "Opening Address" in *Protestants and Catholics on the Spiritual Life.* Edited by Michael Marx. Collegeville, MN: Liturgical Press, 1965.

_____. "Dekumenische Erweckung." in *Aktiver Friede: Gedekschrift fuer Friedrich Siegmund Schultze.* Soest, Netherlands: Macker and Jahn, 1972.

_____. "Development for What?" in *Development for What?* ed. John H. Hallowell. Durham, NC: Published by the Lilly Endowment Research Program in Christianity and Politics by the Duke University Press, 1964.

_____. "The Devotional Literature of Christianity." *The Vitality of the Christian Tradition.* ed. George Thomas. New York: Harper and Brothers, 1945.

_____. "Enomiya Lasalle zum achtzigsten Geburtstag." in *Munen muso: Ungegenstandliche Meditation.* ed. G. Stachel. Mainz: Matthias Grunewald-Verlag, 1978.

_____. "No Final Formula for Retreats." in *Call to Adventure.* ed. Raymon J. Magee. Nashville: Abingdon Press, 1967.

_____. "On the Power of Sustained Attention." *Then and Now.* ed. Anna S. Brinton. Philadelphia: University of Pennsylvania Press, 1960.

_____. "Prayer and Worship." in *The Religious Life.* ed. Georgia Harkness. New York: Association Press, 1953.

_____. "Quaker-Roman Catholic Ecumenical Encounter." in *No Time But*

This Present. ed. Margaret C. McNeill. Birmingham, England: Friends World Committee for Consultation, 1965.

_____. "A Religious Minority in Action: The Society of Friends." in *Group Relations and Group Antagonisms.* Religion and Civilization Series. New York: Institute for Religious and Social Studies, Jewish Theological Seminary of America, 1944.

_____. "Religious Encounter." in *Buddhism and Culture.* ed. Sususu Yamaguchi. Dedicated to Dr. Daisetz Teitaro Suzuki in "Commemoration of his ninetieth birthday. Kyoto, Japan: Nakano Press, 1960.

_____. "A Theology of Practical Mysticism." in *Men Who Shape Belief.* Philadelphia, PA: Westminster Press, 1955.

_____. "The Ultimate Underpinning." in *To God Be the Glory.* Sermons in honor of George Arthur Buttrick. ed. Theodore Gill. Nashville: Abingdon Press, 1973.

_____. *The Very Thought of Thee.* (from three great mystics: Bernard of Clairvaux, Jeremy Taylor, and Evelyn Underhill) Edited and arranged by Douglas Steere. Nashville: The Upper Room, 1953.

INDEX

Allport, Gordon, 2

AFSC 2,3,16,17,19,21,93,181

alternation, 44,45,116,146-47

anthropology, 33,46,71,92

Augustine, St., 115

Barth, Karl, 113

Boehme, Jacob, 116-7

Brinton, Howard, 113,128

Buber, Martin, 15,113

Chapman, Dom, 116

christology, 65,174

Cobb, John, 170

Coburn, John, 117-8

concerns,
    seeds of concern, 52,53,63,96;
    following out concerns, 16-20, 29-
    30,48-50,56,67-69,130
    Steere's key concerns, 16-20

consolations/desolations, 138

costliness, of spiritual journey, holiness
    92,99,101,177

Diekmann, Godfrey, 4,18,60,173

discernment, 53,68-69,127-9,136;
    also, *See* concerns

Eckhart, Meister, 34,116-7

eclecticism, question of Steere's, 117-9

ecumenism, 4,6,17-19,60,64-5

ecumenical spirituality, 169-174

Ecumenical Institute of Spirituality,
    4,21,60,173-4

enthusiasm, 134-6
    evangelical and mystical, 134-5,

evangelicals, 1,2,14

evangelical piety, 1,2,14

existentialism, 3,7,13,57,89,108,
    113,132

existential realism, 13,57,88-90,108-9

Fellowship of Reconciliation, 4

Finnish concern, Steere's, 16-17

Friends World Committee for Con-
    sultation, 4,16,19-21,46,175

Galilea, Segundo, 133

Guardini, Romano, 4,14,15,107

Gutierrez, Gustavo, 133

Harvard Univ., 4,5,11,12,15,31,
    36,148

Hauerwas, Stanley, 139-143,151,152

Haverford College, 4,13-15,17,20, 26,93

Hicksite, (branch of Quakerism), 13

Hinson, Glenn, 6,70,118-9,132,139 170,175

Hocking, William Ernest, 12,116

Holmes, Urban, 1,2

Hügel, Friedrich von, 3,13,14,71,83- 93,101,102,107,108

Holy Spirit, 63

Interfaith initiatives, Hindu-Christian, 18,60 Zen-Christian, 4-5,18-20,60,62, 70,170

Jones, Rufus, 4,12,14-6,26

Jung, Carl, 108

Kant, Immanuel, 116

Kelly, Thomas, 14

Kierkegaard, Soren, 13,15, 25,51,108- 113

Kunkel, Fritz, 15,108

Lacey, Paul, 171-72

lectures, Steere's, 4,5,31,36,37,44,46, 62,94,98

Lewis, C.I., 12

liberalism, 1,2

liberation theology, 133

Macquarrie, John, 109-113, 132

Marcel, Gabriel, 107,108,114,115

Maritain, Jacques, 108,109, 115

Merton, Thomas, 70,139

modernism, 84,85,87

NCC, WCC, 4,18

Niebuhr, Reinhold, 107

nonviolence, 66,67,101

Oxford Movement, 11

Orthodox (branch of Quakerism), 13

Palmer, Parker J., 4,13,16,17,18,118 173

Pascal, 107,109

peacemaking, 18,20

personalism, 12,15,34,58

Pendle Hill, 4,13,16,21,93

quietism, 134-9

Radnor Meeting, 13,21

Rahner, Karl, 113

realism, 83,85,86,89,109

realistic cleft, 38,57

Rhodes Scholarship, 4,12,85

Roberts, Arthur, 118

saint, making and role of, 31,32, 33,34,94,96,100

Sales, St. Francis de, 108,114

Saliers, Don, 139,140,143,152-54

Shalem Institute, 2,157

AUTHOR'S BIOGRAPHICAL SKETCH

John D. Copenhaver, Jr., is assistant professor of religion at Shenandoah University in Winchester, VA where he chairs the Department of Religion and Philosophy. He attended college at Washington and Lee University, majoring in European History. Although planning on a career in law, a single course in comparative religion stimulated a passion for theological understanding that eventually led him to prepare for Christian ministry. He attended Fuller Theological Seminary and completed the Master of Divinity program there before returning to Virginia to be ordained in the United Methodist Church. After serving as a pastor and campus minister for several years, he decided to pursue graduate studies in religion. Convinced that the contemporary Christian Church needed to recover its long neglected spiritual traditions, he chose to attend the Catholic University of America in order to concentrate on studies in the field of Christian spirituality. Concurrent with his studies at Catholic University, he enrolled in the Shalem Institute for Spiritual Formation and completed their Graduate Program in Christian Spiritual Guidance. Shortly after completing the Ph.D. in religion at Catholic University, he joined the faculty of Shenandoah University. He is an active participant in the American Academy of Religion, presenting papers at regional and national meetings. In 1990 he participated as a fellow in the seventh Coolidge Research Colloquium sponsored by the Association for Religion and Intellectual Life at the Episcopal Divinity School in Cambridge, Massachusetts.

Copenhaver has more than an academic interest in the issues that this book addresses. Concerned for a holistic spirituality, he has been actively involved in peace and social justice groups, as well as programs for spiritual renewal. He serves on the National Board of Directors for Methodists United for Peace and Justice and coordinates a local chapter of the Fellowship of Reconciliation, an interfaith peacemaking group. In 1987 he traveled to Nicaragua with a delegation from Witness for Peace. He is faculty advisor to the Amnesty International chapter at Shenandoah University. His involvement in spiritual renewal programs finds expression through service on the Board of Discipleship of the Virginia Conference and through the Disciplined Order of Christ.

He is married to Marsha A. Childs, a substance abuse counselor, and they have a three year old son, Thomas.

DATE DUE